Autonomous Language Learning with Technology

Advances in Digital Language Learning and Teaching

Series Editors: Michael Thomas, University of Central Lancashire, UK, Mark Peterson, Kyoto University, Japan, and Mark Warschauer, University of California – Irvine, USA

Today's language educators need support to understand how their learners are changing and the ways technology can be used to aid their teaching and learning strategies. The movement towards different modes of language learning – from presence based to autonomous as well as blended and fully online modes – requires different skill sets such as e-moderation and new ways of designing and developing language learning tasks in the digital age. Theoretical studies that include practical case studies and high-quality empirical studies incorporating critical perspectives are necessary to move the field further. This new series is committed to providing such an outlet for high-quality work on digital language learning and teaching. Volumes in the series will focus on a number of areas including but not limited to:

- task-based learning and teaching approaches utilizing technology
- language learner creativity
- e-moderation and teaching languages online
- blended language learning
- designing courses for online and distance-language learning
- mobile-assisted language learning
- autonomous language learning, both in and outside of formal educational contexts
- the use of Web 2.0/social media technologies
- immersive and virtual language learning environments
- digital game-based language learning
- language educator professional development with digital technologies
- teaching language skills with technologies

Enquiries about the series can be made by contacting the series editors: Michael Thomas (MThomas4@uclan.acuk), Mark Peterson (tufsmp@yahoo.com) and Mark Warschauer (markw@uci.edu).

Titles in the Series

Autonomy and Foreign Language Learning in a Virtual Learning Environment, Miranda Hamilton

Online Teaching and Learning: Sociocultural Perspectives, edited by Carla Meskill

Task-based Language Learning in a Real-World Digital Environment, edited by Paul Seedhouse

Teaching Languages with Technology: Communicative Approaches to Interactive Whiteboard Use, edited by Euline Cutrim Schmid and Shona Whyte

WorldCall, edited by Ana Gimeno, Mike Levy, Françoise Blin and David Barr

Autonomous Language Learning with Technology

Beyond the Classroom

Chun Lai

BLOOMSBURY ACADEMIC
LONDON • NEW YORK • OXFORD • NEW DELHI • SYDNEY

BLOOMSBURY ACADEMIC
Bloomsbury Publishing Plc
50 Bedford Square, London, WC1B 3DP, UK
1385 Broadway, New York, NY 10018, USA

BLOOMSBURY, BLOOMSBURY ACADEMIC and the
Diana logo are trademarks of Bloomsbury Publishing Plc

First published 2017
Paperback edition first published 2018

Cover design by James Watson
Cover image © shutterstock.com

A catalogue record for this book is available from the British Library.

Library of Congress Cataloging-in-Publication Data
Names: Lai, Chun (Language teacher) author.
Title: Autonomous language learning with technology beyond the classroom / Chun Lai.
Description: London; New York: Bloomsbury Academic, [2017] | Series:
Advances in Digital Language Learning and Teaching |
Includes bibliographical references and index.
Identifiers: LCCN 2016058379| ISBN 9781474240413 (hb) | ISBN 9781474240437 (epub)
Subjects: LCSH: Language and languages–Study and teaching–Technological
innovations. | Language and languages–Study and
teaching–Self-instruction. | Language and languages–Computer-assisted
instruction. | Web-based instruction–Technological innovations. |
Distance education–Technological innovations. | on-line
Classification: LCC P53.855 .L24 2017 | DDC 418.0078/5–dc23 LC record
available at https://lccn.loc.gov/2016058379

ISBN: HB: 978-1-4742-4041-3
PB: 978-1-3500-9472-7
ePDF: 978-1-4742-4042-2
ePub: 978-1-4742-4043-7

Series: Advances in Digital Learning and Teaching

Typeset by Deanta Global Publishing Services, Chennai, India

To find out more about our authors and books visit
www.bloomsbury.com and sign up for our newsletters.

Contents

List of Figures

List of Tables

Part One

Understanding Out-of-Class Autonomous Language Learning with Technology

1

Introducing Key Concepts

Autonomous language learning is firmly grounded in constructivism, which highlights the active roles that learners play in the learning process, and in humanistic and cognitive psychology, which emphasizes the supporting of learners' inherent drive towards self-actualization of their full potential and enabling them to utilize social, psychological and behavioural resources to achieve personal transformation (Benson, 2011a; Gremmo and Riley, 1995). Autonomous language learning intertwines with and is influenced by the ongoing educational reforms aimed at allowing learners freedom in learning and redefining teachers' and students' roles in education. It also aligns with the focus on people's freedom to direct their own lives as propagated in political philosophy, and corresponds with the pursuit of self-directed learning and informal learning as described in the adult education literature (Benson, 2011a). There is a consensus in the literature that autonomous learning is more effective than non-autonomous learning because the former is often associated with greater perceived meaningfulness, personal relevance, emotional investment and a greater likelihood of internalization. As Dickinson (1995) pointed out, 'There is convincing evidence that people who take the initiative in learning learn more things and learn better than people who sit at the feet of teachers, passively waiting to be taught' (p. 14). Griffiths (2008) concurred with Dickinson on the essential role of autonomy in learning after reviewing the existing literature on 'good language learners'. She found that a common characteristic of 'successful' language learners identified in these studies was their willingness to seek out their own learning opportunities and their engagement with the language on their own terms. Autonomy is such an important component in successful language learning that Little (1994) stated 'All genuinely successful learning is in the end autonomous' (p. 431).

Autonomous learning can occur in both formal and informal contexts. Formal learning refers to intentional, compulsory, institutionally sponsored, classroom-based learning that is highly structured and leads to formal credentials, whereas informal learning is learning that takes place outside formal educational institutions (Marsick and Watkins, 2001). Informal learning includes both planned, structured learning on a voluntary basis in flexible learning programmes that do not lead to formal credentials (namely, non-formal learning or informal education) and unplanned learning from everyday life experience (Colley, Hodkinson and Malcolm, 2003; Rogers, 2016). As its title indicates, this book primarily focuses on autonomous language learning that is initiated by learners themselves and takes place outside language classrooms in K–12 schools and universities.

Why such an interest in learning beyond the classroom? Dewey (1966), arguing that all learning is worthwhile, was among the first few educators to recognize the importance of informal learning. According to him, schools, despite being an important means of learning, are 'only one means' of learning (p. 4). Learning takes place in a variety of formal and informal settings across time and space (Colley, Hodkinson and Malcolm, 2003; National Research Council, 2009), and formal institutions are only part of it (Bäumer et al., 2011). These formal and informal settings form 'a complex web of synchronic as well as chronological learning opportunities' (Bäumer et al., 2011, p. 92), which successful learners usually make good use of to enhance their learning experience (Blyth and LaCroix-Dalluhn, 2011). It has also been found that learning experience across these different settings often brings unique yet complementary sets of outcomes (Blyth and LaCroix-Dalluhn, 2011; Lai, 2015a). Formal learning often generates cognitive skills, whereas the non-cognitive skills that are inherent in many successful individuals are commonly acquired through informal learning (Barron, 2006; Blyth and LaCroix-Dalluhn, 2011). Thus, to reach their full potential in learning and make learning more effective, it is important for learners to engage in autonomous learning that goes beyond classroom-based learning (Thornton, 2010), and to utilize different forms of learning to extend personal learning (Hall, 2009). In fact, learners of different ages have been found to construct personally relevant activity contexts with diverse learning opportunities, resources and activities within and across settings in order to meet their learning needs (Barron, 2006; Leander, Philips and Taylor, 2010; Sefton-Green, 2006). Given that students engage in informal learning outside the classroom, it would undermine educators' endeavours to enhance the quality of education if they did not make an effort to understand its nature (Rogers, 2016).

Over the last decade, increasing attention in the field of language learning has been paid to learning beyond the classroom. This enhanced attention comes from the rise and wide acceptance of communicative language-learning theories that highlight extensive language exposure and authentic language use and interaction as necessary conditions for language learning. It has been further augmented by the proliferation and normalization of information and communication technologies in people's lives as technology-enhanced and technology-mediated environments make these critical language-learning conditions easily accessible. In-class language learning is often constrained in its physical and human configurations and by its limited instruction hours, which makes it hard to satisfy critical language-learning conditions. Thus, learning beyond the classroom is much needed so that learners can make use of the human, physical and environmental resources both available in their immediate surroundings and mediated by technological resources to construct ideal language-learning environments. The increased attention has also been boosted by various research studies showing that autonomous out-of-class language learning is positively associated with learners' oral proficiency, vocabulary size and knowledge, and reading and listening comprehension abilities (Sylvén and Sundqvist, 2012; Sundqvist and Wikström, 2015), as well as their overall grades in standardized tests (Lai, Zhu and Gong, 2015; Larsson, 2012). Research studies have further found that the positive association between out-of-class language learning and language-learning outcomes is manifested not only in the cognitive domain but also in the affective domain, such as greater self-efficacy and confidence in and enjoyment of language learning (Lai, Zhu and Gong, 2015; Palviainen, 2012; Sundqvist, 2011). Research also shows that not only do foreign-language learners perceive their out-of-class language-learning experience positively, but they also view it as playing a qualitatively different role from that of learning experience inside the classroom, and that the functions of these two types of learning complement each other (Lai, 2015a). The recent increased attention paid to out-of-class language learning echoes Benson's (2011b) observation that 'after a period in which the pendulum of autonomy has swung towards the classroom, we may be entering a period in which it swings back towards out-of-class learning, or at least towards the ways in which classroom teaching connects with students' self-directed language learning beyond the classroom' (p. 18).

Despite the increased research attention paid to out-of-class language learning, it remains a relatively uncharted terrain, in that researchers are only starting to accumulate knowledge about its nature, its functions, its quality indicators, the interaction between its various elements and constituents, and its relationship to in-class language learning. Benson (2008) argued that 'the bulk of the literature on autonomy in language learning is concerned with institutional settings and pays very little attention to non-institutional learning' (p. 20). At present, researchers' understanding of autonomous out-of-class language learning is still quite limited. This book intends to provide an overview of the current understanding of learners' autonomous language learning beyond the classroom, with a particular focus on their self-initiated use of technology for learning. This interest in understanding language learners' technology use beyond the classroom has arisen partly because the normalization of technology in human life makes it part and parcel of learners' out-of-class learning experience and partly because technology is likely to make the most contribution to the construction of ideal language-learning environments since long-term, frequent language immersion and study abroad are not realistic options for most language learners.

In discussing autonomous language learning with technology beyond the classroom, it is necessary first to understand what autonomy entails. Understanding the different aspects or dimensions of autonomy and the goals of autonomous language learning helps to set the frame of reference for the discussion of autonomous language learning with technology outside educational institutions.

Aspects of autonomy

There have been various definitions of autonomy, the most oft-cited of which is that by Holec (1981), who defined autonomy as 'the ability to take charge of one's own learning' (p. 3). Benson (2001) also highlighted the capacity aspect of autonomy, describing it as 'the capacity to take control of one's own learning', and argued that it 'may take a variety of forms in relation to different levels of the learning process' (p. 47). Dickinson (1987) defined autonomy as 'the situation in which the learner is totally responsible for all the decisions concerned with his learning and the implementation of those decisions' (p. 11), thus adding the situation aspect of autonomy. Dam and colleagues (1990) accentuated the social aspect of autonomy and defined it as 'a capacity and willingness to act independently and in cooperation with others, as a social, responsible person' (p. 102). The various definitions suggest that autonomy is a multidimensional concept, and this multidimensionality is reflected in the duality of meaning in the nature of autonomy, in the sociality of autonomy and in the teachability of autonomy.

Nature of autonomy: Capacity and situational freedom dimensions

When talking about autonomy, a natural question would be: What exactly is it? Benson (2008) reviewed the existent literature and concluded that autonomy entails both a capacity dimension and a situation dimension, which he named 'capacity' and 'situational freedom', respectively. Benson (2011a) elaborated on what he meant by 'the capacity to control one's own learning' (p. 58). According to him, the potential for autonomous action involves three essential components: 1) the ability to engage in self-directed learning (i.e. learners need not only to grasp essential study skills but also to have adequate knowledge of the target language to engage in a learning task on their own); 2) the desire for self-directed learning (i.e. the intensity of learners' intentions with respect to the self-directed learning task); and 3) the freedom to engage in self-directed learning (i.e. the degree to which learners are 'permitted' to control their learning). The first two relate to the capacity dimension and the last one constitutes the situational freedom dimension.

The capacity aspect refers to a set of competencies rather than a unitary capacity for action (Benson, 2001; Lewis, 2013). Wall (2003) described this capacity as an individual's ability to chart 'his own course through life … according to his own understanding of what is valuable and worth doing' (p. 308). The competencies include a set of metacognitive and cognitive abilities associated with the management of one's learning process. Little (1991) referred to this set of abilities as the capacity for 'detachment, critical reflection, decision-making and independent action' (p. 4). The competencies also include learners' attitudinal ability to take responsibility for their own learning (Benson, 1997; Little 1999) and to attribute value to their participation, and learners' 'social-interactive' ability to articulate and exchange their views with others (Hamilton, 2013; Little, 2007). In addition, Lewis (2013) emphasized competencies associated with human sociality, such as collaboration and communication abilities, global awareness, cross-cultural skills and so on. Besides the multiplicity of the competencies involved, essential competencies may also be different in different learning contexts (e.g. solitary interaction with objects vs. interaction with the social world) and at different times (Benson, 2001; Lewis, 2013). Hence, the context of autonomous learning with technology beyond the classroom may demand a unique set of competencies, given the particularities of learners' interaction in such settings.

The situational freedom aspect refers to learners having the right to have control over their learning (Benson, 2009) and the freedom from others' control over themselves (Hamilton, 2013). More importantly, this aspect stresses the importance of structure in creating conditions that help teachers to relinquish their control, offer learners 'access to an environment that provides a wide range of options' (Wall, 2003, p. 308), and empower learners to exercise agency in negotiating and shaping the direction of their learning and voicing their views. Thus, the resources afforded by an environment, and the social and discursive configurations and characteristics of the environment may define the level of autonomy that the environment affords and hence may influence the degree of autonomy that an individual can demonstrate. Moreover, autonomy exists in the interdependent relationship between the individual and the social, discursive and resource realities of the context within which he or she exists (Benson, 2009). Nunan (1996) underlined the fact that the degrees of autonomy depend on both individual factors such as personality, goals in learning and prior educational experience, and contextual factors such as the ideology and philosophy of a culture or community. The influence of cultural values on autonomy through the values and beliefs of individuals and the community is apparent in the sociocultural perspective of autonomy, which accentuates the interaction between learners and the environment (Dang, 2012; Oxford, 2008; Palfreyman, 2003). Accordingly, autonomy is highly variable and may manifest itself differently for different people, in different cultures, and even within the same person across temporal, spatial and contextual dimensions (Benson, 2009; Murray, 2014; Sinclair, 2000). Thus, learner autonomy is situation specific (Holec, 1981; Gao, 2007): learners might be 'autonomous in one area while dependent in another' (Murray, 1999, p. 301). The realities of the contexts for autonomy inside and outside the classroom are different, and the characteristics of learning beyond the classroom may shape individuals' interaction with it and, hence, the levels of autonomy that individuals exhibit and the support they need. For instance, Benson (2011b) argued that the connection between teacher autonomy and learning autonomy may manifest itself differently in classroom settings and out-of-class learning settings. According to him, in the former setting, it is considered important for teachers to be autonomous learners and autonomous practitioners themselves in order to support learner autonomy, whereas in the latter setting, what is valued more is teachers serving as language advisers to help learners make informed decisions about their learning.

When discussing autonomy in any context, educators and researchers need to take both aspects – capacity and the freedom afforded in a given situation – and their interaction into consideration.

Sociality of autonomy: Independent and interpersonal dimensions

Earlier works on autonomy have overemphasized its independent nature, an overemphasis that has gradually been redressed by the recognition that interdependence is an essential component of autonomy in action (Boud, 1988). The duality of autonomy in having both independent and interpersonal dimensions is reflected in Dam et al.'s (1990) definition of learner autonomy: 'A capacity and willingness to act independently and in cooperation with others, as a social, responsible person' (p. 102).

In their self-determination theory, Deci and Ryan (1985) regarded autonomy as the fundamental psychological need of learners to initiate and source their behaviours and self-expression. According to Deci and Ryan, learners often enter a learning situation with degrees of inner motivational resources that could lead to autonomous learning behaviours that they use to engage themselves in the learning situation. The conditions of the learning situation, including human relationships, support or thwart the inner motivational resources that learners bring with them. Deci and Ryan therefore argued that an individual's sense of autonomy relies on two components: competence (i.e. 'abilities to confront and overcome optimal challenges' (Deci and Flaste, 1996, p. 66) and relatedness (i.e. the feeling of being 'connected with others in the midst of being effective and autonomous' (Deci and Flaste, 1996, p. 88). For Deci and Ryan, social connections and relationships mediate learner autonomy. Reasserting Dam's (1995) arguments for the social dimension of learner autonomy, Lewis (2013, 2014) emphasized the fact that social interactions are part and parcel of learner autonomy, particularly so in online settings. He argued that learner autonomy includes both the independent aspect of interacting with objects for goal-driven behaviours and the interpersonal aspect of interacting with the social world, where cooperative attitudes and behaviours are crucial. These two aspects of learner autonomy may demand different capacities and involve different patterns of interaction between individuals and the learning situation.

Taking a developmental perspective, Little (1996) regarded collaboration as essential to the development of autonomy. According to him, 'The development of a capacity for reflection and analysis, central to the development of learner autonomy, depends on the development of an internationalization of a capacity to participate fully and critically in social interactions' (p. 210). This view accentuates the role of social agents such as teachers and peers as well as the redefinition of teachers' and students' roles in the language curriculum in the development of learner autonomy (Voller, 1997; Sinclair, 2000). Thus, the mediation of more capable others (Oxford, 2003; Murray, 2014), and apprenticeship in a community of practice via 'interaction, social construction of knowledge, scaffolding, modelling, goal-setting, peer sharing and learning reflection' (Oxford, 2011, p. 29; Murray, 2014) are critical to the development of autonomy. Equally important is the development of learners' sense of self-efficacy through constant reflective practices, conscious learning from observing others and paying attention to 'social persuasion' (Bandura, 1997).

In sum, autonomy entails both independent and social aspects. Moreover, both aspects need to be taken into account in a discussion of the exercise and development of learner autonomy.

Teachability of autonomy: Natural propensity and development dimensions

Autonomy is regarded as a natural propensity of human beings. Benson (2011b) pointed out that, despite the controversies over the concept of autonomy, researchers generally agree that 'language learners naturally tend to take control of their learning' (p. 16). At the same time, he also pointed out another general consensus in this research field: 'Learners who lack autonomy are capable of developing it' (p. 15), which suggests that autonomy is something that can be taught and developed. Little (2007) concurred with this point of view and identified two senses of autonomy: the biological inner aspect and the behavioural social aspect. According to him, the biological inner aspect refers to individuals' thoughts, emotions, perceptions and responses to the world around them, and this inner capacity is genetically determined. However, this inner capacity is enlarged or suppressed by various individual and external factors, which shape people's individual- and social-oriented autonomous behaviours. This helps to explain observations of learners' not demonstrating autonomous behaviours when left to exercise free choice in some situations (Raz, 1986; Sinclair, 2000). Consequently, Benson (2012) concluded: 'Although the potential for autonomy may be intrinsic [in] the human condition, autonomy itself is something that must be acquired and maintained over the course of a lifetime' (p. 32). Autonomy is not only teachable, it also needs to be consciously supported, fostered and maintained. In fostering learner autonomy, the development of long-term 'dispositional autonomy' needs to be prioritized over sporadic 'occurrent' autonomy (Benson, 2012; Young, 1986, p. 76). In other words, instead of scattering a few autonomous learning activities here and there in their learning experience, a systematic and holistic approach that integrates both the curriculum set-up and intervention arrangements and takes account of the psychological, social, political and technical perspectives of autonomy is needed to foster and maintain learners' natural tendency towards controlling their own learning.

In conclusion, autonomy involves both capacity and situational freedom, includes both independent and interpersonal dimensions, and is a natural propensity that needs to be consciously fostered and maintained. Autonomous learning is 'learning in which a capacity to control learning is displayed or required' (Benson, 2001, p. 110). Consequently, autonomy is both the predispositions towards and the outcomes of autonomous learning. On the one hand, learners 'need to be autonomous in order to be able to learn independently' (Lam and Reinders, 2005, p. 226), and on the other hand, the expected outcomes of autonomous learning are not only cognitive and non-cognitive development but also the development of learner autonomy. What then are the specific forms of learner autonomy that foreign-language educators aim to develop?

Goals of autonomous language learning

The concept of autonomy was first introduced in the field of political science to advocate people's rights to freedom and control over their own lives. When this concept is transferred to the field of language learning, what specific goals should educators focus on achieving through autonomous learning? Littlewood (1996) defined autonomy as the 'capacity for thinking and acting independently that may occur in any situation' (p. 428). Independence in thinking and acting involves different aspects, including independent decision-making and action in language learning, independent use of the target language, and use of the target language to make a difference in oneself and in society – in other words, *autonomy as language learner*; *autonomy as language user*; and *autonomy as person*. Macaro (1997) and Benson (2012) supported these goals in highlighting the autonomy of language-learning competence, the autonomy of language competence, the autonomy of independent choice and action, and personal autonomy.

Autonomy as language learner

Autonomy as language learner involves acquiring the ability to engage in self-directed learning both within and beyond the classroom through collective experience (Littlewood, 1996). Benson (2012) differentiated this goal further into autonomy in language learning and autonomy in learning. The former highlights learners' control over the purposes and goals of language learning, hence the directions and content of learning, and the latter stresses learners' control over the management of the learning process. Thus, learners' control over their own learning involves three components: control of the learning content ('what' and 'how much'); management of the 'where', 'when' and 'how' of language learning; and the cognitive processes involved in learning such as noticing, metacognition and reflection (Benson, 2011a). Developing *autonomy as a language learner* necessarily involves helping students to reflect on the goals and purposes of their language learning and to develop the ability to control the different aspects of learning, and enhancing their ability to perceive affordances in the learning contexts (Huang and Benson, 2013). Oxford (2015) further asserted that control over learning also involves the socio-emotional aspects of learning, including the management of beliefs, emotions, motivations and strategies (Costa and Kallick, 2008; Schunk and Ertmer, 2000), the establishment and management of social relationships (Costa and Kallick, 2008; Goleman, 2006; van Deurzen, 2012), and the ability to persist against adversity (Truebridge, 2014).

Autonomy as language user

Autonomy as language user or communicator refers to learners' capacity for creative language use and their ability to use situation-appropriate communication strategies (Littlewood, 1996). This competence in generating one's own utterances is regarded as an important dimension of learner autonomy since it can free learners from the restriction of input (Macaro, 1997; 2008). In this respect, Macaro (2008) stressed the importance of avoiding a rigid prioritization of grammatical accuracy over risk taking and creative language production. Situation-appropriate communication strategies refer not only to the communication strategies that enhance learners' opportunities to maintain conversations in the target language despite a knowledge gap, but also to the communication strategies in relation to attitudes and behaviours that secure more learning and life opportunities, such as actively seeking help, dealing with cultural challenges and shifts in sociocultural identities, cross-cultural skills and global awareness, and respecting, trusting and relating to others (Lewis, 2014; Oxford, 2011). Benson (2009a) argued that an important aim of learner-autonomy support is to foster 'the emergence of new and relatively stable multilingual "selves" out of potentially disorienting processes of second language acquisition' (p. 23). Macaro (2008) further emphasized, in the multilingual and multicultural contexts, language learners' ability to make independent free choices over what proficiency levels they strive to achieve in the different languages that are used in society and over what language they would use predominantly and what language they would try to maintain. Thus, Macaro stressed the importance of engaging students in reflecting critically on their strategic decisions and behaviours on language learning in relation to the sociocultural contexts in which they live.

Autonomy as person

Littlewood (1996) defined autonomy as a person's ability in a foreign-language learning context to express personal meaning and create personal learning contexts. Acknowledging this personal empowerment goal, Raya, Lamb and Vieira (2007) further added a social goal in their definition of autonomy: 'The competence to develop as a self-determined, socially responsible and critically aware participant in (and beyond) educational environments, within a vision of education as (inter)personal empowerment and social transformation' (p. 1). Thus, there is a strong emphasis in developing autonomy in life through foreign-language learning – the enhanced power of self-expression (Aviram and Assor, 2010; Benson, 2012). It is critical to develop learners' acute perception of sociocultural power relations and discursive resources in support of their autonomous learning behaviour and their critical evaluation of the resource-generation values of this behaviour in enhancing 'cultural capital, identity and future desires' (Oxford, 2015, p. 66; Palfreyman, 2014). It is equally important to encourage, engage and support students' self-expression in the target language and to foster a sense of personal and social responsibility and a sense of criticality.

The section above reviewed the literature on the nature of autonomy and the goals of autonomous language learning. The nature of autonomy forms the essence of autonomous learning and informs educators and researchers of the various dimensions they need to consider in order to understand the exercise of autonomy. The goals of autonomous language learning suggest that there are three aspects of autonomy – *autonomy as language learner*, *autonomy as language user or communicator*, and *autonomy as person* – that educators may want to foster among the learners. Both the nature and the goals of autonomy inform educators of the critical aspects and issues they need to pay attention to in discussing how to support autonomous learning. These insights need to be combined with an understanding of the particularities of learning with technology in informal learning contexts to inform a discussion of autonomous learning with technology beyond the classroom.

Characteristics of autonomous learning with technology beyond the classroom

Learning beyond the classroom involves learning in informal contexts, which is characterized by the possibility of the learning being emergent, contingent and opportunistic since informal learning is both 'reactive, unintended, and also deliberative, intentional' (Hager, 2012; Rogers, 2016, p. 270). Moreover, learning beyond the classroom often involves constant monitoring, making appropriate judgements, and adjusting short-term goals in a continually evolving process (Hager and Halliday, 2006). Thus, in this learning context, learners' flexible mentalities and the ability to perceive the learning affordances in the emergent events and environments are critical for them to seize and take advantage of the ongoing opportunities for learning (Benson, 2013). Furthermore, informal learning often involves collaborative components (Hager, 2012; Rogers, 2016) and various social networks (Palfreyman, 2011), which redefine the roles of teachers and students in learning. This is particularly true with informal learning with technology, as various social networking tools permeate people's lives and technological tools and platforms are becoming highly interactive – even online dictionary sites come with discussion forums. Consequently, in this context, teachers' roles need to be redefined (Benson, 2001) and the influence of and learners' interactions with different social agents need to be taken into consideration. Hence, the abilities associated with human sociality are becoming ever increasingly important for informal learning with technology (Lewis, 2013, 2014; Oxford, 2011; Palfreyman, 2011). In addition, learning beyond the classroom is highly contextual and 'learners themselves are part of the context' (Kelley and Hager, 2015, p. 377). Therefore, theoretical lenses that highlight learners' holistic interactions with various elements within the context would be especially helpful in understanding the nature of informal learning (Hamilton, 2013; Luckin, 2010). Since learning beyond the classroom is relatively unstructured, and the control of learning is in the hands of the learners, learning that takes place in this context is often characterized by motivations, relationships and commitments, and identity and agency are major issues in the context of autonomous learning beyond the classroom (Sackey, Nguyen and Grabill, 2015). Accordingly, the influence of these factors on learning may be increased and needs to be given greater attention in this context. In terms of the outcomes, learning in this context is most often implicit or tacit, which makes it hard to be captured and quantified (Hager, 2012), and it is most often holistic and whole-person embodied, often involving affective outcomes and non-cognitive abilities (Barron et al., 2007; Blyth and LaCroix-Dalluhn, 2011; Lai, Zhu and Gong, 2015). Scribner and Cole (1973) characterized out-of-class learning as a fusion of the intellectual and the emotional aspects of learning. This characteristic calls for the employment of a different set of criteria and measurements in examining the influences of autonomous learning beyond the classroom (Barron et al., 2007; Blyth and LaCroix-Dalluhn, 2011).

When the focus is especially on the use of technology for learning in this context, additional issues are brought into the spotlight. For one thing, technology may transform the specificities of both the goals of autonomous language learning and the aspects of autonomy. The reciprocal relationship between new literacies and learning autonomy and how it redefines learning autonomy deserves attention (Benson, 2013; Blin, 2010; Villanueva, Ruiz-Madrid and Luzón, 2010). Also, when technology mediates the learning experience, what the capacity and the situational freedom dimensions of autonomy entail needs to be reconceptualized as technology-mediated and technology-enhanced environments may demand different sets of skills and conditions for action (Chik, 2014; Oxford, 2008). Additionally, technology may bring with it new factors to complicate the situation further. For instance, learners' culturally shaped views of and approaches to technological tools might influence their autonomous learning intentions and behaviours with different technological tools.

Taking all these issues into consideration, Figure 1.1 synthesizes the discussions above to provide a frame of reference for the discussion of autonomous language learning with technology beyond the classroom in this book. The various aspects of autonomy are placed at the centre of the figure to highlight the major dimensions to consider, while its yin-yang shape and the curved lines connecting the different dimensions signify the fluid interweaving relationship between the duality of meaning of autonomy. The key features of autonomous language learning with technology beyond the classroom are placed in the middle. These key features both interact with the various aspects of autonomy and moderate their interactions in achieving the three goals specified in the outer circle.

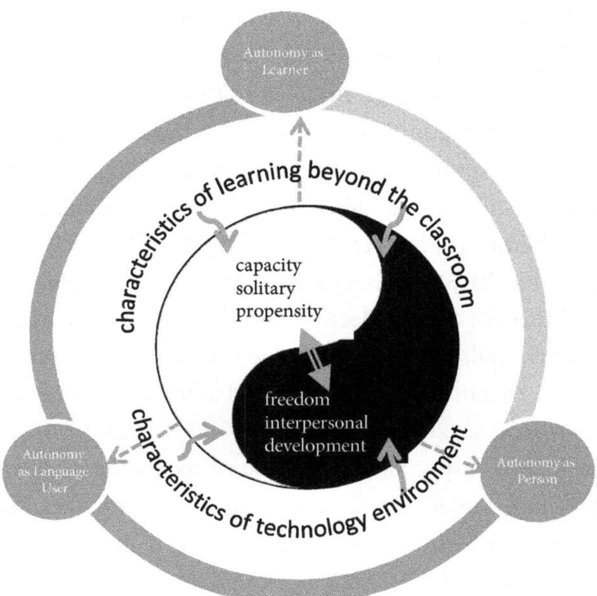

Figure 1.1 A frame of reference for discussing autonomous language learning with technology beyond the classroom.

As autonomy is a complex, multidimensional and variable term, which has often been confused with many other terms, it is important to delineate the relationship between autonomy and other related concepts in this introductory chapter so that readers can have a clear idea of what is meant by 'autonomous learning' in this book (see Table 1.1.).

Related terms

Autonomous learning and self-directed learning

Although autonomous learning and self-directed learning have different origins, with the former originating from the political and philosophical literature and the latter from the humanistic tradition of adult education literature, the two concepts share many similarities. Both terms are characterized by a predominant independent connotation in earlier works and were later conceptualized as containing a strong interpersonal dimension. According to Knowles (1975), 'self-directed learning usually takes place in association with various kinds of helpers, such as teachers, tutors, mentors, resource people and peers' (p. 18), and

Table 1.1 Terms associated with autonomous learning

Association	Term	Relation to autonomous learning
Interchangeable term	Self-directed learning	• Similar dimensions • Similar goals
Related terms	Agency	• Source of origin • Prerequisite • 'Raw material' (Huang, 2011, p. 242)
	Metacognition	• Key capacity
	Identity	• Outcome • 'Direction of development' (Chik, 2007, p. 41)
Confusing terms	Self-instruction/self-study Self-access Independent learning	Partial representation • Solitary and away from the mediation of teachers
	Informal learning	Partial representation of • Context for learning • Characteristics of learning

thus has a strong social component. Self-directed learning is conceptualized as the interaction between process, personal attributes and the context (Bouchard, 2012; Spear and Mocker, 1984; Tough, 1971). As Percival (1996) asserted, the essence of self-directed learning is that learners have control over all educational decisions, and it could be both self-initiated and other-initiated and takes place both in teacher-directed classrooms and beyond (Guglielmino, 2008). Thus, similar to autonomous learning, self-directed learning contains both independent and interdependent components (Guglielmino, 2008; Knowles, 1975; Percival, 1996). Stubbé and Theunissen (2008) maintained that self-directed learning consisted of multiple dimensions: learner control (both the capacity and the freedom to make decisions), self-regulating learning strategies and reflection, and interaction with the social and physical environment. These multiple dimensions of self-directed learning correspond with the key aspects of autonomous learning. Furthermore, self-directed learning has similar goals to those of autonomous learning. The goals of self-directed learning are conceptualized as: 1) development of a learner's capacity to be self-directed; 2) transformational learning that brings changes to how individuals view themselves and the world; and 3) promotion of emancipatory learning and social action

(Merriam et al., 2007). Thus, these two concepts place a similar emphasis on the goals towards learning autonomy and personal autonomy. Given the similarities in their conceptualization, these two terms are used interchangeably in this book.

There are three concepts that are different from autonomy but are closely related to it. These concepts include agency, identity and metacognition.

Agency

Agency has been defined as learners' capacity to choose among alternative courses of action (Giddens, 1984), and learners' intentional efforts to change themselves or their situations through their own actions (Ray, 2009). Thus, similar to autonomy, agency conveys a sense of deliberation and choice (Huang, 2011), the timing and the extent of whose exercise depend on learners' belief systems, motivation, affects, self-regulatory skills, abilities and affordances in specific settings (Mercer, 2011). Agency is theorized as 'a point of origin for the development of autonomy' (Benson, 2007, p. 30) and is a prerequisite for autonomous learning (Gao and Zhang, 2011). However, agency focuses more on self-conscious reflexive actions and not necessarily on realizing one's control over the learning process, although these intentional actions may enhance one's controlling capacity (Huang and Benson, 2013). Furthermore, autonomy is the systematic exercise of control over one's learning, while agency could involve sporadic actions (Huang and Benson, 2013). Thereby, agency serves as the 'raw material' for autonomy (Huang, 2011, p. 242) and helps strengthen learners' autonomy in the technical sense, but it does not necessarily lead to learner autonomy in the psychological and political sense. Thus, according to Huang and Benson (2013), agency is a necessary but not sufficient condition for autonomy.

Metacognition

Metacognition, or learning strategies, is a critical component of the capacity aspect of autonomy. According to Oxford (2008), the exercise of metacognition both reflects and promotes autonomy. Gao and Zhang (2011) regarded agency and metacognition as two sides of the same coin. They defined metacognition as entailing knowledge of oneself, knowledge of the task and knowledge of the strategies that are appropriate in fulfilling the task. They further argued that agency needs to be supplemented with metacognitive operations (e.g. to utilize their knowledge of themselves as learners, their understanding of the task, and the selection and use of the appropriate strategies to tackle the task) to realize autonomy. Aviram and Assor (2010) concurred with Gao and Zhang and regarded self-knowledge as a critical ability to realize autonomy. Thus, similar to agency, metacognition is a necessary but not sufficient condition for autonomous learning.

Identity

Identity is 'our sense of who we are and our relationship to the world' (Kanno, 2003, p. 3). Benson (2007) regarded identity as an important outcome of autonomy. As Little (1996) pointed out, autonomous learning can enlarge learners' sense of identity, and for autonomous language learners, the target language would gradually be integrated into their definition of what they are. Huang (2011) further argued that the relationship between autonomy and identity might not be unilateral, but rather bilateral, whereby identity also serves as a point of origin and the 'direction of development' for autonomy (Chik, 2007, p. 41). So, the development of autonomy and identity go hand in hand, both depending on the exercise of agency and metacognition (Huang, 2011).

There are also a few approaches to learning that are similar to autonomous learning but only reflect partial aspects of autonomy. These include self-study or self-access, independent learning and informal learning.

Autonomous learning is different from terms associated with other types of learning such as self-study, or self-access, and independent learning. These terms often carry an independent connotation and signify detachment from external sources or influence (Ryan and Deci, 2002), whereas autonomous learning has a strong social dimension and entails constant interaction, negotiation, cooperation and so on (Dam, 1995). As Little (1996) pointed out, autonomous learning is not self-instruction or teacher-free learning. In effect, as Dickinson (1977) mentioned earlier, what defines autonomous learning is not the specific forms of learning, namely whether it is self-directed or other-directed, but rather 'the individual specification of functional aims and the free choice of means of achieving those aims' (p. 17). Furthermore, these approaches to learning symbolize only learners' control over the learning environment, which needs to be complemented with their internal capacity, knowledge and motivation for taking control for autonomous learning to happen (Lamb, 2008). Self-study, self-access and independent learning are forms of learning that could be interwoven into learners' autonomous learning experience, but they only represent the independent dimension of autonomous learning. In autonomous learning, different independent and collaborative forms of learning interweave at different times of learning, and the key is being able to make a free choice of different means of learning.

Informal learning refers to learning, intentional or unintentional, that takes place outside formal educational institutions (Colley, Hodkinson and Malcolm, 2003; Rogers, 2016). Theoretical discussions on informal learning focus primarily on its unstructured, unplanned nature (Colley, Hodkinson and Malcolm, 2003) and emphasize the non-institutionalization of the context of learning (Hager, 2012; Rogers, 2016). Informal learning is different from autonomous learning in that autonomous learning is not constrained to informal learning contexts and can take place both within educational institutions and beyond. Another important difference is that autonomous learning places more emphasis on freedom of choice and the capacity to control, regardless of the contexts of learning – informal or formal – and the nature of learning – structured and planned or unstructured and unplanned. Informal learning may satisfy freedom of choice, but it does not necessarily imply intentional learning efforts and the capacity to control. Nonetheless, autonomous language learning with technology beyond the classroom takes place in informal learning contexts and is characterized by the nature of informal learning. The characteristics of informal learning can help researchers and educators gain a better understanding of the nature of autonomous language learning with technology beyond the classroom and the conditions that support its development.

2

Theoretical Backgrounds and Frameworks

The concept of autonomy was introduced into the field of language education in the 1970s with the establishment of Centre for Research and Pedagogical Applications in Language Learning (CRAPEL), and technology has played an important part in learner autonomy since early on. An important initiative in CRAPEL's approaches to autonomous learning has been the establishment of the self-access resource centre. Stand-alone drill and practice software has been an important resource that such centres curate and make available to students. Thus, technology has been affiliated with autonomy since the very beginning, serving as a potential facilitative tool for the exercise and development of autonomy (Motteram, 1997). With the fast development of information and communication technologies and their permeation into people's lives, the reciprocal relationship between technology and autonomous language learning is attracting increasing attention.

Affinity of technology and autonomous learning

Educational technology has demonstrated its effectiveness as a purveyor of learner autonomy.

(Murray, 1999, p. 296)

The development of autonomy is in no sense dependent on IT.

(Benson, 2005, p. 187)

The above quotations represent different views on the relationship between technology and autonomous language learning in current academic discourse. On the one hand, scholars extol the benefits of technology for the development of autonomy in offering important tools to facilitate the exercise of autonomy and in creating new spaces and contexts for autonomous learning

(Murray, 1999; Kessler, 2009; Reinders and White, 2010); on the other hand, scholars caution against the misleading view of technology as an indispensable condition of autonomy and of autonomy as a necessary outcome of immersion in technological environments (Benson, 2005; Kenning, 1996; Reinders and White, 2010). Thus, technology brings both affordances and constraints to the development of autonomy. As Reinders and White (2010) pointed out: 'This tension between affordance and constraint is a recurring theme in the investigation of the relationship between technology and autonomy' (p. 2). Some scholars further argue that technology redefines what autonomy entails and therefore advocate re-examining and redefining the relationship between technology and autonomous language learning (Benson, 2013; Blin, 2010).

Technology and the capacity to control

It is argued that technology can help enhance learners' capacity to control their own learning. For one thing, technology can help learners to monitor and manage their learning process more effectively. Technology documents learners' interaction within technological environments, which can be used as a reference to help learners adjust their learning strategies and process. The wiki is one such example, whereby learners' collaborative writing process is recorded and visualized in the system so that they can have a clear view of their collaboration process. Technology also provides support for learners in exercising some cognitive strategies during learning. Assistive tools such as annotation tools enable learners to take notes and record their thinking processes while reading, and pedagogical agents in technological platforms provide learners with the immediate language, culture and strategy support they need as they interact with materials in the target language. In addition, the access to virtual social communities and the high levels of interactivity in most technological platforms can help learners manage their emotions, motivations and efforts more effectively.

At the same time, technology redefines capacities that are essential to autonomous language learning. In the technological era, learners' ability to deal with copious information is critical to their exercise of autonomy (Qi, 2012). As Saadatmand and Kumpulainen (2012) put it, learning in open and networked environments demands high self-organization skills and the skills to deal with emergent learning opportunities. In other words, learners need to negotiate a huge mass of resources, tools and possibilities; decide what to learn and which tools and resources to use; build connections between the varieties of information; and manage the level of interactions in various learning networks and communities.

Thus, multimodal language-learning technologies require learners to have greater self-knowledge and self-awareness and exercise greater metacognitive strategies such as making choices about tasks and selecting the technological medium that suits both the task in hand and their learning preferences (Shakarami and Abdullah, 2011; White, 1995). The incorporation of technology into the out-of-class language-learning repertoire of learners also demands a new set of knowledge and skills in relation to technology use, that is, learners' understanding of the language-learning affordances of different technological tools/platforms, their knowledge and skills in selecting and mapping appropriate technological tools/platforms for different learning purposes, and their ability to make effective use of these technologies for learning and to navigate across different (learning) environments (Benson, 2013; Lai, 2013; Reinders and White, 2010). For instance, to benefit from learning experience that involves technology-mediated communications, learners need to understand the characteristics of the new discourse practices in such environments and to be able to engage in and make use of these practices for language learning (Villanueva, Ruiz-Madrid and Luzon, 2010). To benefit from the vast amount of information online, learners need to develop the skills to 'understand not only the text on the page, but the whole multimodal ensemble of writing, images, layout, graphics, sound and hypertext links' (Hafner, Chik and Jones, 2015, p. 1). Scholars further highlight the importance of being attuned, and strategically responsive, to technological changes, and seizing and creating opportunities for learning (Benson, 2013).

In addition, technology also reprioritizes learners' capacity to enjoy and succeed in the autonomous learning experience. Due to the prevalence of social networking tools and online interest-based communities, and the enhanced interactivity featured in most technological platforms (i.e. through crowd sourcing, social tagging, commenting and various interaction tools), autonomous language learning with technology beyond the classroom usually involves heavy social components. This enhanced social dimension of autonomous learning mediated by technology has made social competencies more important than ever (Benson, 2013; Chik, 2015; Lewis, 2013). Lewis (2013) argued that, in such collective learning contexts, cooperative attitudes and behaviours, empathy and identifying with other learners and reciprocity in giving and receiving help are critical to a positive autonomous learning experience. Thus, the importance of social competencies (being prosocial and relating to other members of the group) might be heightened in this context as such competencies play a more critical role in determining whether learners can enjoy and learn from the experience and hence in also determining the likelihood of maintaining the learning behaviours (Lewis, 2014).

Technology and situational freedom

Technology provides learners with unrestricted access to language-learning materials and language-use opportunities, and thus has the potential to proffer learners the freedom and choice they need in autonomous learning (Hamilton, 2013). However, situational freedom is not just about offering alternative choices but also about providing structures that facilitate autonomous actions (Benson, 2008; Reinders and White, 2010). Kenning (1996) accentuated the importance of learners having the capacity to take advantage of the alternative choices offered: 'The effective use of electronic tools and resources assumes certain prerequisites and that unless learners already have certain attitudes, skills and strategies, they are unlikely to derive much benefit' (p. 132–3). Thus, Benson (2001) argued that for technology to facilitate freedom of action, two conditions need to be met: 1) it must be structured in ways that provide ample opportunities for learner choice and control; and 2) it must contain mechanisms that help learners to take advantage of these opportunities.

Researchers further argue that technology may redefine the essential characteristics of situational freedom and what it entails. Who are those 'others' from whose control learners are striving to be free in the use of technology in informal learning contexts? Who are the social agents that might facilitate or inhibit freedom seeking in informal learning contexts? What facilitating conditions need to be built into the structures of technology-enhanced learning environments to enable freedom seeking? Scholars argue that online social networks are an important element in, and a means of, boosting situational freedom in informal learning contexts (Palfreyman, 2011; Reinders and White, 2010). As Lewis (2014) observed, with learners increasingly exercising autonomy in social contexts, it is no longer appropriate to view learner autonomy as an essentially self-centred concept; rather, educators need to understand what learner autonomy might look like and what situational freedom means when the operation of learner autonomy changes from 'I-mode' to 'we-mode'.

Technology also reshapes the facilitating structures for situational freedom. As Benson (2013) noted, the advent of information and communication technologies has changed the nature of the supporting structures that facilitate learners' freedom of action. Benson argued that in early work on autonomy, supporting structures for freedom of action had a strong flavour of being 'institutionalized and other-initiated' in the form of collecting and providing resources in self-access centres and equipping students with relevant skills through training programmes. The development of information and communication technologies has resulted in autonomous learning being more self-initiated and taking place in informal contexts not mediated by, and even without the knowledge of, teachers. Thus, the current discussion on supporting structures for freedom of action demands a greater understanding of the complexity of learners' autonomous learning beyond the classroom (Benson, 2013; Benson and Reinders, 2011).

Technology and the goals of autonomy

Technology affords the most effective means of achieving the three goals of autonomy. It offers opportunities and support for learners to manage the socio-emotional aspects of learning. The interactive, social, authentic and entertaining features of technology-enhanced or -mediated learning experience facilitate learners' management of their beliefs, emotions, motivations and strategies, and afford them easy access to opportunities for cross-cultural interactions and social relationship management that are difficult to realize in classroom learning contexts. Technology may also foster the development of a positive attitude towards autonomous language use (Reinders and White, 2010). For instance, technological platforms, such as concordance, digital storytelling sites and social networking tools, also provide safe environments for learners' – even for beginners – creative language use, for their experimentation with various strategic decisions and behaviours, and for their multi-identity development.

Technology also brings new layers of meaning to the goals of autonomy. In terms of *autonomy as language learner*, the goal is to develop not only learners' capacity to manage the direction and process of their learning but also their ability to attune themselves to learning opportunities afforded in various formal and informal contexts and to perceive, employ and coordinate these affordances in different contexts to construct a personalized learning experience (Benson, 2013; Reinders and White, 2010). For the goal of *autonomy as person*, technology brings new elements to what self-expression and social responsibility entail. Meyers and colleagues (2013) argued that in the age of social media and Web 2.0 services, self-expression contains the elements of an active, reflective 'participatory creator' (p. 362) of digital contents to shape and redefine the status quo. Furthermore, digital creation carries the social responsibility for actively engaging in mashups or other forms of creative use of digital contents and 'for maintaining connectability' (p. 363) by offering opportunities for alternation, extension and mashups by others.

Technology and concepts associated with autonomy

Technology may strengthen the link between some concepts and autonomous learning. One oft-discussed concept is identity. Sackey et al. (2015) argued that informal learning with technology 'deepens the importance of identity to learning' (p. 115). On the one hand, such learning is heavily influenced by learners' identity. Fleckenstein (2005) talked about how the spatial distances and 'facelessness' that characterize technology-mediated interactions may challenge online identity construction, which may influence learners' investment and persistence in autonomous learning behaviours in technology-mediated environments. On the other hand, technology imposes demands on the construction of new types of identities. For instance, social technologies such as social networking tools and online communities 'privilege a type of discourse based on the construction and representation of personal and shared identities' that break 'the boundaries between private and public spheres' (Maranto and Barton, 2010, p. 43). It has also been argued that technology facilitates learners' exercise of agency. According to Barron (2006), learning beyond the classroom is often interest based, and the role that agency plays in informal learning is to create learning opportunities by pursuing interests and developing human relationships and to seek material resources to support the pursuit of those interests. Social technological tools allow the proliferation of interest-based communities and boost and support learners' agentic actions in engaging in interest-based learning beyond the classroom (Barron, 2010).

Thus, technology has much to bring to the arena of autonomous language learning beyond the classroom. For one thing, it provides optimal conditions and venues for autonomous learning. For another, it redefines what autonomous learning entails and introduces new elements into autonomous learning. In the section below, I will discuss various theoretical perspectives that could help shed light on how students interpret and make use of the affinity between technology and autonomous language learning beyond the classroom.

Theoretical perspectives in understanding autonomous language learning with technology beyond the classroom

Learners' autonomous language learning with technology beyond the classroom is a complex phenomenon that involves various aspects and dimensions and interactions thereof. Understanding this complex phenomenon relies on the theoretical insights from different research fields, including technology-enhanced learning, lifelong learning, informal learning and so on. This section will draw upon some relevant theoretical models from different research fields that could help researchers and educators to understand this phenomenon better.

Theories that help understand learners' learning experience

Benson (2009b) observed that students' learning experience involves 'a configuration of several settings' (p. 231), and it is hard to interpret the meaning of one setting without considering all the other settings in which learning may take place simultaneously. He argued that it is important to pay attention to 'the "ecology" of settings and modes of practices within the lives of language learners' (p. 233). The proposal to adopt an ecological perspective on learners' learning experience beyond the class has been reinforced in quite a few existent theoretical frameworks on students' learning experience (Barron, 2006; Hamilton, 2013; Luckin, 2010).

Hamilton's ecological perspective of autonomous learning behaviour in a technologically mediated environment

Hamilton (2013) advocated adopting an ecological approach to studying the relationship between technology and autonomy. He emphasized studying learner autonomy in any technologically mediated environment through exploring how the introduction of technology transforms the affordances of a learning environment and influences the totality of relationships in that environment. Affordance is a central concept of the ecological perspective on learner autonomy. Following Chemero's (2003) view that affordances should not be viewed as a property of an environment but as 'relations between the abilities of organisms and features of the environment' (p. 189), Hamilton emphasized that the totality of relationship is embodied in the ways individuals interact with one another and with physical resources in a technology-enhanced or technology-mediated environment. Moreover, this totality of relationships defines the affordances of technology for autonomous action because affordances are dependent on an organism's ability to perceive and take advantage of the totality of relations.

Hamilton's framework of autonomous learning behaviour conceptualizes that a learning environment consists of various activity spaces where learning takes place. Each activity space contains material, cultural and discursive resources and constraints that influence the relationships between individuals and the multidimensional ways in which they engage with one another within the space. The introduction of technology may reconfigure the social dynamics of the activity spaces and change the 'totality of relationships' between individuals, the affordances they appropriate and the language they use in the activity spaces. Hamilton (2013) conceptualized the relationship between autonomy and technology-mediated learning as follows: 1) learners have the potential for autonomous behaviour in technology-mediated contexts; 2) the provision of a well-resourced technological environment mediates potential 'proactive' and 'reactive' autonomy, but there is no guarantee that autonomous behaviours will occur naturally. Therefore, both technological design and learners' psychological reactions need to be taken into consideration when discussing the relationship between technology and autonomy; and 3) the technological element 'transforms the configuration of the learning environment, affecting how students respond to one another, altering the dimensions of affordances for learning, and influencing learners' use of language' (p. 217). Thus, Hamilton underscored the importance of focusing on the affordances reconfigured by technology in terms of learners' autonomous selective use of, or ignorance of, elements of the technological platform during their interaction with it and the nature of individuals' interactions with one another in the environments as they engaged with the technology-enhanced or technology-mediated contents. Consequently, adopting an ecological perspective on autonomous language learning requires a focus on learners' ability to create and perceive the affordances.

Hamilton's framework is helpful in understanding learners' autonomous interaction with technologies within any technological space, namely, how the technology-induced reconfiguration of the totality of relationship within technologically mediated spaces shape learners' autonomous learning behaviours with the technological and non-technological elements in those spaces.

Bennett and Maton's (2010) sociological view of learners' autonomous behaviours within a technologically mediated environment

Bennett and Maton (2010) proposed another perspective to understand learners' autonomous behaviours within any technologically mediated space. They introduced their sociological approach to understanding learners' autonomous interaction with technological resources out of their concern about the educational practice of blindly encouraging the use of more daily-life technologies in academic contexts to enhance the connection between learning across contexts. They argued that superficial adoption of everyday technologies in formal educational contexts may not bring the expected outcomes since the affordances of the technologies and the required skills and knowledge may change while transiting from one context to another. Thus, it is important and meaningful to understand 'what knowledge and assumptions students bring to academic contexts from other aspects of their lives, and what that means to teaching and learning' (p. 11), and to theorize 'the social practices and the forms of knowledge in different contexts' (p. 15).

Bennett and Maton adopted Bourdieu's concepts of 'field', 'capital' and 'habitus' to investigate the social nature of technology for learning and to shed light on learners' technological practices in different contexts. In Bourdieu's (1990) theory, people exist in multiple social fields of practices that have their respective agreed-upon conventions and ways of acting. Fields are structured systems of social networks within which individuals manoeuvre, and different fields have different objectified and embodied aspects (such as social values, ways of acting, interests and social status hierarchies) that mediate social practices. Capital refers to the status and resources that individuals possess and bring to their social participation in the fields. It encapsulates different forms of power, including economic, cultural, social or symbolic resources. Habitus refers to the dispositions (perceptions, values and practices) shaped by experiences that individuals carry across various social fields of practices or contexts. Individuals' habitus is structured by their past and present circumstances and experiences, and helps to shape their present and future perceptions and practices. Social agents' action in the field is critical to understanding individuals' habitus. Bourdieu (1986) summarized the relation of the three concepts as: '[(habitus) (capital)] + field = practice' (p. 101). The three components are interlocking, and individuals' practices and behaviours result from the interaction between an individual's dispositions, his or her material and symbolic assets, his or her position in the social arena and the features of the social fields (Maton, 2008). Thus, to understand learners' autonomous learning behaviours and practices within any technology-enhanced or technology-mediated environment, it is important to analyse the nature of the settings, examining the conventions and practices in the social field of practice, the capital that learners possess and bring to the social field of practice and the habitus that learners may carry with them to the social field. Furthermore, Bourdieu argued that when individuals move between fields, their success depends on whether their habitus and capital are congruent with the norms in the new field and on their ability to utilize and gain capital in the new field. Bourdieu's concepts of field, habitus and capital have been widely applied in research on learners' technological behaviours inside and outside the classroom. The concept of habitus has been used to study the relationship between digital choices and social class (North, Snyder and Bulfin, 2008) and to help examine individuals' current and future technology practices (Beckman, Bennett and Lockyer, 2014). The concept of capital has also been used to explain how family capital informs students' use of technologies for homework (Cranmer, 2006). Johnson (2009) also used Bourdieu's theory of field to investigate students' learning inside and outside the classroom and reveal the discrepancies between students' and educators' understanding of what constitutes learning and the role of technology in the learning process.

Bennett and Maton (2010) further proposed the use of Bernstein's (1999) concepts to theorize the forms of knowledge gained in different settings and students' relationships with technology at school and in their everyday lives. Bernstein differentiated 'horizontal discourse' from 'vertical discourse', and these different forms of knowledge vary in terms of the context specificity/dependency, embedment in social relations, degrees of affective loading and the structure and the coherency of the knowledge and practices. According to Bernstein, horizontal discourse refers to knowledge acquired in everyday life, which is fragmented and context specific, immediate goal oriented, life relevant, embedded in learners' ongoing practices and acquired in interactions with close and intimate social relations. Vertical discourse refers to knowledge acquired in educational settings, which is often coherent and systematic, context independent and explicit. Thus, the learning outcomes of technology use in different contexts may take different forms.

Bennett and Maton suggested that these two theoretical lenses should be used concurrently to provide useful information for conceptualizing 'which "everyday" technology-supported activities have most relevance for which forms of formal education, when, where, how and for which students' (p. 15). The sociological perspective they take could not only help educators understand learners' autonomous learning behaviours with technology within any technologically mediated space, but also enable them to compare technology use and outcomes across different learning contexts. Complementing Hamilton's ecological perspective, which highlights the totality of relationships within any technologically mediated space, Bennett and Maton's sociological approach enriches our understanding of the relationship between technology and autonomy by emphasizing the interaction between learners' capital and habitus and the social fields of practice within the spaces.

White's (2009) learner-context interface

White (2009) proposed yet another approach to examining learners' autonomous interaction with individual technological platforms. She proposed the learner-context interface theory to explain learners' autonomous learning in distance-learning contexts. The theory highlights a learner-centric view and posits that learning within a technology-enhanced or technology-mediated platform is an individual process whereby learners construct 'a personally meaningful and effective interface between themselves and the learning context' (p. 7). Thus, the integral interaction between the learning context and the learner is the essence of the relationship between technology and autonomy.

The theory consists of three dimensions: the learner, the context and the interface. The learner dimension refers to learners' beliefs, motivation, affect, skills and needs that influence how they perceive, relate to and respond to the learning context in order to construct a learning interface that is meaningful to them. Learners' learning experience at the interface in turn affects their beliefs, affect and identity. The context dimension includes not only the features of the platform and related learning sites but also the affordances and constraints individual learners perceive and respond to. The interface is the learning experience constructed through the dynamic interaction between the affordances of the learning context and the needs, preferences and abilities of the learner, which in turn informs and shapes future learning experience. Thus, the construction of the interface relies on learners' knowledge of themselves and of the affordances and constraints of the context, and is shaped by learners' metacognitive knowledge and beliefs in identifying, selecting and engaging with opportunities for interaction and learning. The construction of the interface involves the process of learners adjusting and adapting themselves to new roles and identities, and enhances metacognition. Furthermore, the construction of the interface is subject to the influence of individual attributes, the characteristics of the technological platform and the social, personal and learning environment.

White's learner interface theory complements the previous two perspectives by highlighting the role of the metacognitive process in learners' autonomous interaction within technologically mediated spaces and adopts a dynamic view of the interaction as an ongoing process of learners constantly adjusting and adapting to their changing roles and identities in the interaction.

Barron's (2006) learning ecology framework

Barron took a broader and more holistic approach to examining learners' autonomous behaviour in constructing their personalized learning ecology. Arguing that interest is the essence of self-initiated, self-sustaining learning, and that interest-based learning often spans different settings, Barron (2006) combined sociocultural and ecological theories of human development to develop a learning ecology framework that captures the developmental process of self-sustained learning and illustrates how learning is distributed across different settings and resources. This framework pre-assumes that individuals are simultaneously involved in multiple settings and are actively appropriating the resources distributed in various contexts to engage in interest-driven learning. It highlights interest as a trigger for students' self-directed learning beyond the classroom, and focuses on documenting the genesis of interest in learning (the pathways of participation – the kinds of events, activities and process), the strategic moves learners take to create activity contexts across settings and to construct their learning ecology, and the changes in their learning ecology as their learning transits through different settings.

Barron defined learning ecology as the set of physical or virtual contexts that provide opportunities for learning, with each context comprising a 'unique configuration of activities, material resources, relationships and the interactions that emerge from them' (Barron, 2006, p. 195). She further conceptualized a learning ecology as 'a dynamic entity that can be characterized by the diversity and depth of learning resources and activities' (p. 217). Barron's framework contains three conjectures: 1) Learners' interest in learning is triggered and sustained by a variety of ideational and relational resources that are available in a learning ecology, including ongoing activities of other people, interactions with social networks, books, computer programmes, assignments and so on, and can develop in different contexts. Therefore, the diversity of resources in one's learning ecology is critical to sparking off self-sustaining learning; 2) Once their interest is ignited, people employ a variety of strategies to create learning opportunities and further their development, such as seeking out informational resources, finding learning companions, creating new informal activity contexts, developing knowledge networks and so on; and 3) These interest-driven learning activities are boundary crossing, with interests originating in one context and being followed up in many other contexts, and there are 'fertile bi-directional flows of knowledge between contexts' (p. 218). The changing relationships between individuals and the social contexts contribute to boundary crossing. As a result, learners' identity development, engagement and competency development intertwine closely with one another.

Barron's learning ecology framework goes beyond analysing the nature of learners' autonomous interaction with technology within individual technological spaces to shed light on how learners coordinate and traverse different technological and non-technological spaces to construct their learning ecologies and engage in self-sustaining learning. This theoretical framework highlights the significant roles individuals play in sustaining their own knowledge and identity development, and helps identify critical factors and processes that make learning beyond the classroom self-sustaining. It also suggests an expanded view of outcomes, focusing on the potential of educational experience for preparing students for future learning and on its contribution to competency development. This theoretical framework calls for research work on the configurations of people, ideational resources and activities in learners' interest development, taking into account learners' prior history and sense of self. It also highlights the interconnections between formal learning experience and informal learning experience, and calls for research to unravel various strategic moves that learners engage in across settings to sustain their interest-driven learning. Barron (2006) further suggests using it as a framework for the design and evaluation of intervention programmes that focus on supporting informal learning through developing interest.

Luckin's (2010) ecology of resources framework

Luckin's (2010) framework also theorizes learners' construction of an ecology of learning but with a specific focus on the support mechanisms that help them to make use of the different resource elements and interactions that contribute to their construction of the ecology of learning. Her ecology of resources model discusses how to design educational experiences to help learners be aware of and select the various forms of assistance available in their environments so as to construct a personalized learning experience that meets their learning needs.

According to Luckin (2008), an ecology of resources is 'a set of inter-related resource elements, including people and objects, the interactions between which provide a particular context' (p. 451). The *zone of collaboration* is the essence of the ecology of resources and refers to learner appropriation of assistances in one's environment. It is 'the relationship between the identification of a learner's collaborative capability and the specification of the assistance that needs to be offered to the learner in order for them to succeed at a particular task' (Luckin, 2010, p. 28). This *zone of collaboration* is full of forms of assistance that, depending on learners' capabilities, their motivation and their understanding of their own knowledge and competency, could potentially be utilized as resources to support learning. The *zone of collaboration* consists of the *zone of available assistance* (ZAA) and the *zone of proximal adjustment* (ZPA). The ZAA refers to the resources that are available to learners at particular points in time, and the ZPA refers to the subset of resources that are actually appropriated by the learners to meet their needs. The resources that comprise the ZAA include the knowledge and skills to be learned, the tools, the people who know more about this knowledge and these skills, and the environment – physical or virtual – with which learners interact. According to this model, learners are surrounded by various resources that could potentially provide assistance, of varying degrees, to their learning (ZAA). Within these resources, there are subsets that are appropriate to the learner's needs at different stages of development (ZPA). Learners actively construct these resource subsets to meet their learning needs (the move from ZAA to ZPA) through an active negotiation process filtered positively or negatively by the enablers or constraints around them. The filters include the 'more able partners' (e.g. teachers, parents, peers, technological tools) and their inherent characteristics and cultural roles, and learners' cognitive, affective, metacognitive and epistemological resources such as their learning motivations, epistemological beliefs, history of experience and so on. These filters and the interactions between them affect learners' interactions with the various elements in the ecology.

Luckin's (2010) ecology of resources model builds on Barron's concept of learning ecology to focus on the internal and external factors and processes that mediate learners' construction of their learning ecologies. It highlights the identification of the elements of resources available to learners and the filters and interactions that facilitate or constrain their utilization of these resources. Luckin proposed this framework to map out the complexity of learner-centric contexts. Based on the ecology of resources model, Luckin (2010) further developed the ecology of resources design framework, which helps to situate and 'support the dynamic process of developing technology-rich learning activities' that 'take a learner's wider context into account' (Luckin et al., 2013, p. 36). This framework consists of three phases. Phase 1 involves identifying the forms of assistances that could act as resources for learning and the filters and their potential interactions. Phase 2 involves identifying the relationships within and between the resources and their suitability with learners' needs. Phase 3 involves developing the scaffolds and adjustments to support learning and enable the conversion of ZAA into ZPA. This framework is useful in guiding the development of support mechanisms to facilitate learners' construction of a learning ecology.

Wong's (2012) learner-centric view of mobile seamless learning

The above theoretical frameworks help explain how learners interact with technology-mediated contexts to construct personalized learning experiences and how they can utilize resources distributed across different settings to create their own ecology of learning. In addition to these frameworks, there are also other theoretical frameworks that could add to our understanding of learners' construction of seamless learning experience across different contexts. Wong's (2012) learner-centric view of mobile seamless learning is one such example.

Focusing specifically on the seamless integration of learning experiences across different contexts, scenarios and formats mediated by personal mobile devices, Wong and Looi (2011) and Wong (2012) identified ten dimensions that delineate what 'seamlessness' in mobile-assisted seamless learning (MSL) entails. Among the ten dimensions, two stress the connection of learning experiences across temporal (MSL3) and spatial (MSL4) aspects. Three dimensions pertain to the 'learning space' aspect: the seamlessness of formal and informal learning (MSL1); the seamlessness of personalized and social learning (MSL2); and the seamlessness of the physical and digital worlds (MSL6). A further three dimensions are related to the connection of facilitating resources and experiences that learners have access to in both formal and informal contexts to construct knowledge: the ubiquitous access to and utilization of learning resources acquired in different places – both teacher supplied and learner self-initiated (MSL5); the multiplicity of pedagogical or learning models that are facilitated by the teachers (MSL10); and the connections between multiple learning tasks (MSL8). Two last dimensions emphasize the connections and integration of different learning resources, experiences and knowledge: learners integrate all the personal learning tools, resources and self-created artefacts and selectively take advantage of their affordances to construct a personalized learning hub to support learning (MSL7); and learners synthesize prior and newly acquired knowledge and multiple skills across disciplines (MSL9).

Wong (2012) further derived a model of mobile seamless learning from the learner's perspective – learners construct knowledge through perpetual learning across contexts – to illustrate the relationship between these ten dimensions. In this model, connections across time (MSL3) and across locations (MSL4) are two universal dimensions that encompass all the other eight dimensions. MSL5 and MSL10 are facilitating resources that learners acquire in formal and informal contexts to facilitate their performance and seamless switch between multiple learning tasks (MSL8), which leads to knowledge synthesis (MSL9). MSL9 may then feed back to MSL 8 and initiate subsequent learning activities. The three dimensions of the learning spaces – informal/formal (MSL1), social/individual (MSL2) and physical/virtual (MSL6) – represent the continuum of learning contexts where the learning experiences and facilitating resources reside. The ultimate goal of seamless learning is not only to achieve knowledge synthesis but also to develop the habits and skills for seamless learning.

Wong's learner-centric mobile seamless learning model identifies various dimensions that could be used to examine how learners identify, seize and connect the technology-mediated opportunities and resources for learning that abound in their daily living spaces to bridge their learning experience across both formal and informal learning contexts. The model could also be utilized to guide the set-up of instructional arrangements and the provision of support mechanisms to realize seamless learning.

Emirbayer and Mische's (1998) temporal view of agency

The various theoretical models discussed above touched lightly, if any, on the temporal dimensions of learning ecology construction. For instance, Barron (2006) pointed out that the construction of a learning ecology is an ongoing process in response to different stages of interest development. Luckin (2010) noted that the construction of the ZPA is subject to learners' needs at different times of development, while Wong (2012) regarded learning across time as an overarching dimension of seamless learning. However, none of these models gave a detailed account of the temporal dimensions of the relationship between technology and autonomy.

Emirbayer and Mische's (1998) temporal view of agency could help enhance our understanding of the influence of temporal dimensions on learners' interactions with technological spaces and their construction of learning ecologies. Emirbayer and Mische defined agency as 'a temporally embedded process of social engagement informed by the past (in its habitual aspect), but also oriented toward the future (as a capacity to imagine alternative possibilities) and toward the present (as a capacity to contextualize past habits and future projects with contingencies of the moment)' (p. 963). They introduced the concept of 'the chordal triad of agency' (p. 970), which consists of three elements: 1) the iterational element, which refers to learners' selective reactions to 'past patterns of thought and action'; 2) the projective element, which refers to learners' vision of the future projection of the action in relation to their expectations, desires and fears for the future; and 3) the practical-evaluative element, which refers to learners' evaluative judgements and decision-making with respect to several alternative routes of action. Emirbayer and Mische pointed out that all three temporal elements exert influence – although in varying degrees – on an individual's decision-making concerning agentic actions, and that these three elements may exert dissonant influences on agentic behaviours, with one's temporal orientation usually dominating in any given situation. Moreover, the 'chordal composition' is relational and may change as learners react to different situations and environments.

Thus, Emirbayer and Mische's (1998) temporal view of agency elaborated on and shed useful insights into how different temporal dimensions might work together to affect both learners' autonomous interaction with individuals' technologically mediated spaces and their construction of learning ecologies.

Theories that help explain the factors affecting learners' technological experience

Understanding the factors that affect learners' technological experience is critical since it helps explain the variations that exist in language learners' autonomous use of technology for learning (Lai and Gu, 2011; Winke and Goetler, 2008), and also helps identify areas of support that educators could provide to foster autonomous language learning with technology. There are a few theoretical frameworks that can provide insights.

Technology adoption models

Autonomous learning with technology involves individuals' decision-making in regard to technology adoption. The theory of planned behaviour by Ajzen (1985; 2005) has been commended for explaining individual behavioural intentions. This theory builds on the theory of reasoned action by Fishbein and Ajzen (1975), which stipulates that individuals' behavioural intentions are predicted by their attitudes (i.e. perceived usefulness and enjoyment) towards the given behaviour and the subjective norm (i.e. social influence and expectations) associated with a behaviour. The theory of planned behaviour acknowledges the predictive power of the two components posited in the theory of reasoned action – attitude and subjective norm – but includes an additional construct: perceived behavioural control, (i.e. a user's perceived control in performing a given behaviour). This construct has two underlying determinants: control beliefs and perceived facilitation. Control beliefs refer to perceived availability of capacities and opportunities. Perceived facilitation refers to the perceived availability of resources and support to achieve a given outcome. Thus, the theory of planned behaviour hypothesizes that attitude, subjective norm and perceived behavioural control work together to predict an individual's behavioural intentions, which in turn predict individual behaviours.

Two technology adoption models, Davis's (1989) technology acceptance model (TAM) model and Venkatesh and colleagues' (2003) united theory of acceptance and use of technology (UTAUT) model, build on the theory of planned behaviour and elaborate on the components of each construct in the context of technology adoption and conceptualize the interactions of these variables in predicting individuals' technology adoption behaviours. These two models have been found to work well in explaining teacher and student adoption of technology in educational contexts (McGill and Klobas, 2009; Šumak, Polancic and Hericko, 2010; Teo, 2009; Teo and Schaik, 2012). The TAM model includes three attitudinal factors that explain an individual's intention to adopt any given technological solution: perceived usefulness, perceived ease of use and attitude towards technology. Perceived usefulness is 'the degree to which a person believes that using a particular system would enhance his or her job performance' (Davis, 1989, p. 320). Perceived ease of use refers to 'the degree to which a person believes that using a particular system would be free of effort' (p. 320). Attitude towards behaviour is 'an individual's positive or negative feelings (evaluative affect) about performing the target behavior' (Fishbein and Ajzen, 1975, p. 216). This model hypothesizes that perceived usefulness and perceived ease of use influence users' behavioural intentions through attitude towards behaviour. Perceived ease of use also influences perceived usefulness.

Integrating TAM and several other prominent technology acceptance models, UTAUT has been validated in predicting technology adoption in various organizational contexts, including instructional contexts (Taiwo and Downe, 2013; Williams, Rana and Dwivedi, 2015). The UTAUT model includes four endogenous variables: *performance expectancy* (i.e. a user's expectation regarding the efficacy of the technological solution in enhancing performance), *effort expectancy* (i.e. a user's expectation concerning the efforts needed in using the technological solution), *social influence* (i.e. a user's perception concerning the social pressure to adopt the technological solution), and *facilitating conditions* (i.e. a user's perception of the support available to use the technological solution). Performance expectancy, effort expectancy and social influence are conceptualized to influence users' intentions to adopt technological solutions, which in turn predict usage behaviours. Also, facilitating conditions are hypothesized to influence usage behaviours both directly and indirectly through users' intentions to adopt. Venkatesh et al. (2012) further suggest adding *price value* (i.e. the cognitive trade-off between the perceived benefits of technology behaviour and the monetary costs), *hedonic motivation* (i.e. user-perceived enjoyment of technology use), and *habit* (i.e. the extent to which users automatically engage in the technological behaviour) into the model in the context of individual consumer use of technology. It is hypothesized that hedonic motivation and price value influence usage behaviours through users' intentions to adopt technological solutions, and habit predicts usage behaviours both directly and indirectly through users' intention to adopt.

Existent technology adoption models can be used to identify the critical factors that influence language learners' autonomous use of technology for learning and to unravel the intricate interactions among these factors. More importantly, researchers point out that despite the usefulness of the TPB in explaining an individual's acceptance of technology, the underlying structures of and psychological antecedents to its key constructs are context- and domain specific (Straub, 2009; Venkatesh, Davis and Morris, 2007). Thus, it is essential to unravel the antecedents to the key determinants of autonomous technology adoption for language learning. The literature on autonomous language learning can offer insights into factors that are critical to this domain and the relationships thereof. Mercer (2011) points out that autonomous language-learning behaviour is contingent on 'a learner's sense of agency involving their belief systems, and the control parameters of motivation, affect, metacognitive/self-regulatory skills, as well as actual abilities and the affordances, actual and perceived in specific settings' (p. 9). Thus, to Mercer, autonomous behaviour is a product of the interaction between individual psychological factors and contextual characteristics. This view is concurred in several models of autonomous learning (Weinstein, Woodruff and Awalt, 2002; Winnie and Hadwin, 1998). Individual psychological factors include learner motivation, learner beliefs, dispositions and styles, knowledge of learning strategies, skills and so on, while contextual characteristics include the context of learning, resources, time, teacher influence and so on. Thus, this body of literature could serve as a frame of reference for identifying various key factors and relationships within and across these two categories that may influence language learners' autonomous use of technology for learning.

Social network theories

Today's learners are networked individuals who are connected not only with various community networks in their immediate surroundings but also with geographically dispersed virtual communities (Castells, 2001). Learners' interactions in different social networks shape their learning and development. Social network is of particular importance in the context of autonomous learning beyond the classroom, and its impact deserves special attention. Highlighting the characteristics of informal learning as being interest based, Barron (2010) deemed it important to understand how learners develop and sustain engagement across settings, time and networks of support. She further asserted that the focus on engagement accentuates learning as a process of becoming, and thus memberships in affinity groups are particularly relevant. Consequently, Barron (2010) argued for 'a key role for persons in learners' social networks who can serve as learning partners that bridge contexts, settings, and learning opportunities and support interest and identity development' (p. 115). Similarly, Palfreyman (2011) pointed out: 'Understanding the patterns and nature of the different relationships in an individual's network will help us to understand what s/he has to work with in learning beyond the classroom' (p. 33). Thus, in the context of autonomous learning beyond the classroom, it is important to refer to social network theories to understand the social factors that affect learners' autonomous technology use for learning.

Social network theories can help conceptualize how social factors could influence learners' autonomous learning with technology beyond the classroom. Social network theories view people as living within networks of relationships and regard human actions as facilitated or constrained by their social networks (Palfreyman, 2011). Krackhardt and Hanson (1993) distinguished three types of relationship networks: 'advice networks', 'trust networks' and 'communication networks'. Palfreyman (2011) argued that these three types of relationship networks could serve different functions in supporting learning beyond the classroom. The advice networks share guidance and advice for action, the trust networks afford venues for emotion sharing and help seeking and the communication networks provide opportunities for learners to discuss and clarify the learning process. An associated concept of social network is social capital. Social capital refers to the resources accrued by learners through their relationships with others (Coleman, 1988), as well as the norms, relationships and trusts that facilitate action (Putnam, 1993). The shape of the social network determines the availability of social capital and the kinds of support that it could provide to individuals. It is argued that networks with weak ties or bridging social capital (i.e. lots of loose connections) lend themselves to providing new ideas and useful information to their members, but not emotional support (Putnam, 2000). Networks with strong ties or bonding social capital are a good venue for emotional support and bonding (Putnam, 2000). Technology and social capital have a reciprocal relationship. On the one hand, technology – the internet in particular – can not only broaden learners' bridging social capital and afford the establishment of new forms of social capital and relationship building, but also affect bonding social capital (Bargh and McKenna, 2004; Resnick, 2001). On the other hand, learners' bonding and bridging social capital may influence their access to technological ideas and support for learning and the intensity of their engagement in such activities.

Thus, social network theories could provide in-depth insights into the influence of social forces on autonomous technology use for learning beyond the classroom, delineating the influences of different types of social network and associated social capital. These theories could also help conceptualize how social capitals could be utilized to support autonomous learning with technology beyond the classroom.

Theories that help explain the development of autonomous learning with technology

Educational research has two major purposes: to document a particular phenomenon and to come up with interventions to improve the phenomenon. In terms of autonomous language learning with technology, on the one hand, educators are interested in charting out this less explored terrain to understand learners' autonomous learning behaviours with technology, and on the other hand, they hope to enhance learners' technological experience. There are a few theoretical models that could inform their intervention endeavours.

Self-regulated learning models

Self-regulated learning refers to learners' utilization of strategies to control their cognition, motivation, behaviour and emotions in order to achieve various learning, performance and avoidance goals (Panadero and Alonso-Tapia, 2014). Self-regulated theories theorize how various cognitive, motivational and contextual factors influence the learning process (Greene and Azevedo, 2007). The current literature contains two types of self-regulated learning models that reflect different perspectives on self-regulated learning: component models and process models.

Component models highlight learning strategies and regard them as learner traits. Boekaerts's (1999) and Pintrich's (2000) self-regulation models are two widely accepted component models. Boekaerts's (1999) model underscored the influence of three kinds of information on learners' appraisal that directs their learning behaviours. The three aspects include the cognitive (i.e. conceptual and procedural knowledge and perception of the learning situation), the metacognitive (i.e. the learning process and learners' knowledge and skills to regulate this process) and the motivational (i.e. learners' goals, needs and expectancies) aspects of self-regulation. Motivational regulation influences learners' metacognitive regulation, which in turn affects cognitive regulation. There are corresponding self-regulation strategies for each aspect. Cognitive strategies include organization, elaboration and problem-solving strategies. Metacognitive strategies include planning, monitoring and evaluation strategies. Motivational strategies include resource management, causal attribution, action control and feedback. Pintrich (2000) further pointed out that self-regulation involves four key aspects: cognition, motivation, behaviour and context. The cognition aspect includes goal management, metacognitive knowledge, dynamic metacognitive judgements, adapting and adjusting cognitive activities and self-evaluation. The motivation aspect refers to the awareness, management and constant adjustment of goal orientations, self-efficacy, interest, task value, emotions and causal attributions. The behavioural aspect includes time and effort management and adjustment, persistence, help seeking and so on. The context aspect refers to learners' perceptions, evaluation and monitoring of the task and context, and their efforts to eliminate or reduce distractions and renegotiate task requirements. Moreover, Pintrich conceptualized that the specific components of the four aspects may vary at different stages of self-regulation (forethought, monitoring, control and reaction and reflection).

Process models conceptualize self-regulated learning as both personal attributes and an event. Winnie and colleagues' four-stage model describes self-regulated learning as an event (Winnie and Hardwin, 1998; Winne and Perry, 2000). The four sequential stages include task definition, goal setting and planning, enacting tactics and strategies and adaptation of future study techniques. Each stage contains the same general structure: conditions, operations, products, evaluations and standards. Conditions refer to both task conditions (i.e. available resources, social contexts, time constraints) and cognitive conditions (i.e. interest, task knowledge, goal orientation). Operations are the processes of utilizing tactics and strategies during the task. Products are the outcomes of operations. Evaluations comprise internal and external feedback on the products. Standards are the criteria used to evaluate the products. Zimmerman (2000) further conceptualized self-regulation as a cyclical process in which metacognitive and motivational processes and beliefs interact in successive feedback cycles. Zimmerman and colleagues (Schunk and Zimmerman, 1997; Zimmerman, 2000) proposed a four-stage developmental model to illustrate the development of self-regulatory skills and strategies. At the first stage, the observation level, learners induce a skill through observing more capable agents' behaviours; at the second stage, the emulation level, learners perform the skill with the assistance from peers and more capable agents; at the third stage, the self-control level, learners practice the skill independently, without receiving any assistance; and at the fourth stage, the self-regulated level, learners make adjustments to the skill in response to the outcome. Zimmerman (2000) further proposed a three-phase cyclical model that threads together the four developmental stages. Phase I is the forethought phase, which corresponds with the observation level. At this phase, the focus is to get learners cognitively and motivationally prepared for the activities and to help them set the goals and plan strategies for them. Phase II is the performance control phase, which targets the emulative and the self-control level. At this phase, learners perform the activities, and self-instruct and -monitor their progress. Phase III is the self-reflection phase, which corresponds with the self-regulation level. At this phase, learners evaluate their performance against the goals they set, and adjust their strategies based on the evaluation.

The above models contribute to an understanding of self-regulation processes during events but yield limited information on how educators can facilitate the development of self-regulation. To understand the facilitation of this development, greater attention needs to be given to the social aspects of the regulation of learning (Hadwin and Oshige, 2011). Hadwin and Oshige (2011) reviewed the current perspectives on the interaction of individual and social factors in developing self-regulated learning. According to them, there are three perspectives: *the self-regulated learning perspective, the co-regulated learning perspective* and *the socially shared regulation perspective. The self-regulated learning perspective* focuses on learners becoming strategic learners through active monitoring and regulation of different aspects of their learning process. In this perspective, the social context is considered an independent variable that could work to facilitate individuals' strategy repertoire and utilization. This perspective is represented in Cleary and Zimmerman's (2004) self-regulation empowerment programme (SREP), which suggests first assessing students' study strategies and motivation and then increasing their self-awareness and self-efficacy through engaging them in self-recording their strategies. This is followed by tutors demonstrating and verbalizing context-specific strategies and students practising the modelled strategies. The programme ends with the examination of the cyclical process of strategy exercise. *The co-regulated learning perspective* emphasizes that self-regulated learning is appropriated during the interaction between learners and their more capable partners. This perspective accentuates that the activities, engagement and mutual relationships in the learning context shape co-regulation (McCaslin, 2009). *The socially shared regulation perspective* stresses the processes whereby multiple others regulate the learners' collective activity. For instance, Yowell and Smylie (1999) conceptualized the development of self-regulated learning as residing at the microsystem level (in interpersonal interactions through scaffolding and intersubjectivity), the mesosystem level (interactions between individuals and their immediate environment such as friends and their schools that connect them with other microsystems), and the exosystem level, where the sociocultural values and norms afford and constrain the development.

These self-regulation models provide important information on the various aspects and processes involved in autonomous learning. Educators and researchers can use these models to inform the construction, implementation and evaluation of intervention programmes aimed at enhancing learners' autonomous learning with technology beyond the classroom.

Hubbard's (2004) CALL learner-training principles

Building on the cyclical self-regulated learning model, Hubbard (2004) proposed a learner-training framework in the context of computer-assisted language learning (CALL). His CALL learner-training framework consists of five practice-based principles. The framework underscores learner centricity in the training process and language-specific technological knowledge in the training components. The five principles include 1) trainers experiencing CALL themselves; 2) giving learners teacher training and enhancing their knowledge of language-learning models and principles; 3) using a progressive, cyclical approach that gives learners a chance to explore before detailed training; 4) using collaborative debriefings; and 5) teaching exploitation strategies that are specific to language learning.

Hubbard accentuated going beyond equipping students with general computer literacy and taking a more domain-dependent approach. He conceptualized that the cognitive and metacognitive components should be more than just general computer literacy and/or lists of technological resources available; rather, these components should feature learners' cognitive and metacognitive knowledge and skills concerning the contextualized 'pedagogical' application of various technologies and an awareness of the psychological and social factors involved (i.e. the interaction between technology, metacognitive knowledge and content). Mishra and Koehler's (2006) technological pedagogical content knowledge framework (TPACK) serves as a useful theoretical framework in defining the technological knowledge learner's need. This framework was developed in the context of teacher-technology adoption and specifies the levels of knowledge teachers need to possess for the effective integration of technology into teaching. The essence of the framework is that knowledge about technology cannot be treated as context-free but should be related to and interact with an understanding of the pedagogy and the specific learning content. Although this approach was developed to delineate the essential knowledge and skills for technology integration into instruction, it applies just as well to promoting learner integration of technology for learning. The metacognitive technological content knowledge learners need for active and effective use of technology for learning should include an understanding of the useful technologies that permeate their everyday lives, the ability to judge what technology to use for what particular learning needs and to benefit what particular language skills, knowledge of the cognitive and socio-affective factors and processes involved in the use of a particular technology or technologies for the various learning purposes, and how to use a particular technology or technologies in ways that maximize their claimed potential for a particular learning content, purpose and need.

This chapter has introduced some theoretical frameworks that might provide useful insights into understanding the different facets of autonomous language learning with technology beyond the classroom. The theoretical frameworks introduced here are far from being a comprehensive list; rather they are examples of a potential theoretical lens for a better understanding of the phenomenon. For organizational purposes, these frameworks are categorized under different facets of autonomous technology use for learning. However, this does not mean that the categorization is mutually exclusive. Theoretical frameworks categorized under one facet could and should be used to shed light on the other facets so as to gain a well-rounded understanding of the complexity of the issue.

Figure 2.1 conceptualizes a framework of out-of-class autonomous language learning with technology in terms of the various spaces with which it interacts and the dynamic relationships in which it is situated. The out-of-class technological spaces consist of various technological fields that interact with each other. Within each technological field, the package of dispositions, capacities, past experiences and future aspirations that learners bring with them interact with the social relationships that are embodied in the field and the sociocultural practices that are associated with technology in shaping learners' interaction with the technology. Learners' interaction with technology is also shaped by the various internal and external aspects of autonomy. This interaction is further constrained or enabled by the interaction of one technological field with others within the out-of-class technological spaces. Learners' coordinated interaction with the various technological fields within the out-of-class technological spaces is further influenced by the non-technological spaces that are available outside the classroom, and this influence is bi-directional. The availability of

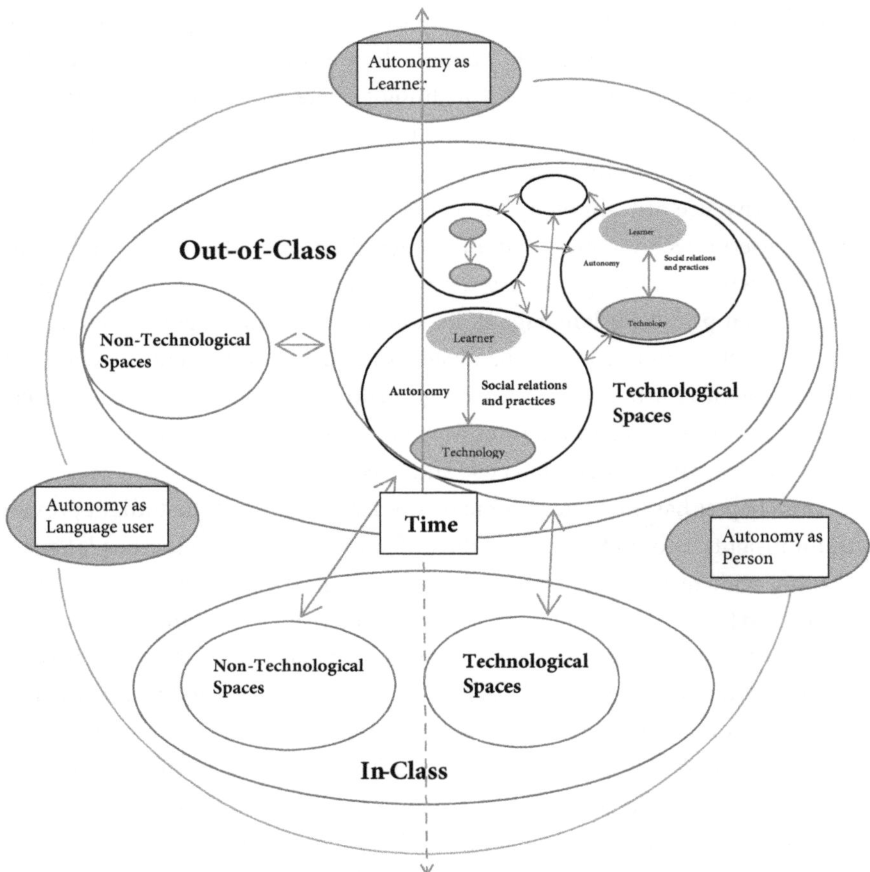

Figure 2.1 Theoretical framework of autonomous language learning with technology beyond the classroom.

physical and human target-language resources outside the classroom can shape learners' selection and use of technological resources for learning, which in turn can influence their selection and use of these physical and human resources. Learners' construction of out-of-class technological spaces is further shaped by the constituents and conditions of the technological and non-technological spaces (such as pedagogical practices) inside the classroom, and, at the same time, influences their expectations concerning the configurations and situation of the technological and non-technological spaces thereof. Thus, the construction of out-of-class autonomous language learning with technology is relational and interactive, characterized by the intertwining relationships of learners' psychological, affective and cognitive resources, and the affordances and social interactions within and across various technological and non-technological spaces both inside and outside the classroom.

In addition, the construction of out-of-class autonomous language learning with technology is a dynamic and evolves in response to the over-time changes in technological and non-technological spaces inside and outside the classroom and the interactions thereof, the changes in learners' dispositions and capacities, and the changes in social relationships and practices within technological spaces and their interaction with learners' dispositions and capacities. Moreover, the ultimate outcomes of out-of-class autonomous language learning with technology are autonomy as language users, autonomy as learners and autonomy as persons.

3

The Nature of Out-of-Class Autonomous Language Learning with Technology

Understanding the nature of learning is the key focus of educational research. However, research on learning has primarily taken place in instructional contexts. Realizing that language learning more and more frequently takes place in out-of-school contexts, Benson (2009b) called for researchers to go beyond the predominant focus on understanding learning that takes place in instructional contexts to map out the terrain of language learning beyond the classroom. He advocated research efforts to document the nature of different settings and the learning processes they each support. Since then, an increasing number of research studies have been dedicated to charting the landscape of autonomous language learning with technology beyond the classroom, eliciting language learners' accounts of their out-of-school practices and their construction of personalized learning ecologies with technology, and analysing the efficacies of learner-generated learning ecologies.

The nature of autonomous out-of-class language learning with technology

Learner engagement in technology-mediated autonomous language learning

The use of technology to engage in autonomous language learning beyond the classroom has been found to be a common phenomenon among K–12 and university students, although the frequency of student engagement in such activities varies. For instance, Swedish upper-primary-school

English-as-a-foreign-language (EFL) learners have been found to spend around seven hours a week engaged in English-related computer use (Sundqvist and Sylvén, 2014), while a study of lower-secondary-school EFL learners in China found that the learners spent an average of 2.21 hours each week using technological platforms and tools to explore extra English-language learning opportunities and resources beyond the classroom (Lai, Zhu and Gong, 2015). Furthermore, 90 per cent of the 374 Flemish sixth-grade EFL learners who participated in Kuppens's (2010) study reported listening to English music at least three times a week, more than half of them reported watching subtitled English TV programmes at least three times a week, and 58 per cent of them reported visiting English websites at least once a week. Thus, primary and secondary school students in different parts of the world are using technologies, to a varying degree, to support their language learning. Similar phenomena were observed among the tertiary students. Lai and Gu (2011) studied HK undergraduate foreign-language students' self-initiated and self-directed use of technology for learning, and noted that 54 per cent of the participants reported spending more than four hours a week using technologies for language learning outside the classroom. Another study of a similar population in Hong Kong reported that learners spent an average of 1–3 hours a week on autonomous use of technology for language learning beyond the classroom (Lai, 2013). In a survey study conducted among 225 university students in France, only two students reported that they did not access English online in their free time at all. Sixty per cent of the participants reported regularly watching films and TV series, and thirty per cent reported regularly corresponding with English users on Facebook (Toffoli and Sockett, 2010). Thus, language learners are using technologies for language learning outside classrooms on their own, and the frequency of their technology use ranges from as much as fourteen hours a week or more to as little as less than one hour a week (Lai, 2013; Lai and Gu, 2011; Sundqvist and Sylvén, 2014; Wong and Nunan, 2011).

Researchers have also documented the type or dimension of learning that learners use technology to support during their autonomous language learning beyond the classroom. In a survey study I conducted with 681 university foreign-language learners in Hong Kong, the United States and China on their use of technology in the target language and for language learning beyond the classroom, the learners responded most positively on their use of technology for instructional purpose (M = 4.23, SD = 0.89; 6-point Likert scale with 6 indicating strongly agree). Thus, they responded positively on using technology to help them to memorize the vocabulary and grammar learned in class and to engage in individual learning. They responded less positively on the use of technology for entertainment and information purposes (M = 4.13, SD = 0.93), including using the language to pursue personal interests and for everyday life purposes. Also, the participants responded the least positively on their use of technology for social connection purposes (M = 3.61, SD = 1.20), such as communicating with native speakers or other learners of the target language and using technologies to engage in social learning. This finding on the learners' limited use of technology for social purposes corroborated the findings from Lai and Gu's (2011) survey study of 279 HK university foreign-language learners, in which the learners reported positive perceptions, and actual use, of technology to regulate goal commitment, learning resources, cultural learning and their emotion and motivation (i.e. persevering, despite obstacles, to fulfil language-learning goals, expanding and enriching their language-learning resources, maintaining interest in learning the language, etc.). However, their responses concerning the use of technology to connect with native speakers and to seek help from peers around the world were the least positive and showed the most variation among all the technology-use categories.

Researchers have further found that autonomous language learning with technology beyond the classroom is characterized by being emergent, interest-based, predominantly receptive and involving a heavy proportion of incidental learning. Cabot's (2014) case studies of six upper-secondary-school students in Western Norway revealed that the students' out-of-class English-language learning with technology was often of an implicit or incidental nature. Similarly, Jones (2015) reported that adult Welsh learners tended to engage in a lot of creative and opportunistic use of mobile devices while multitasking and during small, emergent periods of time. Furthermore, several studies (Ekşî and Aydin, 2013; Hyland, 2004) found that most of the activities that language learners engaged in outside the classroom were of a receptive nature. The predominance of such receptive activities has been confirmed by studies in various contexts, including among upper-secondary-school English-language learners in Sweden (Larsson, 2012), upper-secondary-school EFL learners in Japan (Barbee, 2013), primary and secondary school students in Spain (Olmedo, 2015), and university foreign-language learners in France, Cyprus, Turkey and Hong Kong (Çelik, Arkin and Sabriler, 2012; Ekşî and Aydin, 2013; Toffoli and Sockett, 2010; Wu, 2012). In these studies, watching online movies and videos and listening to music were the most popular activities reported by learners. For instance, Çelik, Arkin and Sabriler (2012) found that Cyprus university EFL learners in their study engaged more frequently in activities such as watching movies, reading books, magazines and newspapers and listening to music, and that they engaged the least in communicating with people using chat programmes. Ekşî and Aydin (2013) found that Istanbul university students in their study reported listening to music and watching films the most frequently. They also reported a high frequency of dictionary use and video and TV viewing. On the other hand, engaging in speaking (e.g. online chatting) and writing (e.g. emails, writing stories) were least frequently reported. Wu (2012) surveyed HK English-as-a-second-language (ESL) learners on their out-of-class language-learning activities and found that listening (e.g. watching films/news/TV, listening to songs/radio channels) and reading were the two most frequent categories of activities, accounting for about 60 per cent of the total number of activities the learners engaged in. The participants reported engaging in limited activities related to speaking and writing. Similar research findings were reported in Toffoli and Sockett's (2010) survey study among 222 French university EFL students. More than half of the participants claimed to listen to English at least once a week, and their online listening activities included not only listening to music but also watching TV series in English. Around 25 per cent of the participants reported that they read English on the web at least once a week, with the most frequent context for reading being social networking sites. Although the participants did report engaging in writing on the web, these writing activities were generally very short and personal and often involved commenting on others' posts. They seldom participated in thematic forums; hence their writing was rarely informative. In terms of speaking, the participants very rarely took advantage of verbal interaction in English on the internet. In another study conducted in the French context, Bailly (2010) initiated a language-advising programme in several French high schools whereby students studied selected foreign languages without formal language instruction, assisted only by language-advising sessions. She found that when given total freedom in their language learning, students tended to engage in a conventional set of learning activities such as grammar and vocabulary drills, using dictionaries and translating sentences. They also engaged in activities that were connected to their personal lives and environments, such as watching TV and movies, watching Japanese animes, reading mangas and listening to songs by their favourite singers. However, these activities were mainly of a receptive nature and shaped largely by students' current personal interests and hobbies.

In addition, listening and vocabulary are mentioned in various studies as the top two aspects of language study that learners focus on improving through autonomous use of technology for learning beyond the classroom. The majority of the 177 Istanbul university students surveyed in Ekşî and Aydin's (2013) study reported that their out-of-class English learning focused primarily on acquiring new vocabulary, reviewing learned vocabulary and increasing the amount of language input. The Norwegian upper-secondary school EFL learners in Cabot's (2014) study predominantly listened to English in the out-of-class learning context and rarely engaged in writing in their out-of-school learning. Çelik, Arkin and Sabriler (2012) found that 70.7 per cent of the Cyprus university EFL learners in their study reported using information communication technologies (ICT) to practise their listening skills, followed by vocabulary (59.1 per cent) and writing (58.1 per cent). Only 38.3 per cent of the participants reported using ICT to practise grammar. The same emphasis on listening and vocabulary was also reported in Trinder's (2016) survey study of Austrian advanced EFL learners, in which the learners reported valuing the use of technological resources to improve their listening skills and expand and reinforce their vocabulary and informal language use.

Language learners also utilize a variety of technological resources for language learning beyond the classroom. Steel and Levy (2013) surveyed 587 university undergraduate foreign-language students in Australia on their use of technologies outside the classroom and found that discipline-specific technologies (e.g. online dictionaries, web-based translators, conjugation websites) were the most frequently used technological tools, and that students valued the tools that helped them acquire the basics through repeated practice. In addition, YouTube and online movies, social networking sites and mobile-phone applications were also reported being used by over 50 per cent of the participants, although very few learners perceived communication technologies as beneficial to language learning. Students reported low usage of technologies provided by institutions, such as forums, wikis, blogs and video conferencing, and valued these technologies less. Li, Snow and White (2015) surveyed 623 sixth–eighth graders in the United States on their preferences for different technologies in developing language and literacy, and found that YouTube was most favoured among the students for its potential in developing vocabulary. Trinder (2016) surveyed Austrian advanced EFL learners on their use of technology and found that social media was quite frequently used (38 per cent of learners used social media daily and 20 per cent frequently), whereas Skype and instant messaging sites were used regularly by only a minority of the participants. Also, blogs and discussion forums were rarely used. Seventy per cent of the participants reported watching online films and video clips daily or frequently. As for disciplinary technologies, 94 per cent of the participants used online dictionaries on a daily or frequent basis, but only 5 per cent of them regularly visited grammar or language-learning websites. The participants viewed online dictionaries, online videos and online news sites/journals as very helpful for language learning and regarded communication technologies as less helpful in general; they seemed to favour input/content media with rich visual and aural elements.

Thus, current research has found that second/foreign-language learners use technology for language learning beyond the classroom on a weekly basis. They frequently use specific language-learning platforms and tools such as online dictionaries, translation tools and online drill and practice sites, and, at the same time, utilize some authentic language sources, such as online audio and video materials. Although they do use social networking tools in learning the second/foreign language, they tend to have negative perceptions of the language-learning potential of these tools. The online activities they engage in are mainly of a receptive nature, with their primary focus being on listening and vocabulary development.

Learner interaction with technology-mediated resources

In addition to charting the landscape of learners' use of technology for language learning beyond the classroom, researchers have also documented how learners interact with these various technology-mediated resources and platforms during their self-initiated, self-directed learning outside the classroom. As listening to songs is one of the most mentioned out-of-class activities that learners engage in, researchers have examined what learners pay attention to while listening to songs. Olmedo (2015) found that learners pay more attention to meaning than to the language form when processing English media. The majority of the primary and secondary EFL learners/participants in her study reported that they tried to understand the meaning of the songs in general rather than paying attention to the lyrics. They also attended to the soundtrack first before reading the subtitles when watching films. This primary focus on meaning was also reported in Sockett and Toffoli's (2012) study, in which the participants reported listening to songs for gist. Only in the case of the songs they liked, would they follow this up by listening to the songs again while referring to written lyrics websites. Rosell-Aguilar (2013) surveyed users of iTunes U at the Open University in the United Kingdom on their use of podcasts offered at the site. He found that the majority of the language learners (around 60 per cent) listened to them while engaged in other activities such as exercising, doing housework or travelling, and only around 40 per cent listened to the podcasts as their sole activity. The majority of the users preferred listening to the podcasts on mobile devices. Only around 10 per cent of them took notes while listening, more than half of them rarely or never took notes, and around 33 per cent of them frequently used the transcripts while listening. The author concluded: 'The transfer to and use on mobile devices, the low use of transcripts and the fact that many respondents listen as part of another activity suggests that many of the learners are listening to the language materials as a casual activity' (p. 86). He further pointed out that this unfocused approach to listening might have its own virtue in terms of familiarizing learners with the rhythm, sounds and intonation patterns of the target language. Ala-Kyyny (2012) surveyed ninety-seven Finnish EFL upper-secondary-school learners aged between sixteen and twenty and found that the majority of them did not perceive listening to English music as a means of English learning despite their extensive engagement with English songs. The author suggested that these students did not consciously think of learning when choosing music for listening. However, 59 per cent of the participants did claim paying attention to lyrics often, and 86 per cent reported they sometimes checked song lyrics from different sources. Thus, learners' learning via online songs is mainly incidental rather than intentional. However, online songs, if they match students' interests, do have the potential to lead to intentional learning.

To understand learners' use of the internet for learning, Sockett and Toffoli (2012) conducted an eight-week activity-log study with five undergraduate students from a French university on their online activities in English. The students' logs showed that their interaction with the internet indicated the 'user' status, whereby they accessed the internet mainly to research areas of interest, obtain information, listen to music, watch TV series and chat with friends and acquaintances. Moreover, their interaction with the internet was of a durable nature, characterized by high frequency and long duration. Using internet resources often involves encountering unknown words, and learners' help-seeking behaviour in relation to unknown words has attracted researchers' particular attention. Olmedo (2015) found that the learners in her study preferred searching for the meaning of single words to using online translators to obtain the meaning of the whole text when surfing the internet. Levy and Steel (2015) examined university foreign-language learners' use of online dictionaries in particular. They found that students valued online and mobile app-based dictionaries, as they are time efficient and easy to use. Students learning character-based languages valued the functionality of the mobile app-based dictionaries that enabled them to input character-based search through handwriting on screen. Many students reported locating high-quality mobile app-based dictionaries to take advantage of the portability and mobility they offered. Students commented that electronic dictionaries helped them to extend their vocabulary and improve their understanding of word choice and appropriate contexts of use. They favoured the complementary tools in the electronic dictionaries, including their ability to store vocabulary, to make flashcards, to create quizzes, to generate personalized vocabulary lists and to enable recording, and the incorporation of video, audio and other multimodal functionality and learning tools such as stroke order animations, blog entries, discussion forums and communities. Furthermore, in an interview study I conducted with a group of intermediate Chinese-as-a-second-language (CSL) learners in Hong Kong, the learners reported using electronic dictionaries on both laptops and mobile phones: checking dictionaries on laptops for the serious study of words and checking dictionaries on mobile phones for quick translations and assistance for language use. The participants also reported some difficulties with the input method on mobile dictionaries because of the small screen, but they felt that the scan function of some mobile dictionary apps helped solve the problem.

With regard to language learners' use of social networking sites for out-of-class language learning, researchers have found that this aspect of use is quite limited. Li, Snow and White (2015) found that the K–12 students in their study expressed little interest in using Facebook as a medium for learning. This observed hesitancy in using social networking tools for learning concurs with Davis and James's (2013) findings where middle school students in the United States perceived Facebook as a space for peer interaction and a main venue for non-intervened communication. Thus, learners demonstrated some hesitancy in embracing social networking tools for language-learning purposes. Despite this general negative tone, researchers have compared learners' preferred social networking tools. Sockett et al. found that French university EFL learners preferred Facebook to Twitter and Myspace when corresponding with English users on social networking websites (Toffoli and Sockett, 2010). Studies have also examined learners' interaction with social networking sites designed specifically for language-learning purposes. Stevenson and Liu (2010) documented learners' interaction with Babble, a language-learning social networking site, and found that learners held ambivalent views towards it: on the one hand, they welcomed the opportunities to interact with native speakers, and on the other hand, they questioned the trustworthiness of peer feedback and the site's function to establish social relationships. Stevenson and Liu further found that 54 per cent of their participants stopped using Babble within less than one month, and 26 per cent of them stopped using it after one to three months. Lin, Warschauer and Blake (2016) surveyed 4,174 Livemocha users and interviewed twenty case-study participants. The survey responses suggested that the participants felt that the site increased their motivation and self-confidence in learning the target languages, and that the majority of the participants took advantage of the site's online chat rooms to practise the foreign languages. However, they observed the same attrition phenomenon in learners' engagement with the platform as reported in Stevenson and Liu's (2010) study.

Research has also examined learners' use of mobile devices. Studies have shown that in naturalistic settings and when given the choice, learners are far more likely to opt to work on personal computers (PCs) than on mobile phones (Stockwell, 2013). Stockwell (2013) developed a vocabulary-learning system that could be accessed via both PCs and mobile devices, and the learner-tracking data indicated that over 70 per cent of the students chose not to use mobile devices at all, with only 15 per cent of the mobile activities taking place in transit. Stockwell's study focused specifically on learners' interaction with different digital devices when introduced to an online vocabulary-learning system. In contrast, Chen (2013) studied university students' interaction with mobile devices when given access to the equipment. In that study, tablets were given to ten freshmen English majors ranging from seventeen to twenty years old who were of intermediate English-proficiency level, and the participants were requested to keep a log of their daily usage. The participants reported spending an average of 0.61 hours per day on learning English with the device, but they also engaged in a lot of incidental English learning through engaging in activities carried out in English, such as watching movies, playing games and surfing the internet. Most of the activities were carried out individually, and the participants spent little time engaging in interactive activities on their tablets. Studies have also examined language learners' perceptions and use of mobile devices for language learning in general. Steel (2012) found that the university language learners in her study favoured mobile apps because they allowed them to practise language anywhere and anytime. The mobile apps they most often used included mobile dictionaries, translators, mobile flashcards and vocabulary-learning games. The participants reported benefiting most from mobile apps in vocabulary learning and in reading, writing, grammar and translation tasks. Few participants mentioned using mobile devices for communication purposes. Similarly, Demouy et al. (2016) found that adult distance-language learners in the United Kingdom most often used mobile devices to watch videos and listen to the target language, and that dictionaries and online translation tools were the most popular resources and apps used by the learners. Furthermore, their use of mobile devices was both planned and spontaneous, making use of otherwise 'dead' time such as daily commutes and lunchtimes at work. The adult Welsh learners of different proficiency levels interviewed by Jones (2015) reported that listening to the target language was the most convenient activity with mobile devices. Viberg and Grönlund (2013), focusing specifically on the use of mobile devices for different dimensions of language learning, surveyed 345 university language learners' attitudes towards mobile-assisted language learning, and found that 83 per cent of the students reported positive perceptions of using mobile devices for individualization, 74 per cent reported positive perceptions of using mobile devices for collaboration and 73 per cent reported positive perceptions of using mobile devices for authenticity. I conducted a survey study of intermediate-to-upper-level undergraduate CSL learners' perceptions and use of mobile devices for Chinese learning, and found that the forty-five participants' most positive perceptions were of the use of mobile devices for personalization (e.g. ubiquitous access to learning and obtaining immediate support and help), and their least positive perceptions were of the use of mobile devices for collaboration (e.g. to connect with speakers of Mandarin) and to bridge in-class and out-of-class learning (e.g. bringing authentic materials into the classroom). Furthermore, the learners used mobile devices more often for assistive functions such as dictionary and translation tools, and for listening to authentic materials such as podcasts, songs and online videos (0.5–1 hr/day). They reported using mobile devices less for material generation in the target language through video recording and photo taking, for authentic reading such as reading online news and researching information authenticity, and for communication via text messaging and short message service (SMS) (less than 0.5 hr/day). Byrne and Diem (2013) surveyed 3,739 users of the free English grammar Android app that they had developed and found that the users of the app were heavily skewed towards the beginner level. In addition, Kukulska-Hulme and de los Arcos (2011) also revealed the strategies language learners use when interacting with mobile devices. They found that in the mobile environment, learners kept some effective strategies such as repetition and self-monitoring, but felt constrained on the employment of other strategies such as visual mnemonics. At the same time, they developed some new strategies such as drawing on more diverse social networks for learning and aligning their language-learning practice in response to the emergent and segmental nature of mobile learning.

Learner construction of personalized learning ecology with technology

Learning involves the accumulation of experience across different formal and informal learning contexts, in which learners actively seek out new learning resources and create learning opportunities (Barron, 2010). Whitworth (2009) argued that informal learning network technologies open up possibilities for learners to generate their own learning contexts. Language learning involves strategic efforts whereby learners employ their 'sociocultural capacity' to critically reconfigure social, discursive and material resources to create favourable language-learning environments (Gao, 2010, p. 26). Benson (2009b) pointed out that 'in describing an individual's learning we are likely to be concerned not with one setting, but with learning within a configuration of several settings' (p. 231). Ethnographic and biographical studies confirm that language learners do actively manipulate various physical and non-physical resources to create learning opportunities outside the language classroom (Hyland, 2004; Lamb, 2004; Inozu et al., 2010). Learners also perceive learning in different contexts as serving different functions (Lai, 2015a; Lamb, 2004). The realization that language learners exert agency in constructing their language-learning experience outside the classroom means that a systematic investigation and documentation of the holistic ecology of language learning is needed: the constitution of places for learning, the various ways in which learners exert agency to selectively appropriate various settings in order to construct and develop a personalized learning ecology and the (re)configuration of resources and interactions within and across a set of contexts as well as the potential synergies or barriers of learning across contexts (Barron, 2010; Benson, 2009b; Borreno and Yeh, 2010; Gao, 2010). Considering that various formal and informal learning experiences constitute learners' holistic learning experience, scholars are calling for research efforts to understand learners' construction of language-learning ecology across in-class and out-of-class learning contexts (Bäumer et al., 2011; Leander, Phillips and Taylor, 2010; Benson and Reinders, 2011).

In response to this call for research, Lai (2015a) interviewed a group of university foreign-language learners in Hong Kong on their strategic use of in-class and out-of-class language-learning experiences. The learners reported that their in-class and out-of-class learning experiences were closely connected. On the one hand, they reported continuing exploring, outside the classroom, the materials used during in-class learning and related materials, searching for additional information associated with classroom topics and incorporating in-class activities and related resources to their out-of-school activities. On the other hand, they felt that their out-of-class learning experiences gave more purposes and goals for their in-class learning, and they brought the materials that they acquired from their out-of-class experience to their language classes to enrich their in-class learning, making it more authentic, meaningful and interesting. Furthermore, their selection and construction of out-of-class experiences were often influenced by their perceptions of the limitations of in-class learning, which were individually defined and mediated by their language-learning beliefs. For instance, the participants reported preferring out-of-class learning experiences that are fun and relaxing so as to compensate for the typically serious nature of in-class learning.

Other research studies have also tapped into language learners' construction of a learning ecology while traversing spatio – temporal situations. For instance, Gao (2010) documented how material, discursive and social interactions in different contexts at different times shaped learners' selective use of strategies for English learning. All the four English-language learners in his study constantly configured and reconfigured their English-learning strategies in response to the opportunities and setbacks arising out of the changes in their living contexts and experiences. He used the story of Liu, one of the students, to illustrate the dynamic strategy-construction process. Liu opted to adopt a lot of social-learning strategies (e.g. listening to English radio or watching English TV programmes, implementing a rule to use English for all academic matters, making friends and socializing with local students) to make good use of the abundance of material and social resources in English upon moving to Hong Kong. However, subsequent setbacks in integrating into the local community and the resulting greater affiliation and interaction with Putonghua-speaking mainland Chinese students exposed her to the popular discourse of achieving high academic results and a pursuing postgraduate degree at an overseas university, which influenced her into adopting more memorization strategies. Gao came to the conclusion that learners actively (re)construct their language-learning strategies through (re)configuring the social, discursive and material resources in their immediate learning settings. Benson et al. (2003) gave a vivid account of how a Korean English learner configured and reconfigured her language-learning experience in response to the sociocultural contexts at different stages of learning. Her high school English-learning environment was dominated by memorization and achieving good grades, and she tried to eliminate the damaging effect of the stifling and demotivating learning environment on her English-learning motivation by partitioning her learning goals into a proximal one (achieving good grades through memorization) and an ultimate one (communicating with and understanding native speakers of the language), and keeping a balance between the two. As she moved to university, she took advantage of the abundance of opportunities and time in this learning setting to construct a learning ecology consisting of writing articles in English as a campus reporter, reading books and magazines, listening to English pop music and watching Hollywood and educational programmes on TV. She voluntarily enrolled in an English-language course taught by native speakers of English to move closer to her ultimate goal, but the teaching methods there (an overemphasis on pronunciation and error correction) were in conflict with her ultimate goal, a dissonance she tried to bridge through creating a new context for learning: studying overseas. Her language-learning process was a dynamic one that entailed creating and recreating 'new ways of learning and new situations' (p. 35) in response to the cultural norms and resources in different sociocultural contexts so as to move closer to her ultimate goal. Cabot (2014) took a longitudinal approach to examine six French upper-secondary students' construction of English-learning ecologies over time. The study found that the conventions concerning the use of particular digital artefacts and the content and the evolving functionalities in them served as triggers for the learners' selective use of and sustained engagement with them. More importantly, the author found that the participants' agency in learning ecology construction in the past – namely, in primary schools – was driven by both digital (e.g. Facebook, Instagram, Minecraft, League of Legends) and non-digital (e.g. vocabulary tests, the blackboard, homework) artefacts, while their agency in their present and future construction of a learning ecology seemed to be primarily influenced by digital artefacts. Furthermore, girls seemed to go through an evolution from a playful-artefact-dominated past to an expressive-artefact-dominated present, whereas the boys' ecology evolution showed a reverse pattern: from an expressive past to a playful present. Cabot further found that the participants' agentic moments (e.g. facing a new challenge in target-language use; discovering the functionalities of a digital artefact) instigated ecological transitions.

The quality of out-of-class autonomous language learning

Describing learners' out-of-school practices is just the first step; what is now needed is the evaluation of the contributions of these practices to the overall learning experience (Arbelaiz and Gorospe, 2009). Understanding the quality of learners' out-of-class practices is useful for teachers to support the creation of quality learning experiences (Barron, 2010). At present, most empirical studies have remained at the stage of describing the nature of autonomous learning with technology beyond the classroom, and only a limited few can inform our understanding of the quality of learner self-initiated out-of-class learning with technology.

The quality of different types of learning activities

Studies have attested to the positive association between out-of-class learning with technology and various language-learning outcomes. Larsson (2012) examined the association of Swedish learners' out-of-school English-language activities with their scores in the National Test of English and found that students who actively engaged in out-of-class English-language learning tended to obtain higher grades in the test than those who were not involved in out-of-school learning. Olsson (2011) found that frequent engagement in out-of-class learning – especially via digital games – was positively associated with nineth-graders' performance in writing of letters and news articles and with their final grades in the English class. The Swedish National Agency of Education (2012) also found that heavy involvement in autonomous English learning beyond the classroom might have explained the higher levels of English-language proficiency among the fifteen- and sixteen-year-olds in Sweden compared to those of their counterparts from fourteen other European countries. Focusing specifically on the impact of gameplay on ninth-graders' English vocabulary outcomes, Sundqvist and Wikstrőm (2015) found that the frequency of gameplay was positively associated with different English vocabulary measures. Also, Kuppens (2010) found in her study with Flemish Dutch-speaking sixth-grader participants that the frequency of watching subtitled English TV programmes and movies was positively associated with primary-school pupils' performance in two oral translation tests. Sundqvist (2009) further argued that the positive association between out-of-class learning with technology and various language-learning outcomes is manifested not only in cognitive but also in affective learning outcomes. Her study found that the higher the frequency of autonomous English-learning activities that learners engaged in beyond the classroom, the larger their vocabulary size was and the less anxious they appeared when speaking in English. Sundqvist (2011) examined the association between the frequency of Swedish English-language learners' out-of-class learning and their oral proficiency, and found significant positive associations with oral proficiency (0.31) and with vocabulary size (0.36). There was also a positive correlation between the amount of out-of-class learning and self-efficacy in English learning. Lai, Zhu and Gong (2015) concurred with the learning effects at the affective domain, and found a positive correlation between autonomous out-of-class learning with technology and learners' grades in English class, their enjoyment of English learning and their confidence in learning English. Thus, there is sufficient research evidence supporting the positive link between autonomous out-of-class learning with technology and various language-learning outcomes.

Barron (2010) highlighted the fact that different life contexts entail different configurations of tools, relationships and activities, thus affording different learning opportunities. Consequently, assessment of the quality of different learning ecologies and their contributions to the 'holistic ecology of learning' is critical (Arbelaiz and Gorospe, 2009, p. 55; Bäumer, Preis and Guner, 2011). Research studies have shown that different types of out-of-class learning activities have different affordances for language learning. Lindgren and Muñoz (2012) surveyed 865 upper-primary-school students' (aged 10–11) out-of-school activities and found that watching subtitled films was the most powerful type of exposure in predicting students' listening and reading performances. Participants in Sockett and Toffoli's (2012) study also perceived watching TV series and films as the most helpful in improving listening skills. Sundqvist (2009) found that digital gaming and internet browsing were the two most important activities for enlarging vocabulary size. Sundqvist (2011) took a more general approach and examined the association between the receptive and productive out-of-class English-learning activities that Swedish English-language learners engaged in and their English-learning outcomes. She found that activities that required learners' active utilization of their language skills in the target language to engage in productive participation contributed more to the enhancement of learners' oral proficiency and vocabulary size than did activities of a receptive nature, which allowed learners to play a more passive role. The former category included activities such as reading books, reading newspapers/magazines, surfing the internet and playing video games, while the latter category included activities such as watching TV and films, and listening to music. Thus, different types of technology-enhanced out-of-class activities have differential language-learning affordances.

The quality of language-learning ecologies

In addition to examining the language-learning efficacies of specific types of autonomous out-of-class activities, researchers have also investigated the potentials of different learning ecologies that language learners construct.

Palvianien (2012) surveyed first-year Swedish university students who majored in either English or Swedish on their K–12 experience of learning English and Swedish. The participants reported that their Swedish-learning experience was primarily of a receptive nature, such as watching TV and movies and listening to music, but that their English-learning experience consisted of a combination of receptive and productive activities. The two groups of learners exhibited different degrees of confidence in their language skills, with the English majors feeling more confident about their language abilities than the Swedish majors. The former perceived themselves as active English users, who utilized both material and social resources to create opportunities to use the language in real situations, and felt that such language-use opportunities increased their confidence in their English skills. Fagerlund (2012) examined six Finnish learners' out-of-class learning activities for learning English and Swedish. She found that these learners engaged in both receptive and productive activities for English learning, but mostly in receptive activities for Swedish learning. And correspondingly, the learners expressed different perceptions of the efficacy of out-of-class learning for improving English and Swedish, respectively. Specifically, they perceived their out-of-class English-language learning as positive and empowering, but expressed doubts about whether they had gained anything from their out-of-class Swedish-language learning experiences. Thus, the different types of out-of-class activities that learners engaged in when learning English and Swedish provoked different perceptions of the value of out-of-class learning. Palfreyman (2011), focusing especially on the strength of learners' social networks (i.e. networks of relationships facilitating or constraining the transfer of informational and material resources and learning activities), accentuated the importance of a diversity of social networks in out-of-class learning. According to Palfreyman, advice networks (i.e. relationships with people whereby a learner receives or provides guidance), trust networks (i.e. relationships in which feelings and difficulties are shared and support is sought) and communication networks (i.e. relationships that support the discussion and clarification of one's learning) are different types of social networks that learners can and need to rely on in facilitating their out-of-class learning experience. Wiklund (2002) found that for adolescent immigrants in Sweden, the more varied networks these learners utilized, the higher proficiency they demonstrated in the second language. All these studies demonstrate the importance of diversity in language-learning experiences.

The observations of the above researchers align with arguments for the importance of diversity for an effective and healthy ecology. Nardi and O'Day

(1999) highlighted the fact that diversity is essential to the health of any ecology, and a healthy information ecology needs to involve different kinds of people, resources, materials, technologies and relationships that allow for 'individual proclivities and interests' (p. 52). Brown (2000) adopted ecology as a metaphor to describe a learning environment and also pointed out that diversity is critical to the powerfulness of an ecology. Malcolm, Hodkinson and Colley (2003) argued that there are aspects of formality and informality in any learning situation, and that a productive balance between the two needs to be sustained. Richardson (2002) concurred that effective learning ecologies need to 'balance the many resources and methods people may apply to their learning' (p. 48). Lai, Gong and Zhu (2015) took the holism of learners' in-class and out-of-class learning experiences into consideration in discussing the quality of out-of-class learning. They examined the quality of the learning ecologies that a group of lower-secondary-school EFL learners' constructed outside the classroom. Considering that their in-class English-learning experience focused heavily on formal linguistic features, the authors hypothesized that the number of different types of meaning-focused activities that each participant engaged in outside the classroom could serve as an indicator of the balance between a focus on form and a focus on meaning in the learners' holistic learning experiences (i.e. the variety of meaning-focused activity types). The authors also examined the degree to which technology-enhanced out-of-class learning helped to meet the participants' different socio-psychological needs – including goal commitment needs, metacognition needs, resource needs, social connection needs and attitudinal needs – in language learning (i.e. diversity of purpose of technology use). Regression analyses showed that the variety of out-of-class meaning-focused activities and the diversity of purpose of technology use significantly predicted the participants' English-learning outcomes. The variety of meaning-focused activities was a significant predictor of the participants' cognitive (i.e. English grades) and affective outcomes (i.e. confidence and enjoyment in learning English), and the diversity of technology use was a significant predictor of the affective outcomes only. The authors concluded that the degree to which out-of-class activities contributed to the diversity and balance of the attentional focus (focus on meaning and on form) in the holistic language-learning experience and to satisfying various psychosocial needs was a critical indicator of the quality of out-of-class language learning. Specifically, in the contexts where in-class instruction is heavily form focused, the proportion of meaning-focused activities among the out-of-class learning activities that learners engage in is an important characteristic of quality out-of-class learning experiences. Furthermore, the diversification of learning experiences in striking a balance in meeting various psychological and socio-affective learning needs is another important quality indicator for the construction of out-of-class learning ecologies.

Constructing a diversity- and balance-oriented quality framework

Researchers have proposed various frameworks to differentiate types of out-of-class learning. Benson (2011c) was among the first to devise such a framework, and conceptualized four key dimensions to differentiate various out-of-class learning activities: location, formality, pedagogy and locus of control. Location refers to the relationship of the learners (the physical, social and pedagogical relationships) with the human and material resources in the learning contexts (e.g. classroom based or non-classroom based). Formality refers to how educationally structured and organized the learning experience is or whether the learning experience is qualification granting (i.e. formal, non-formal or informal). Pedagogy refers to the extent to which the learning experience involves educational processes such as the sequencing of contents, explicit explanations and assessments (i.e. self-instruction pedagogy or naturalistic pedagogy). Locus of control refers to the degree to which learners perceive their learning to be controlled by other people or instructional materials or by themselves (i.e. other directed or self-directed). Bäumer et al. (2011) reviewed educational research that discusses the learning opportunities of learning experiences and identified four basic factors that determine quality learning experiences: 1) structure (the educational processes that are involved in the learning experience), 2) support (various forms of support, including pedagogical, social and emotional support, available in the learning experience), 3) challenge (whether the difficulty level of the learning experience could lead learners to their 'zone of proximal development'), and 4) orientation (whether the learning experience induces shared values, norms and favourable attitudes). Bäumer et al. argued that although these four core factors were originally generated from the classroom-instruction context, they may apply just as well to other learning environments and experiences. These two frameworks espoused by Benson and Bäumer et al., in a nutshell, have identified three core aspects in categorizing out-of-class learning activities: 1) pedagogy/structure – the psychological processes and the social relationships involved in the activity;

2) functions/support – the language-learning needs that are addressed by the activity; and 3) spaces/medium – the learning affordances and constraints of the activity space. With the key categorizing dimensions generated, the next step is to identify important features of quality language-learning experience and map quality dimensions on the three categorizing aspects of out-of-class learning activities.

In order to understand what dimensions of language-learning experience learners need to balance in each of the three aspects, insights may be found from three bodies of literature: literature on optimal language-learning environments, literature on the strategies of effective language learners, and literature that categorizes the dimensions of out-of-class learning activities.

Over the years, a number of frameworks on optimal language-learning environments have been proposed, which highlight key principles critical to successful language learning. Influential frameworks from the psycholinguistic perspective include Ellis (2005) and Doughty and Long (2003). For example, the following were the ten principles generated by Ellis (2005): 1) instruction should help learners accumulate both a rich collection of formulaic expressions and develop a rule-based competence; 2) instruction should induce a primary focus on meaning by the learners; 3) instruction should also direct learners' attention to language forms; 4) instruction should prioritize helping learners acquire implicit knowledge of the second language (L2) but at the same time support them to develop some explicit knowledge of the language; 5) instruction should be learner centred, respecting their development needs and progression; 6) instruction should provide learners with extensive L2 input; 7) instruction should provide learners with abundant opportunities for productive language use; 8) instruction should ensure sufficient opportunities for interaction in the L2; 9) instruction should consider individual differences; and 10) the assessment of L2 proficiency should target both free language production and controlled language production. Although when Ellis (2005) proposed this framework, he was thinking of language-instructional contexts, some of the principles apply to the construction of language-learning experiences across different settings. The principles that Ellis proposed highlighted several dimensions of balance: the balance between focus on form and focus on meaning; the balance between explicit, rule-based learning and implicit, incidental acquisition; the balance between receptive, input-focused activities and productive, output-based activities; and the balance between the development of fluency and the development of accuracy. Ellis (2005) also stressed the importance of the individualization of learning.

Lantolf, Thorne and Poehner (2015) discussed the interpretations of an optimal language-learning environment from the sociocultural perspective of L2 development, which highlights the dualism of the autonomous learner and the social environment. This perspective highlights the fact that learning takes place through learners' 'interaction within social and material environments' and participation – both direct and vicarious – in different 'cultural, linguistic and historically formed settings' mediated by cultural tools – physical and symbolic – and other- and self-regulation (p. 207). It also stresses the importance of helping learners internalize age-appropriate holistic concepts through concrete experiences, practical activities and explicit verbalization of the concepts. Thus, the sociocultural perspective of language learning adds the dimensions of a balance between individual and social learning and a balance between different social and material contexts to the dimensions of balance emphasized in the psycholinguistic theories.

The psycholinguistic and sociolinguistic frameworks list the essential dimensions in the aspect of learning activity and pedagogy that need to be balanced in a language learner's learning experience. A learner-centred approach needs to be taken into account in a discussion of these dimensions. An activity might be meaning focused in its format but might be approached in a form-focused manner by learners. Thus, it is learners' perception and selective attention during the experience that actually matters when we talk about striking a balance along the dimensions.

The literature on effective language-learning strategies has accumulated since the early 1970s. Rubin (1975) was among the earliest scholars who examined the learning behaviours of successful language learners. She listed seven essential learning strategies and techniques that were employed by good language learners: 1) willingness to, and effectiveness in, guessing unknown words; 2) strong motivation to communicate; 3) willingness to make mistakes to communicate; 4) constant attention to categorization and synthesization of patterns in the language; 5) seeking of opportunities to use the language; 6) active learning from their own and others' mistakes; 7) attention to the communication contexts, the relationships of the participants and the rules of speaking. Stern (1983) went beyond the list of specific learning techniques and proposed four basic sets of strategies exhibited by good language learners: 1) active planning strategy (long-term and immediate goal setting and adjusting); 2) explicit learning strategy (focusing on the relationship between language forms and meanings); 3) social-learning strategy (seeking communication opportunities and coping with communication difficulties); and 4) affective strategy (coping with emotional and motivational problems of language learning). Similarly, Oxford (2008) focused on learning strategies essential in independent learning contexts and synthesized four general categories based on functions: 1) metacognitive strategies such as planning, organizing, monitoring and evaluating, which are considered extremely important for independent L2 learning; 2) affective strategies such as building positive motivation, maintaining positive volition and dealing with negative emotions, which address the lack of immediate social support and interaction in the independent learning context; 3) cognitive strategies such as noticing, analysing, combining, categorizing and synthesizing; and 4) social-interactional strategies such as communication, collaboration and noticing sociocultural factors. Thus, this body of literature highlights the necessity of learning experience to balance different learning needs and functions. Quality learning experience depends not only on the incorporation of activities that help meet or support these different learning needs and functions but also on learners' abilities to exercise the tactics and strategies along these different dimensions.

In addition, scholars have conceptualized the types of learning that can take place in out-of-class contexts. Richards (2015) recommended categorizing out-of-class activities along several dimensions: location, modality (oral or written, synchronous or asynchronous), learning aims (intentional or incidental, general or specific), control (learner managed, other managed or teacher managed), type of interaction (one-way or two-way), language register (scripted or unscripted, casual or formal, native speaker or non-native speaker), task demands (repeat, rephrase, respond, summarize, question, react, etc.), manner (individual, pair or group), and means (computer, mobile phone or TV). He further suggested that out-of-class activities could be categorized in terms of benefits: learning benefits (e.g. the development of linguistic, communicative and pragmatic competence, the use of communication strategies, the use of multimodal sources of learning, the improvement of both accuracy and fluency, the adjustment of language in response to the change of purposes, norms and expectations of communication in different contexts); learner benefits (e.g. flexibility in terms of place, time, mode and manner of learning; reflecting learner needs and interests; allowing for social interaction with others); and teacher benefits (e.g. allowing for learning opportunities that class instruction does not afford, bridging classroom and out-of-class learning). Wong and Looi (2011), in their seamless learning framework, put forward several dimensions of balance in terms of learning spaces: informal/formal, social/individual, physical/virtual, and different personal learning tools and device types. These discussions have suggested dimensions that need to be balanced in terms of learning spaces and media.

Based on the literature above, a diversity and balance-oriented framework for quality out-of-class learning experience with technology can be constructed. This framework (shown in Figure 3.1) conceptualizes the quality of out-of-class learning experience in light of in-class experience, with the aim that the holistic in-class and out-of-class learning experience could strike a delicate balance along different dimensions. Three aspects are focused on in this framework: pedagogy/structure, functions/support and spaces/media. Each aspect contains different dimensions that need to be balanced. Learner-experienced activity, learner-skill repertoire and the social and material support that learners can gain access to are all important factors to consider in determining whether balances can be struck along different dimensions.

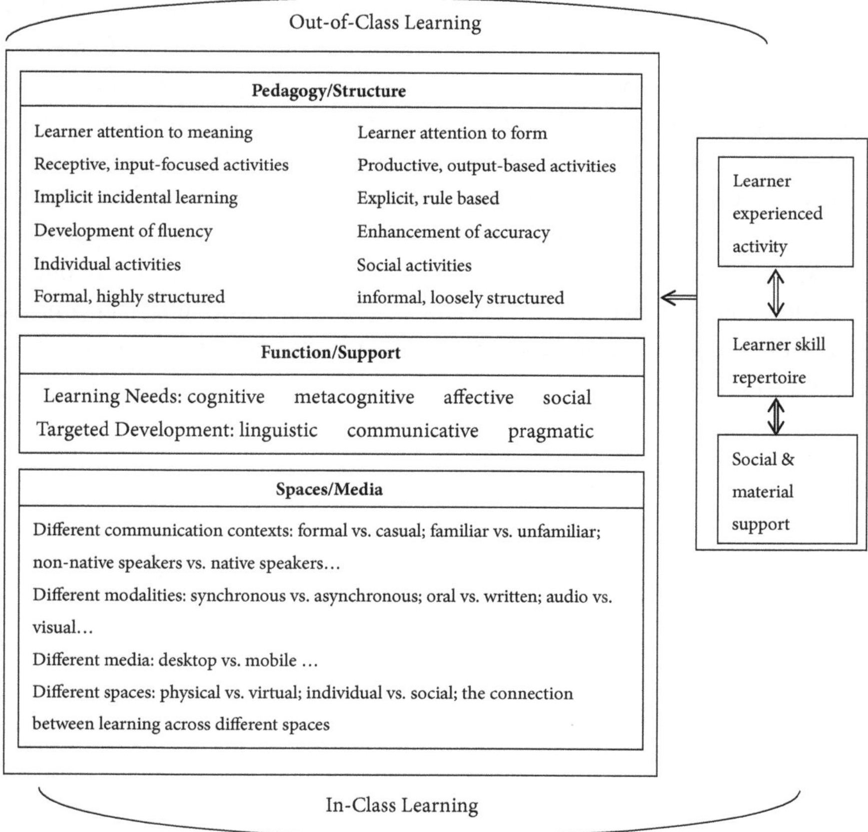

Figure 3.1 A framework of quality out-of-class language learning.

This framework does not prescribe achieving diversities and balances in all the dimensions listed for learning ecologies to be healthy and effective; rather it suggests some dimensions that can be considered when assessing the quality of one's learning experience outside the classroom.

The dimensions listed in the framework are far from being all encompassing but are listed as potential directions or examples that can be considered along the three aspects. Are there important dimensions missing from this framework? What intensity of diversity and balance is needed to ensure the quality of out-of-class learning? Is it a case of the more dimensions the better? Are the different dimensions equally important to the quality of out-of-class learning, or are some dimensions more important than others? There are more questions than answers. However, this framework can potentially serve as a starting frame of reference for an exploration into the quality of autonomous out-of-class language learning.

More importantly, the quality of the learning process is context-sensitive and subject to the influences of the valued practices in the contexts of teaching and learning (Crabbe, 2003; Gieve and Miller, 2006). The quality framework constructed above is based on an assumption that language learning is universal, and fails to consider the influence of the learners' valued practices and the local context of learning (Crabbe, 2003; Gieve and Miller, 2006). Gieve and Miller (2006) argued that the expert formulations of quality out-of-class learning experience need to be redefined in light of what learners value and appreciate. Thus, it is important to take a relativist approach towards the quality of out-of-class learning and take account of the mediation role of what is valued in the specific contexts of teaching and learning when understanding the quality of the learning experience.

4

Factors that Affect Out-of-Class Autonomous Language Learning with Technology

The review of the nature of students' autonomous language learning with technology beyond the classroom has shown that language learners do, to varying degrees, use technological resources in the target language or for language learning on their own. Considering the empirical studies that attest to the positive association between the autonomous use of technology for language learning and various language-learning outcomes, it is critical to understand which factors influence whether and how language learners use technologies for learning outside language classrooms. A clear understanding of these factors could help language educators identify areas of support that they could provide to enhance students' technology use for language learning.

To understand human behavioural intentions, we can refer to the theory of planned behaviour (Ajzen, 1985). According to this theory, three key constructs influence human behavioural intentions. They include learner attitudes, learner perception of behaviour control, and social influence. Thus, this theory suggests that both internal and external factors are influential forces that may affect an individual's intentions to engage in certain behaviours. The current literature has identified various factors that influence language learners' selective use of technological resources for language learning: 1) internal factors such as the learners' views of the language and their personal identity, their language-proficiency levels, and their L2 motivation (Chusanachoti, 2009; Hyland, 2004; Lai and Gu, 2011); 2) a set of external factors such as how the language is viewed and valued by the society and community, the language profiles of learners' immediate living environments and the requirements of the study situation (e.g. assessment regime), and social networks and social norms (Chusanachoti, 2009; Hyland, 2004); and 3) the nature of the resources, such as the transparency, usability, expense and affectivity, and the mode of the resources (face-to-face or non-face-to-face) (Chusanachoti, 2009; Hyland, 2004). In this section, we will review how these internal and external variables influence the nature of language learners' use of technology for language learning or in the target language beyond the classroom.

Learner internal factors

Current research has found that variations in the frequency of technology use are manifested in various learner-related factors, such as gender, proficiency level, learning beliefs and preferences.

Gender and autonomous language learning with technology beyond the classroom

Gender is an individual variable that has attracted researchers' attention when discussing the use of technology for learning. Researchers have explored the relationship between gender and computer use in general. Some studies have found that males generally hold more positive attitudes towards the use of technology and possess higher computer self-efficacy than females (Coffin and MacIntyre, 1999; Li and Kirkup, 2007; Winke, Goetler and Amuzie, 2010), whereas others have reported no gender differences (Compton, Burkett and Burkett, 2003; Volman et al., 2005). Thus, the general educational technology literature has yielded mixed findings on the relationship between gender and technology use.

Against the backdrop of no definitive answers, some researchers have examined gender influences on the frequency of language learners' autonomous use of technology for learning beyond the classroom. These studies have also yielded mixed findings. For instance, Ekşî and Aydin (2013) examined a group of Istanbul university students' out-of-class learning and found no significant gender differences in the frequency of their out-of-class English learning. Çelik, Arkin and Sabriler (2012), focusing specifically on learners' use of technology for language learning beyond the classroom, did not find any significant gender differences between male and female North Cyprus university students in their use of ICT for self-regulated English learning either. In the context of Hong Kong, Lee, Yeung and Ip (2016) also found no significant gender differences in university students' use of technology to seek advice, find answers, solve language problems and improve their language skills. In contrast, Sundqvist and Sylvén's (2014) study of Swedish fourth graders found that the boys reported spending more time (11.5

hours a week) learning English outside the classroom than the girls (5.1 hours per week). The study further found that the boys spent more time (3.4 hours a week) playing digital games than the girls (0.4 hours a week) and more time (1.8 hours a week) watching films than the girls (0.6 hours a week). Boys' greater engagement with digital games in the target language has been confirmed in several other studies. Kuppens (2010) found that, among her Flemish Dutch-speaking sixth-grader participants, boys reported a greater frequency of playing computer games and visiting English websites. Olmedo (2015) examined the amount of out-of-school exposure to English among K–12 English learners in a small town in Spain and found a significant gender difference in the frequency of video game playing in the target language among secondary school male students: the male students spent more time (1–3 times a week) playing video games than the female students (less than once a month). This gender difference in the frequency of game playing was found not salient among the primary-school participants but was significant among the secondary school participants. Thus, the current literature has yielded conflicting findings on the influence of gender on the frequency of learners' technology use for out-of-class language learning.

Despite the inconclusive findings on the gender differences in the frequency of language learners' use of technology for learning, research studies have yielded consistent findings on differences in the ways male and female students use technology outside the classroom. Studies have found that male and female students select different types of technological resources and activities for learning. For instance, Cabot (2014) examined the types of digital resources that a group of upper-secondary-school female and male students in Western Norway engaged with outside the classroom. He found that male students tended to select playful artefacts such as various types of games including Minecraft, League of Legends, Pokémon and so forth, whereas female students opted for more expressive artefacts such as songs, Facebook, Instagram and so on. He further found that there had been an evolution from the use of playful artefacts in the past to the predominant use of expressive artefacts in the present in the case of the girls, whereas, the evolution of the boys' language-learning ecology seemed to follow a reversed pattern. Furthermore, the girls focused more on receptive skills in their out-of-class learning, while the boys engaged much more in activities that involved the use of productive skills. In addition, Viberg and Grönlund (2013) found significant gender differences in Chinese and Swedish university foreign-language learners' attitudes towards the use of mobile devices for personalized learning, authentic learning and collaboration. The female learners expressed more favourable attitudes towards the use of mobile devices for language learning. Moreover, research studies have also found that technology use has differential effects on male and female learners, which has been attributed to the difference in the ways male and female learners interact with technological resources. For instance, Kuppens (2010) found that exposure to media, watching subtitled TV series and movies in particular, had slightly stronger learning effects for the Flemish Dutch-speaking sixth-grade girls in her study than for the boys. Kuppens hypothesized that the differential learning effects indicated that female and male learners might have processed the digital artefacts differently. This hypothesis has been supported by Ala-Kyyny's (2012) study, which examined how a group of Finnish upper-secondary-school language learners interacted with English-language music. Ala-Kyyny found significant differences in female and male students' perceptions and use of music for English learning. Specifically, 72 per cent of the female participants in the study reported paying attention to lyrics often when listening to music in the target language. In contrast, only 47 per cent of the male participants reported doing so. In short, females showed more interest in the lyrics while listening to English songs. Furthermore, female respondents were most interested in referring to the lyrics word by word so as to sing along, whereas male respondents mainly preferred to process the lyrics of songs in their entirety and focused on the general meaning of the songs. Neither group chose to check written lyrics for spelling. Female participants were also found to use lyrics intentionally for English-language learning: as many as 60 per cent of the female participants sometimes used dictionaries to translate songs.

Thus, the current literature has yielded research evidence suggesting that gender differences exist not only in the selection of technologies for learning but also in the processing of technological resources and tools. However, the findings on the influence of gender on the frequency of technology use are mixed. The conflicting findings might have been due to the different research populations involved in the studies, such as the different schooling contexts in which these studies were conducted. For instance, Whitley's (1997) meta-analysis showed that gender differences in attitudes towards computer use tend to decrease from high school to university. The conflicting findings might also have been due to the fact that the biological sex of individuals is not a measure refined enough to serve as a reliable predictor of human behaviours (Aguirre-Urreta and Marakas, 2010; Huffman, Whetten and Huffman, 2013). Researchers are questioning the validity of using the biological sex of individuals to examine gender differences in technology behaviour. Instead, Huffman, Whetten and Huffman (2013) argued that the social roles that individuals subscribe to 'are more important variables because they provide a better designation of one's sexual identity and they better describe attitudes and behaviors' (p. 1780). Aguirre-Urreta and Marakas (2010) also pointed out that the observed gender effects might be attributed more to culturally shaped personality traits, such as locus of control, neuroticism and risk propensity. Thus, research efforts to understand the potential influence of gender on technology use might be more productive and meaningful if they delved deeper into these more fundamental constructs behind the biological sex of individuals.

Proficiency level and autonomous language learning with technology beyond the classroom

As another important individual variable in language learning, the potential influence of language proficiency on autonomous language learning with technology has attracted the attention of researchers. Researchers have examined the frequency of out-of-class autonomous language learning among learners of different proficiency levels. For instance, Wong and Nunan (2011) compared autonomous language learning between high achievers and low achievers. They found that 40 per cent of the high achievers reported spending 1–5 hours per week on English outside the classroom, and 20 per cent reported spending more than 10 hours per week, whereas 70 per cent of the less effective learners reported spending less than an hour per week on English outside the classroom. Wong and Nunan concluded that there might be a positive association between language proficiency and language learners' engagement in self-directed learning. This positive association was partially supported in Ekşî and Aydin's (2013) study, where they found that university English-language learners in Istanbul who were at the B1 (intermediate low) language-proficiency level reported a greater frequency of out-of-class English learning than learners at the A2 (beginner high) level. However, they did not find any significant differences between learners at the A1 (beginner low) and B1 (intermediate low) language-proficiency levels. Thus, current research suggests that there might be some correlation between learners' proficiency levels and their self-directed language-learning behaviours beyond the classroom.

Specifically with regard to language learners' autonomous language learning with technology, research studies have found more consistent findings on the positive association between language learners' proficiency levels and their perceptions and selective use of technological resources for learning. For instance, Ala-Kynny's (2012) study of the Finnish upper-secondary-school language learners found that learners of different proficiency levels reported different perceptions of the language-learning potential of music. Students with higher proficiency showed more confidence in understanding song lyrics and used them more frequently while listening to English songs. They also perceived music much more positively in terms of its benefits for improving different language skills. Marefat and Barbari (2009) examined the relationship between out-of-class language-learning strategies and students' reading-comprehension abilities among a group of Iranian EFL learners. They found that there were no proficiency differences in learners' employment of formal, functional and monitoring learning strategies in general. However, learners of different proficiency levels engaged with different learning resources: students with higher levels of proficiency mostly engaged in reading activities; students at the intermediate level of proficiency engaged more in speaking and listening activities that involved demanding resources such as news on the radio; and students at the lowest level of proficiency mostly selected listening activities with fewer cognitive demands, such as music. The differential utilization of various technological resources was corroborated in Jones's (2015) study, in which she examined the autonomous use of mobile devices for language learning among adult learners of Welsh. Jones found that language-proficiency levels affected what technological resources were accessed and how they were used. She also found that learners with lower levels of proficiency focused more on conversational Welsh and did not engage extensively in reading and writing. Their engagement in reading and writing was often in small chunks such as writing and receiving emails, text messages and/or tweets. In contrast, learners with higher levels of proficiency reported extensive use of digital resources for writing. Furthermore, although listening to Welsh radio was a common activity across the participants, learners at different proficiency levels used this activity for different functions: learners at the beginner level tended to listen to Welsh radio to strengthen their sense of the language rather than to engage in conscious learning with the resources as learners of higher levels of proficiency did. Furthermore, the participants were also found to use Welsh of different difficulty levels for different purposes, such as listening to lighter chat programmes to understand the meaning and listening to news to get used to the rhythm of the language. Lai and Gu (2011) further found that language-proficiency levels may affect learners' selective use of technological resources to meet different language-learning purposes. They found that the HK university foreign-language learners who had been studying their target languages for more than four years reported more positive (although not statistically significant) perceptions of the use of technology to regulate their social connections and support than those with less than four years of learning experience (t = 1.73, p = 0.08). They further reported that language learners' technology use changed over time with an increase in their proficiency level or in their confidence in their language learning. She reported the account of a Spanish language learner's experience of using technology during two years of learning Spanish. The learner did not use any technology in the first semester since she could not understand Spanish songs and thus lost the motivation to seek other technology-delivered authentic materials. In the second semester, she started to use online dictionaries and translators a lot to help her to comprehend texts. Then, starting from the second year, she began using online chatting resources when her confidence in her Spanish proficiency increased after a summer study-abroad programme. Not only did the types of technologies she opted to use change, but the nature of technology use changed over time as well: at the beginning, she used technology just for entertainment and to get a taste of what the language was really like, and it then evolved into more intentional learning plans. Li et al. (2015) surveyed 531 sixth–eighth graders in US public schools on their use of technology for English activities, including 133 English-language learners. They found that English-language learners with higher self-reported English skills used technology for surfing the internet, researching, reading, blogging and photo sharing more than did learners with perceived lower English skills. They also used technology to engage in more diverse activities concerning social networking and schoolwork, whereas learners with lower English skills tended to use technology more for entertainment. The researchers further found that students' use of technology for writing activities was related to their perceptions of their oral proficiency levels: English-language learners with higher oral skills were more likely to use public writing media technology such as blogging, whereas learners with lower oral skills tended to opt more for technology that supported private written communication such as emails.

Learner beliefs/values and autonomous language learning with technology beyond the classroom

Studies have shown that language learners' learning beliefs influence their perceptions of and engagement in out-of-class learning activities. Wu (2012) found that HK ESL learners' self-efficacy in English learning was associated with their positive perceptions of the usefulness of out-of-class learning activities and their engagement in them. Another study conducted with HK university foreign-language learners (Lai and Gu, 2011) further found that language learners who held a stronger belief in seeking language-use opportunities in daily life tended to be more likely to use technology to support their language learning beyond the classroom. Specifically, they found that the stronger the learners held the belief, the more positively they reported using technologies to expand their learning resources (r = 0.30) and to commit themselves to language-learning goals (r = 0.33). In contrast, they found that the correlations between a knowledge-oriented belief (i.e. what was learned in the language classroom was sufficient, and language learning was about grasping the linguistic system) and different categories of technology use were negative and approaching zero. Lai (2015a) further found that different language-learning beliefs influenced learners' ability to perceive the affordances of technological resources. She discussed how a participant who believed in language learning through interaction perceived online resources and language labs as useless for language learning since they did not enhance her opportunities to interact with others in the target language. Lai further contrasted how different language-learning beliefs led to different ways to approach the same resources. One participant, Shiu, believed in the importance of systematic grammar learning and thus visited online French grammar sites frequently for self-study of the grammar. In contrast, another participant, Jie, did not perceive the need to study Japanese grammar systematically and used Japanese grammar websites simply as on-demand aids when watching Japanese soap operas to facilitate comprehension. Kalaja et al. (2011) compared 116 university students' experiences of learning two languages – English and Swedish – outside school, and found that with similar materials and semiotic artefacts in both languages available to these students, they actively constructed their learning ecologies in English but failed to expand their learning ecologies in Swedish. They further identified that the different profiles of ecology construction in these two languages were subject to learners' beliefs about the social status and usefulness of the languages and about the approaches to learning the languages, which shaped the learners' ability to perceive affordances and learning opportunities in the environment, and their ability to utilize these affordances and learning opportunities.

In addition to specific language-learning beliefs, researchers have also examined the influence of fundamental values that learners cling to during their technology-enhanced learning behaviours. Cultural values shape human identity and ways of thinking, and form the basis of human attitudes and behaviours (Cutler, 2005; Markus and Kitayama, 1991). The influence of cultural values on students' learning preferences and approaches to learning has been well established (Parrish and Linder-VanBerschot, 2010; Zhang and Sternberg, 2011).

It has also been found that individuals' preferences for and use of information and communication technologies are closely intertwined with cultural values (Ford, Connelly and Meister, 2003; Leidner and Kayworth, 2006). Building on these research bases, Lai et al. (2016) examined how individual-espoused cultural-value orientations influenced language learners' self-directed use of technology for language learning beyond the classroom. They surveyed 661 university foreign-language learners from three different regions – Hong Kong, the United States and China – on four cultural-value orientations – collectivism (the degree to which individuals conform to group norms and expectations), power distance (the degree to which individuals perceive and accept power difference and abide by superiors' opinions), uncertainty avoidance (the degree to which individuals tolerate unstructured or uncertain events and ambiguous situations) and long-term orientation (the degree of importance that individuals attach to future events) – and the frequency of learners' use of technology for language learning and/or in the target language beyond the classroom. Structural equation modelling (SEM) analysis of the survey data revealed that individual cultural orientations had significant direct effects on learners' use of technology for informal language learning. Specifically, they found significant positive influence of long-term orientation ($\beta = 0.20$, $p < 0.001$), collectivistic orientation ($\beta = 0.07$, $p < 0.05$) and power distance ($\beta = 0.16$, $p < 0.001$) on the frequency of technology use, which suggested that language learners with long-term, collectivistic and high power-distance orientations had greater likelihood of engaging in autonomous use of technology for learning beyond the classroom. Uncertainty avoidance negatively influenced technology use ($\beta = -0.09$, $p < 0.05$). In addition, long-term orientation was found to have a significant positive influence on learners' performance expectancy ($\beta = 0.30$, $p < 0.001$). Thus, the findings showed that learners' long-term orientation and uncertainty avoidance played the most significant roles in influencing the frequency of their language learning with technology, which, the authors argued, corresponded with the uniqueness of informal language learning with technology. In the informal learning contexts, long-term orientations are essential because the outcomes of informal learning are often intangible and do not show up in the short term. Thus, it is critical for learners to be far-sighted and to think forward so as to be able to perceive informal learning as useful and actively take advantage of technological resources for informal learning. Uncertainty avoidance is also essential in informal learning contexts because informal learning often takes place in authentic life experiences, which are often complex, full of ambiguity and without immediate and structured support from instructors and more capable peers (Callanan, Cervantes and Loomis, 2011). The situation is further compounded when the use of technology is involved in informal learning contexts since technology often brings extra layers of uncertainty and challenge. Thus low uncertainty avoidance is particularly important in this context.

Hence, the current research findings suggest that it is not only learners' beliefs about learning and language learning but also the fundamental values they hold that may influence both the frequency of their technology use beyond the classroom and the way they interact with technology.

Learner dispositions/orientations/abilities and autonomous language learning with technology beyond the classroom

The current literature has identified various disposition, orientation and ability factors that influence learners' autonomous language learning with technology beyond the classroom, including learning preferences, goals and needs, habitual practices and learners' ability to perceive and utilize the affordances of technologies for learning.

Lee, Yeung and Ip (2016) examined the relationship between students' learning style preferences and their use of technology for language learning. They used Reid's (1987) four innate and perceptual learning styles to measure students' preferences: visual, auditory, kinaesthetic and tactile learning styles. Running a path analysis on the survey responses of 401 ESL learners from two universities, the authors found that the visual learning style ($\beta = 0.28$, $p < 0.05$) and the kinaesthetic learning style ($\beta = 0.31$, $p < 0.05$) were significant positive predictors of students' use of technology for self-directed English learning. The researchers called for efforts to help students increase their awareness of their own preferred learning styles so as to help them select the technology-enhanced activities that matched their learning preferences.

Learners' language-learning goals have also been found to influence their selective use of technology for learning. Bailly (2010) initiated a foreign-language learning programme in which a group of French upper-secondary-school students studied a self-selected language with only the support of consular sessions. She found that the students mainly engaged in two types of out-of-class learning activities: 'serious' activities that involved learning techniques that were often used at school – such as doing grammar and vocabulary drills, taking notes and so on – and 'lighter', more entertaining activities, which were strongly related to their lives, personal interests and environment, such as chatting, watching TV and playing games. More importantly, she found that learners who approached learning with a very dedicated goal, such as seeking a diploma or pursuing an interest in manga, tended to engage in serious activities more frequently, whereas learners who were learning the language with the purpose of socialization with others or to seek their own identities were more likely to engage in lighter activities.

In addition, learners' learning histories and habitual practices have also been found to influence their technology selection. Lai (2015a) reported that learners' prior language-learning experience mediated their ability to perceive and act on the affordances of technological resources for language learning. The participants in her study tended to transfer their successful experience of using technological resources to learn one language, such as listening to music, into the experience of learning a subsequent language. There were also participants who did not engage much in autonomous learning of a language beyond the classroom but gained good grades, and hence, subsequently opted not to engage in technology-enhanced language learning beyond the classroom when learning another language.

In addition to these non-technology-related individual factors, learners' ability to perceive and take advantage of the affordances of technological resources for language learning is also a critical factor that may influence students' self-directed language learning with technology. Computer self-efficacy has been found to influence students' intention to use technology (Chang and Tung, 2008; Hsu, Wang and Chiu, 2009). It consists not only of generic information, communication literacy and digital literacy (Kennedy et al., 2008), but also of discipline-specific competencies in terms of learners' awareness of the language-learning potentials of technological resources (Alajmi, 2011; Clark et al., 2009) and their knowledge and skills in selecting particular technologies to match their particular learning purposes, needs and strategies and in making effective use of these technologies for learning (Ertmer and Ottenbreit-Leftwich, 2010; Lai, Wang and Lei, 2012). Rahimi and Katal (2012) found that whether English-language learners would use podcasting for English learning on their own was subject to their experience and familiarity with podcasts. Lai and Gu (2011) contrasted the interview responses of learners who reported higher levels of engagement with technology for learning with those of learners who reported little use of technology, and found that active users of technology often reported a higher level of digital literacy. For instance, these learners reported employing strategies to reap the benefits of online chatting but at the same time ensured the quality of their online interactions by using triangulation in information evaluation. They demonstrated metacognitive knowledge and strategies on how to learn a language through online chatting, being attentive to the language used and appropriating the language critically and selectively. These learners also exhibited certain levels of intercultural competence that are needed for cross-cultural online communication.

Learner external factors

The section above reviewed various individual variables that have been reported to influence language learners' self-directed use of technology for learning beyond the classroom. This section will focus on the social and technological factors that affect learners' selection and use of technology for language learning. The oft-cited external factors include teacher, parent and peer support, institutional expectations and instructional arrangements, and the characteristics of the technological resources.

Social influence and support

Peers are one of the major social forces that influence students' learning behaviours. They are reported to be a major motivator for students to go online (Gray et al., 2010). The university foreign-language learners in Lai's (2015a) study reported that peers helped raise their awareness of potentially useful resources. Sharing technological resources among friends and classmates was common and helped them enlarge their language-learning ecology. A Korean learner in the study reported habitually surfing Korean websites and blogs, and he attributed this habit to his best friend from another university who shared with him the benefits of such activities for learning Korean and encouraged him to do the same. The students reported being influenced not only by immediate peer circles but also by virtual communities. Learners reported using the Music Television (MTV) in Spanish that they came across on Facebook postings to enrich their Spanish-learning experience. They also reported selecting English movies to watch online based on online recommendations. Sun, Franklin and Gao (2015), in support of the role of virtual communities in providing affective and cognitive support for students, analysed the postings in an informal English-learning discussion forum and found extensive evidence of social presence, with a high proportion of postings dedicated to personal-experience sharing and distributed teaching presence among the users through facilitating discourses and feedback.

In addition to peers, parental influence has also been reported as one potential factor that affects learners' learning behaviours. For instance, the Chinese lower-secondary-school EFL learners in Lai, Zhu and Gong's (2015) study reported that their parents played a critical role in influencing their engagement in autonomous language learning with technology. These participants reported that their parents shaped their learning approaches through sharing English-language learning strategies, encouraging or discouraging the types of activities that they engaged in, controlling their access to computer-assisted activities and arranging learning resources and venues. As one participant pointed out, his parents introduced him to online English dictionaries, which motivated him to explore other digital resources for learning, including online English books and videos. But at the same time, the researchers found that parental influence also shaped students' interaction with technological resources. For instance, parents' emphasis on grammar influenced students into focusing primarily on grammar and vocabulary even when the students engaged in meaning-focused activities such as watching videos and listening to songs, which turned apparently meaning-focused activities into largely form-focused interaction.

For K–12 and university foreign-language learners, one major social influence comes from teachers. Teachers are important social agents who shape students' intellectual and social experiences and the quality thereof (Davis, 2003; Farmer, Lines and Hamm, 2011): Teachers exert direct and explicit influence on students through their instructional practices, and influence students indirectly and implicitly through role modelling (Katyal and Evers, 2004). Carson and Mynard (2012) argued that teachers could influence students' autonomous language learning outside the classroom through various aspects: 1) raising their awareness of the process and the key metalinguistic and metacognitive concepts of language learning; 2) providing them with methodological information about resources and strategies and guiding them to experiment with these resources and strategies and discover what works for them and what does not; and 3) providing affective support. Teachers' encouragement and support have been found to influence both the quantity and the quality of students' autonomous use of technology for language learning outside the classroom (Lai et al., 2012; Margaryan and Littlejohn, 2008). And the encouragement and support could be in the form of explicit expectancies in the curriculum arrangements and instructional practices (Selwyn, 2008) or in the form of recommendations and guidance (Lai and Gu, 2011; Lai, Zhu and Gong, 2015; Castellano, Mynard and Rubesch, 2011; Deepwell and Malik, 2008). For instance, the lower-secondary-school EFL students in Lai, Zhu and Gong's (2015) study reported that teachers' recommendation of resources raised their awareness of the benefits of technology-enhanced English-language learning and broadened the range of their out-of-class learning experiences. They also reported that teacher guidance on how to use different out-of-class learning activities influenced how they interacted with the technological resources. They further pointed out that teachers also influenced their out-of-class learning indirectly through their parents: teachers' acknowledgement of a certain learning activity or venue would directly determine whether their parents would encourage and support the use of that learning activity or venue. The university foreign-language learners in Lai's (2015a) study reported extending the technological resources their teachers used in-class to out-of-class contexts. They talked about how they continued to watch the videos/movies they viewed in class and started searching for additional videos/movies on their own. Fagerlund (2012) also found that when teachers incorporated into their in-class instruction some technological activities that learners could follow up at home, such as listening to songs and watching videos, students' language-learning experiences beyond the classroom became richer and more diversified. Thus, the current literature points out various roles that teachers can play in influencing language learners' autonomous language learning with technology beyond the classroom.

To understand how these different teacher roles interact with other psychosocial factors to affect language learners' self-directed use of technology, Lai (2015b) collected interview and survey responses from a group of university foreign-language learners. She conducted interview studies with fifteen foreign-language learners in order to understand how different teacher behaviours influenced their out-of-class use of technology for learning, and constructed a conceptual model based on her participants' interview responses. Then she tested the model against 160 survey responses. Students' interview responses revealed three types of teacher behaviours that influenced their self-directed out-of-class use of technology for language learning: affective support in terms of teacher encouragement; capacity support in terms of teacher resource recommendations, metacognitive tips and strategy sharing; and behaviour support in terms of teacher use of technological resources in class. The path analysis of the survey responses showed that the three types of teacher behaviours exerted different influences on the language learners' frequency of technology use for learning beyond the classroom. Specifically, affective support influenced the frequency of technology use through enhancing learners' perceptions of the benefits of technological resources for learning. Capacity support and behaviour support influenced technology use by strengthening learners' perceptions of the availability of support for technology use, which boosted their self-efficacy in using technology for language learning. Lai concluded that different types of teacher support have different functions and need to be concurrently utilized and coordinated to enhance language learners' autonomous use of technology for language learning beyond the classroom.

Institutional expectations and instructional arrangements

Students' situated interpretations of the instructional expectations – expressed through in-class discourse and course requirements – and instructional arrangements – in the form of the curriculum set-up, instructional practices and assessment regimes – shape their learning behaviours (Goodyear and Ellis, 2008), and is found to be related to the frequency and nature of students' technology use (Selwyn, 2008). Whether learners perceive of the use of technology as aligning with their interpretations of the demands of the study situations has been found to be a critical factor influencing their self-initiated use of technology for learning (Chen, 2011; Goodyear and Ellis, 2008). Research findings support a significant association between course requirements and the frequency and nature of student technology use (Kennedy et al., 2008).

Assessment is one component that is highlighted in the current literature. Zhan and Andrews (2014) conducted a longitudinal study of three university EFL students, following them from the day they entered university to the day they took the College English Test Band 4 test through diary entries and interviews. They examined the potential washback effects of the assessment on students' out-of-class learning and found that the learners' interpretation of the assessment expectations shaped the skills that they focused on practising outside the classroom. Saad, Yunus and Embi (2013) collected the out-of-class language-learning strategies of nine EFL learners in Malaysia and triangulated their weekly entries and interviews on their out-of-class learning experience with teacher interviews and document analysis of the module description. The participants reported that assessment had the most influence on their out-of-class learning activity arrangements among all the in-class activities. Furthermore, the authors found that the nature of the assessment for different modules was a major determinant of the types of out-of-class activities that students engaged in. For instance, the assessment for the reading module consisted of tests and quizzes, whereas the assessment for the writing and oral communication modules was in the form of assignments and oral presentations. Consequently, learners reported engaging in the least amount of out-of-class learning for the reading module and largely restricting their learning materials to those used in class. Although these two studies did not examine the use of technology for language learning per se, they did suggest that assessment influences the focus and nature of learners' out-of-class learning.

Characteristics of technological resources

The features of a particular technological resource and its match with the characteristics of informal learning contexts determine its likelihood to be selected and incorporated into language learners' out-of-class learning resource repertoire. Conole (2008) found that students in her study placed greater value on technologies they had 'discovered' or selected for themselves. Personalization was a key factor in technology selection in that the students tended to select technologies and adapt their use to suit their learning needs and preferences. Learners' preference for self-selected technological resources over institution-provisioned ones was also observed in Steel and Levy's (2013) study in the Australian context. In a similar vein, Doyle and Parrish (2012) found that learners tended to choose easier, leisure-typed activities, such as listening to music and songs and watching movies, where personal choice and enjoyment were the major criteria. Barbee (2013) surveyed 151 Japanese EFL secondary school students aged between sixteen and seventeen, and found that the students' selective engagement with technological resources was dependent more on how enjoyable the sources were than on how effective they considered the sources to be. Lai (2015a) further found that the features of out-of-class learning contexts (e.g. segmented periods of short durations, lack of prompt assistance and feedback from teachers) constrained how her participants constructed their learning ecologies. The participants preferred out-of-class experiences that did not require a lot of time, tended to choose the resources that were easy to locate and use, and favoured resources that contained learning support that facilitated their use. Olmedo (2015) also found that Spanish secondary school students in her study tended to select the activities that did not involve a large amount of time, and, thus, they reported watching films with or without subtitles as the activity they least engaged in due to its cognitive and time demands. The Austrian advanced EFL learners in Trinder's (2016) study reported a list of factors that influenced their preferences regarding, and their evaluation of the usefulness of, resources and environments. These factors included the robustness of the technological resources, the multimodal nature of the channels (auditory and visual channels were favoured over text-only media), the ubiquitous and anytime access to the resources, the immediacy and trustworthiness of the help offered, the affective value, target orientation, opportunities for corrective feedback, learning potential as defined by access to native speakers, the use of complex language and exposure to new language and the authenticity of the input, situation or context. Trinder (2016) argued that these factors interacted with learners' 'subjectively experienced quality of particular resources' and their individual learning goals to shape their construction of personalized learning ecologies (p. 98).

Interaction of internal and external factors

The internal and external factors reviewed above do not exist alone and exert influence independently; rather, they coexist to influence language learners' autonomous learning with technology. Thus, it is important to understand how these psychosocial factors interact with one another to affect students' self-directed technology use. Lai (2013) adopted the theory of planned behaviour as the theoretical frame of reference to identify various factors that are relevant to self-directed technology use for learning along the attitudinal, perceived behaviour-control and social-influence dimensions and to conceptualize the interrelationships between these factors. In her study, she examined a number of internal factors, including perceived usefulness (learners' belief in the usefulness of technological resources for language learning), educational compatibility (learners' perceptions of the compatibility between using technology for learning and their own learning preferences and values), language-learning motivation (learners' perception of the value of the language and their interest in learning the language), language-learning approaches (learners' views of language learning that favour active engagement in out-of-class language learning and value language-use opportunities), computer self-efficacy (learners' perceptions of their capability to select and use technology for language learning), and self-regulation (learners' ability to regulate their own learning). She also included some external factors, including learners' situated interpretation (their perceptions of the requirements concerning technology use for learning in the learning contexts), facilitating conditions (their perceptions of the availability of support in their surroundings that encourages and facilitates the use of technology for learning), and subjective norm (their perceptions of whether or not significant others encourage the adoption of technology). She constructed a conceptual framework to hypothesize the interactive relationships between these key predictors in influencing the frequency of various dimensions of technology use. A total of 373 university foreign-language learners were surveyed, and SEM analysis was conducted to test the conceptual model. It was found that, among all the factors included in the model, three variables played major roles in influencing learners' autonomous use of technology. These three variables were language-learning motivation, perceived usefulness and facilitating conditions. Language-learning motivation ($\beta = 0.50$, $p < 0.001$) and perceived usefulness ($\beta = 0.20$, $p < 0.01$) had significant direct influence on learners' technology use. The other independent variables all influenced technology use indirectly through either perceived usefulness or educational compatibility. Facilitating conditions were the main indirect predictors of technology use, and their influence was mediated by perceived usefulness, self-regulation and computer self-efficacy ($\beta = 0.10$, $p < 0.01$). Thus, in addition to its strong direct impact, perceived usefulness was the major mediator of other factors' influence on technology use. Referring back to the three major determinants of individuals' behavioural intentions conceptualized in the theory of planned behaviour – attitude, perceived control of behaviour and social influence – Lai further argued that the three constructs of the attitudinal component included in the study (perceived usefulness, language-learning motivation and educational compatibility) seemed to play major roles, either as dominant predictors or major mediating venues of other variables' influence on technology use or in shaping language learners' digital choices, while the perceived control and social-influence components affected technology use mainly through their influence on these attitudinal factors. Thus, Lai concluded that technology use was the direct product of learners' buy-in of the benefits and necessity of using technology for language learning and their personal will to take advantage of these benefits, and the indirect product of social support. She further highlighted the need to focus on the attitudinal component in developing educational interventions to enhance students' self-directed learning with technology. Figure 4.1 illustrates the internal and external factors investigated in Lai's (2013) study and their interrelationships.

In another study, Lai et al. (2016) integrated cultural-value orientations into the theory of planned behaviour framework in order to understand how the cultural values that individuals espoused may interact with other internal and external factors to influence language learners' autonomous use of technology for language learning beyond the classroom. In that study, they only included the four key predictors of technology adoption listed in the UTAUT model (Venkatesh et al., 2003). The UTAUT model is one of the most influential

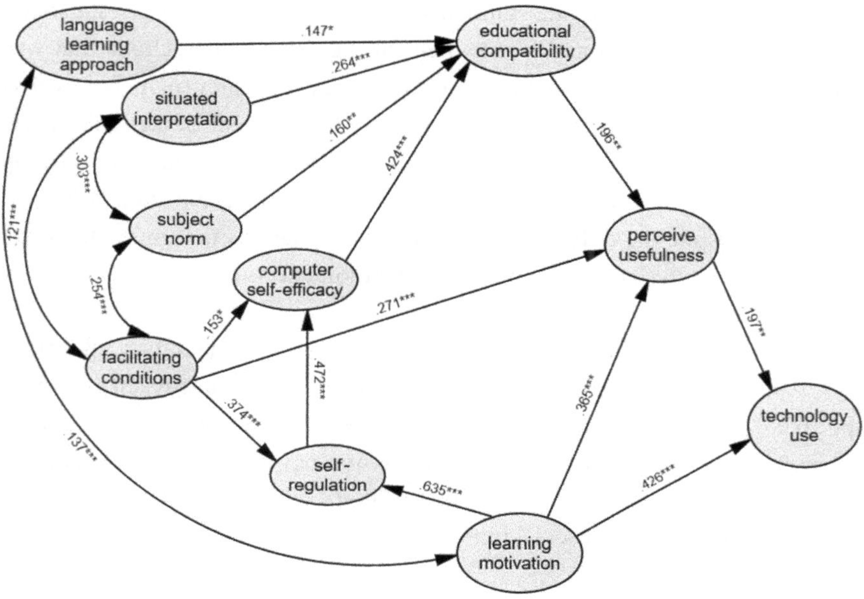

Figure 4.1 The interaction of internal and external factors in Lai's (2013) study.

technology adoption models built upon the theory of planned behaviour – which underscores the influence of learners' attitudinal beliefs on their behavioural intentions in relation to technology adoption – as the theoretical foundation (Oliveria and Martins, 2011; Straub, 2009). The study examined the direct, mediated and moderating influences of individual-espoused cultural values, as conceptualized in Hofstede's typology of dimensions of national culture, on language learners' technology adoption. The conceptual model included four cultural-value orientations (long-term orientation, collectivism, power distance and uncertainty avoidance) and five psychosocial predictors of technology use (performance expectancy, effort expectancy, facilitating conditions, social influence and hedonic motivation). Testing the model on 661 survey responses of university foreign-language learners from three countries, the researchers found that the UTAUT model plus hedonic motivation had high explanatory power on university language learners' autonomous learning with technology beyond the classroom, explaining 71 per cent of the variation in learners' intention to use technology in different cultural settings. Furthermore, individual-espoused cultural-value orientations were found to have significant direct effects on technology adoption in informal learning contexts, since adding cultural-value orientations into the model doubled its explanatory power with respect to technology use. Figure 4.2 summarizes the factors that were investigated in Lai et al.'s study (2016) and highlighted the significant interactions that were discovered in that study. Specifically, performance expectancy (namely perceived usefulness) and hedonic motivation (perceived enjoyment of technology use) were found to have the strongest direct influence on learners' intention to adopt technology for language learning outside the classroom, and their influences remained despite the different cultural-value orientations that individuals held as suggested by the lack of significant moderation effects of such orientations on these two variables (See Figure 4.2).

As for the influence of cultural values, long-term orientation ($\beta = 0.20$, $p < 0.001$), power distance ($\beta = 0.16$, $p < 0.001$) and collectivism ($\beta = 0.07$, $p < 0.05$) positively influenced technology use, whereas uncertainty avoidance ($\beta = -0.09$, $p < 0.05$) negatively influenced technology use; long-term orientation influenced performance expectancy ($\beta = 0.30$, $p < 0.001$), uncertainty avoidance moderated the impact of social influence on technology use ($\beta = 0.07$, $p < 0.05$)

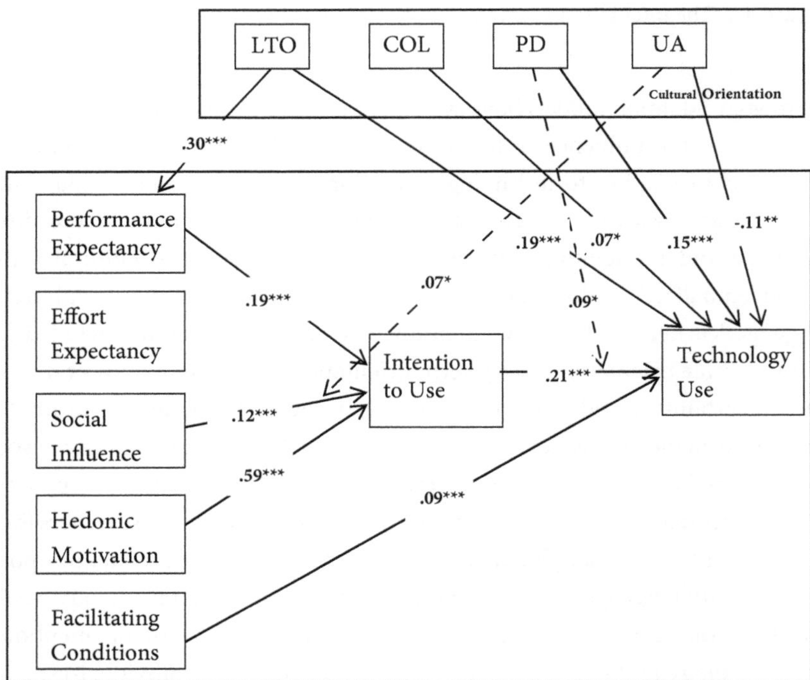

Figure 4.2 The significant interactions in Lai et al.'s (2016) study.

Note: The bold paths were paths that were statically significant. The dotted lines were moderating effects and the solid lines were direct effects. ***p<.001; **p<.01; *<.05; ^p<.10.

and power distance moderated the impact of learners' intention for technology use on actual technology use ($\beta = 0.09$, $p < 0.05$). Therefore, this study added individual-espoused cultural-value orientations as an important internal factor to the list of factors influencing language learners' autonomous learning with technology and revealed the intricate interaction between cultural orientations and other psychosocial factors in influencing technology use in informal language learning.

I also conducted another study to examine how various teacher practices interacted with performance expectancy, effort expectancy, social influence and facilitating conditions to influence language learners' use of technology for learning across two cultural contexts. The study surveyed 418 university foreign-language learners in two regions (190 in Hong Kong and 228 in the United States). It was found that the three types of teacher practices exhibited differential levels of influence, with teacher capacity support having the most influence: teacher affective support did not have a significant influence on students' intention to use technology ($\beta = -0.00$, $p = 0.85$); teacher capacity support had a significant positive influence on students' intention to use technology indirectly via facilitating conditions and social influence ($\beta = 0.21$, $p = 0.007$); and teacher behaviour support influenced students' intention to use technology indirectly via social influence ($\beta = 0.06$, $p = 0.01$). Comparing the predictive model of the HK sample with that of the US sample, the researchers found that teacher capacity support had a similar significant influence on students' intention to use technology for both the HK ($\beta = 0.19$, $p = 0.00$) and the US cohorts ($\beta = 0.24$, $p = 0.00$). In contrast, teacher affective support significantly influenced students' performance expectancy in the HK cohort but not in the US cohort, and teacher behaviour support influenced students' perception of social influence significantly in the HK cohort ($\beta = 0.35$, $p = 0.00$) but not in the US cohort. The study thus concluded that teacher influence on students' intention to engage in self-directed out-of-class learning with technology varied across cultural contexts. It also suggested the importance of teachers providing recommendations on technological resources and sharing cognitive and metacognitive strategies on how to select and use technological resources effectively, given the consistent significant influence of teacher capacity support across cultural contexts. Figure 4.3 summarizes the findings in that study.

The above studies are some initial steps towards unravelling the interaction between various internal and external factors for learners that are identified in the current literature as influencing language learners' autonomous language

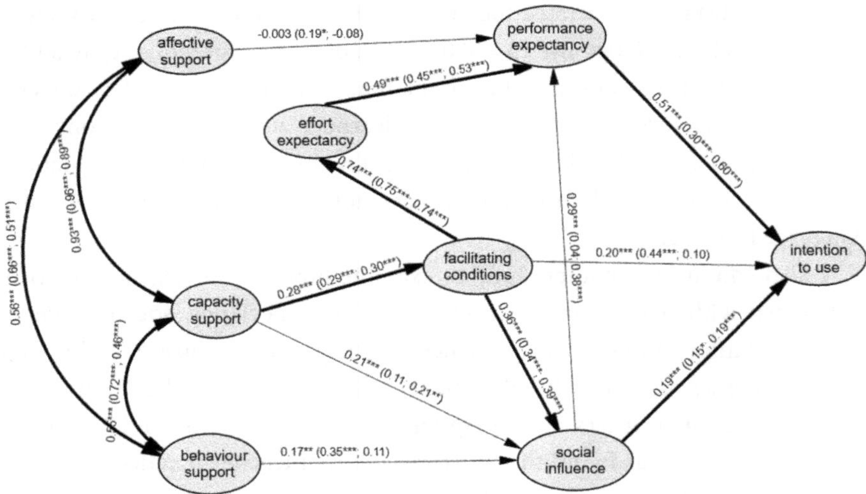

Figure 4.3 The influence of different teacher-practice variables and their interaction paths.

Note: The number in the brackets represented the path weights of HK sample and US sample respectively. The bolded paths were the ones with consistent findings across the two samples and the unbolded paths were those with inconsistent findings.

learning with technology beyond the classroom. These studies only examined a subset of factors and interactions and there are much more to be investigated. More studies are needed to identify key predictors, their antecedents, as well as interactions thereof in influencing language learners' digital choice so as to inform the design of educational interventions aimed at enhancing language learners' use of technology beyond the classroom to enrich their language-learning experience.

Part Two

Promoting Out-of-Class Autonomous Language Learning with Technology

5

Promoting Out-of-Class Autonomous Language Learning with Technology: Learner Training

The previous chapters have discussed the importance of autonomous language learning with technology beyond the classroom and students' varied engagement in such learning behaviours. This discussion led to an essential issue – that is, how can language educators foster and support learners' autonomous language learning with technology beyond the classroom. To understand this issue, language educators need first of all to hear learners' views on what support they need and how they could be supported.

Learners' perceptions of autonomous learning with technology beyond the classroom

The current literature suggests that language learners in general perceive out-of-class learning as essential to successful language learning, and they tend to regard in-class and out-of-class learning as serving different yet complementary functions. For instance, Conole (2008) reported that UK university foreign-language learners in her study valued their out-of-class learning experience and, at the same time, considered in-class learning as vital to building a sense of community. Lamb (2004) obtained similar findings in his study in the Indonesian context, where, although they felt that much of their learning took place outside their English classes, the EFL participants valued the relationships they established with teachers in class. The Norwegian participants in Cabot's (2014) study felt that out-of-class learning provided greater language input, but that in-class learning was particularly essential in serving the metalinguistic function of output and consequently contributed greatly to the development of productive skills such as writing and speaking, at least in the case of the female students. Lai (2015a) interviewed a group of HK university foreign-language learners on their perceptions of the contribution of in-class and out-of-class learning to their language-learning experience. The learners described in-class language learning as compulsory and primarily engaging them in studying the linguistic aspects of the language in a systematic way, which, despite being a passive activity, helped them to build a basic understanding of the language and to focus on and persevere in learning the language. Thus, the learners tended to perceive in-class learning as primarily serving metacognitive and cognitive functions. In contrast, they characterized their out-of-class learning experiences as voluntary, fun and spontaneous, and serving a wide range of functions, including enabling them to acquire language by using it in real life, helping them sustain interest and motivation in learning, giving them access to how the language is actually used by native speakers in daily life and thus strengthening their sense of the language, enhancing their connection with the target culture and peer learners and allowing them to self-assess their language abilities that gave them a sense of accomplishment, boosted their self-efficacy and motivated them to set goals for further study. Therefore, for these learners, out-of-class language learning served different cognitive and metacognitive functions from those served by their in-class learning experience. Furthermore, they felt that out-of-class language learning helped them to meet a wider array of language-learning needs, not only cognitive and metacognitive, but also affective and social needs.

It has been shown that language learners further perceive that they themselves have the greatest responsibility for out-of-class learning. In a number of research studies, the majority of learners were found to believe that they themselves were the ones who should decide the learning objectives and learning contents outside the classroom (Chan, Spratt and Humphrey, 2010; Yildirim, 2008). For instance, Gamble and colleagues (2012) surveyed 399 language learners from seven universities in Japan and found that, regardless of motivation levels, the majority of the participants felt that they needed to assume the responsibility for learning beyond the classroom. At the same time, however, they also expressed a lack of confidence about their ability to engage in learning outside the classroom. Similarly, the HK ESL learners surveyed in Chan and colleagues' (2010) study believed that they themselves should assume the most responsibility for their learning outside the classroom, including deciding what to learn and making sure that they made learning progress outside the class. On the other hand, they perceived that teachers' responsibilities involved setting learning objectives, managing their in-class learning and evaluating their learning. At the same time, they rated themselves low on their ability to engage in learning outside the classroom and reported a general lack of motivation to engage in out-of-class learning.

Learners' reservations about their ability to assume responsibility for their language learning beyond the classroom have been reported in studies conducted in different parts of the world. Holden and Usuki (1999) found that although their Japanese EFL participants were aware of the importance of out-of-class learning and the various means they could utilize for learning, they did not know how to turn this awareness into action. The Cyprus EFL learners in Çelik et al.'s (2012) study also expressed concerns about their skills in using ICT to improve their foreign-language learning ability. Moreover, language learners' concern about their inability to assume their responsibilities for out-of-class learning manifests itself at different levels. First, students lack confidence in their ability to arrange learning activities outside the classroom. Farahani (2014) found that their Iranian EFL learners rated themselves poorly in their decision-making ability in relation to choosing learning materials and activities and setting learning objectives outside the classroom. The student participants in Stolk and colleagues' (2010) study reported challenges in terms of their ability to deal with the uncertainties associated with language learning and expressed concern about whether they were approaching learning in the right way or were learning the 'right thing'. Second, students do not know how to select appropriate technologies and use them effectively for language learning. For instance, Castellano, Mynard and Rubesch (2011) examined Japanese EFL learners' use of a self-access learning centre and found that the learners showed a general trend of high interest but low usage in the technology-enhanced learning materials. They found that this discrepancy was due to learners' lack of awareness of the tools that could be utilized and their reported lack of ability and confidence in making effective use of the technological tools for language learning. Li (2013) studied thirty-two undergraduate English majors in China, who reported a high level of English-learning motivation, and found that most of them had difficulty in engaging in informal learning using Web 2.0 tools. The students attributed their limited use of these tools for language learning primarily to the lack of effective learning methods of using these tools, their inability to locate and access related material and human resources, and their limited self-management skills in terms of setting clear learning goals and managing distractions on the internet. Similarly, Bailly (2010) reported that her French participants were unaware that they could use fun materials for learning and encountered difficulties in gathering appropriate and reliable resources. The participants also lacked knowledge of how to use these materials effectively for learning: they tended to set unrealistic and unreachable objectives, they lacked the criteria for finding and selecting resources that matched their learning needs and preferences, and they did not know how to measure their learning progress and assess their skills. Some of the participants even used inefficient learning strategies. Furthermore, the HK university students in Chan et al.'s study (2010) reported having difficulty in choosing appropriate learning materials that matched their proficiency level. Third, students also seem to have difficulty transferring the strategies acquired in-class to out-of-class learning contexts. For instance, Hussein and Haron (2012) found that around half of their Arabic-language learners in Malaysia were not confident about their ability to apply efficient reading, listening and writing strategies when engaging with materials outside the classroom, and they were particularly uncertain about applying communication strategies to engage in conversations in Arabic.

Learners' feelings of uncertainty about their ability to engage in out-of-class language learning have led to their expectation that teachers should play some role in their out-of-class learning. Cotterall and Reinders (2000) found that the degree of counselling support that students received was the most significant determinant of success in language learning at self-access centres. Learners have expressed specific aspects of the support they expect to receive from teachers. For instance, the HK EFL learners in Chan et al.'s (2010) study perceived that it was their teachers' responsibility to identify the learning weaknesses that they needed to focus on in out-of-class learning. The Chinese EFL learners in Wang's (2007) study expected their teachers to provide advice on language-learning tactics and strategies, and help them to sustain motivation and confidence in autonomous learning of the language beyond the classroom. Lai, Yeung and Hu (2015) further revealed that learners' expectations for teacher involvement and support for out-of-class learning were not reflected in teachers' current practices. They interviewed fifteen undergraduate foreign-language learners and ten foreign-language teachers at a university in Hong Kong on how teachers could influence and support students' self-directed technology use for language learning beyond the classroom. They found that, despite holding similar positive views of the necessity and importance of autonomous language learning with technology beyond the classroom, teachers and students differed in their views on whether teacher involvement was needed: in contrast to the passive and reactive approaches that teachers tended to take, students expected teachers to take a more proactive approach in introducing them to useful technological resources due to their difficulties in selecting the appropriate resources.

The students felt that teachers' general guidance and orientation regarding approaches to language learning was not helpful, but they valued teachers' recommendations concerning specific technological resources for learning. Rather than expecting the gatekeeper role of teachers in providing teacher-made and teacher-adapted online materials for them, the students expected teachers to provide them with metacognitive tips and cognitive strategies on how to select appropriate resources and use them effectively for learning. Furthermore, the learners perceived that teachers' in-class use of technological tools and resources had the potential to develop their mentality for and equip them with the knowledge necessary to use technological resources outside the classroom. Unfortunately, the teachers reported that their in-class integration of technology was mainly driven by the intention to provide audiovisual language and cultural information and stopped short at YouTube videos. Teachers tended to utilize a greater variety of technological resources into the assignments they gave to students; however, students tended to view technology-enhanced language assignments as compulsory work, and these technological resources, if dull, were less likely to be incorporated into their out-of-class learning repertoire. In summary, studies on learners' perceptions of autonomous language learning with technology beyond the classroom show that learners want to be supported in their experimentation with technology for language learning.

Supporting language learners' autonomous learning with technology beyond the classroom

Refuting the belief that, over time, learners will acquire the ability to use technology effectively on their own, Hubbard (2013) argued that such skills would not come naturally to learners, and that explicit training on the principles behind the effective use of various technological tools for language learning is much needed. Various studies have attested to the efficacies of learner training and support in enhancing autonomous language learning with technology. Researchers have found that targeted pedagogical training in the metacognitive strategies of interacting with technological platforms could enhance learners' ability to realize their language-learning potential. O'Bryan (2008) found that three ten-minute pedagogical training sessions on how to use glossing, and the rationale thereof, induced more positive perceptions of the advantage of glosses for enhanced reading performance and significantly greater use of glosses during online reading among learners. Zenotz (2012) found that a training programme on metacognitive reading strategies for online reading in general helped learners to improve their reading comprehension of online texts. Similarly, Ranalli (2013) found that a five-week online strategy instruction programme on web-based dictionary skills led to significantly greater vocabulary gains. Prichard (2013), focusing on learners' use of social networking sites, developed a training programme to inform them of the norms and communication conventions of Facebook interaction, to enhance their awareness of how Facebook could be used in culturally appropriate ways for socialization, and to develop their strategies for using Facebook in ways that could benefit language learning. He found that the training programme helped to enhance learners' use of Facebook to build social capital and raised their awareness of the language-learning potentials of Facebook. Lai, Shum and Tian (2016), focusing on developing language learners' general skills to utilize technological tools for language learning, developed an online training programme that targeted learners' willingness to engage in self-directed uses of technology for language learning and their pedagogical, strategic and technical knowledge of various technological tools for language development. The researchers found that the learners who participated in the online training, in general, expressed more positive attitudes towards and perceptions of self-directed use of technology for language learning. These learners also reported a significant increase in the frequency of their engagement in such behaviours. These studies have shown that intervention programmes have the potential to enhance language learners' autonomous learning with technology beyond the classroom. On such a promising note, this section will discuss in detail various aspects of the support learners need and showcase some current approaches to providing this support.

What to support?

Various conceptualizations of the necessary components for autonomous language learning beyond the classroom have been proposed in different research fields. In the field of out-of-class language learning, Bailly (2010) listed three conditions necessary for success: motivation, learning resources and learning skills. In the field of autonomous and self-regulated learning, Mozzon-McPherson (2007) argued that the development of autonomy involves a process of 'transformation within the individual' (p. 70). Chateau and Zumbihl (2012) further argued that this transformation involves a change in individuals' views regarding their responsibility for learning and their pedagogical roles, and requires the necessary pedagogical knowledge on the part of learners. Loyens, Magda and Rikers

(2008) highlighted three types of information essential to students' autonomous learning: 1) conceptual information in terms of metalinguistic and metacognitive understanding of learning; 2) methodological information, including materials and resources, work techniques and the planning and management of one's learning; and 3) psychological support. Bouchard (2009) further identified four dimensions that influence learners' autonomous learning strategies: 1) the conative (or psychological) dimension, which concerns learners' motivation and confidence; 2) the algorithmic (or pedagogical) dimension, which relates to learners' selection and use of autonomous learning activities; 3) the semiotics dimension, which refers to learners' ability to evaluate and navigate the resource landscape; and 4) the economic dimension, which concerns learners' evaluation of the value of the autonomous behaviour. Dimensions 1 and 4 pertain to the affective aspect, while dimensions 2 and 3 refer to learners' skills in perceiving the affordances of resources and making use of these affordances to engage in autonomous learning.

In the field of learning ecology, Barnett (2011) conceptualized some critical elements that determine the potency of any learning space, that is, the possibility of learners engaging with a particular learning space. According to Barnett (2011), any learning space contains three domains: 1) physical and material spaces; 2) curricular and pedagogical spaces in terms of the relations and conditions; and 3) learners' interior spaces in terms of their will and preferences. Barnett further conceptualized that the potency of a learning space is a function of the following formula: 'Ability (of learning spaces) + a will to explore + pedagogical encouragement' (p. 172). Thus, whether learners incorporate a learning space into their learning ecology and realize its potency depends on the combination of these three essential elements. Whitworth (2009), in discussing learners' generation of a learning ecology in general, identified a list of conditions for learner-generated contexts. Taking the theoretical basis of activity theory, whereby a learner's activity system is mediated by a variety of mediators, including technological artefacts, cognitive structure (prior knowledge and experience) and procedural rules and divisions of labour, Whitworth conceptualized that the genesis of learner-generated learning contexts relies on the following conditions: 1) learner agency in identifying learning needs; 2) learner ability to recognize the technological and other resources available, to understand the affordances of the resources and their match with their learning needs, and to appropriate the resources to meet these needs; and 3) learning experience that is personally meaningful and well supported and affords the widening of interactions across locations and learners. In a similar vein, Luckin (2010) discussed the scaffolding that is needed for learner-generated contexts and emphasized that the scaffolding should embrace and expand not only learners' cognitive resources but also their affective, metacognitive and epistemic resources.

These conceptualizations from different research fields, although addressing different aspects of autonomous learning beyond the classroom, all suggest that learners' out-of-class engagement with technological resources for learning is subject to their will, interest and motivation, their perceptions of the affordances of technological resources and associated activities, and their ability to make effective use of the resources. Consequently, these three elements should form the core of the support that learners need in order to engage in successful autonomous language learning with technology beyond the classroom.

The affective aspect

Selwyn (2011) argued that the chief obstacles to the use of technology for learning are a lack of interest and motivation, and that motivation and dispositions are precursors to learners' engagement in educational opportunities afforded by digital technologies. Moreover, according to Garrison (1997), learners' willingness to engage in self-directed learning, or the affective aspect, consists primarily of learners' intention and motivation to initiate the learning behaviour (i.e. initial motivation), and learners' sustained interest in the behavioural intention (i.e. maintenance of intention).

Entering motivation is determined largely by learners' perceptions of the necessity and usefulness of the behaviour in enhancing their language-learning performance and by their perceptions of their ability to engage in the behaviour (Ajzen, 2005). Learners' perceptions of the necessity and usefulness of autonomous language learning with technology relies foremost on their learning propensity and dispositions. Strong beliefs about the importance of and interest in learning are the necessary conditions to spark off self-initiated efforts to learn (Weinstein, Woodruff and Awalt, 2007; Winnie and Hadwin, 1998; Zimmerman, 2011). Learners' learning propensity has been found to influence both foreign-language learners' engagement in autonomous learning and their self-regulated use of technology for learning (Ferede, 2010; Hyland, 2004; Lai and Gu, 2011). Therefore, learners' beliefs about the value of learning a language in general may influence their willingness to exercise agency in planning and managing their language-learning experience. And such positive beliefs are precursors to learners' perceptions of the worthiness and value of using technology for learning and thus, boost their likelihood to pursue such after-school endeavours. Benson (2011c) further pointed out that helping learners to gain the locus of control is also critical to boosting the perceptions of learners that autonomous language learning with technology is both useful and necessary. It is fundamental for learners to proactively seek opportunities to learn and use the language (Kormos and Csizér, 2014; Lai, 2013; Wong and Looi, 2012). Research studies have found that language learners who believe in taking control of their own learning and who actively seek language-use opportunities beyond the classroom are more likely to self-direct and -manage their language learning and to utilize technologies to regulate their language-learning experience (Lai and Gu, 2011; Mercer, 2011). Karlsson and Kjisik (2011) emphasized that this 'ownership of learning' is not something that comes to students naturally; rather, it needs to be fostered through supportive structures and events accompanied by constant reflections. In addition, learners' perceptions that technological resources are both useful and necessary for language learning also depend critically on their perceptions of the match between the use of technological resources and their language-learning beliefs and approaches, on the one hand, and their learning needs and preferences, on the other hand (Chen, 2011; Lai, 2013; Lai and Gu, 2011). Learners' perceptions of the usefulness of technological resources also rely on their awareness of the potentials of technological resources for language learning. In addition, their self-efficacy in autonomous learning and their perceptions of choice and control of learning afforded by technological resources also shape their entering motivation for autonomous language learning with technology beyond the classroom (Stolk et al., 2010).

The maintenance of intention has much to do with learners' ability to deal with the complexities and uncertainties that characterize learning with technology. Learners' open mindset and the cognitive flexibility to deal with the uncertainties and complexity of interacting with technology (Kop and Fournier, 2011) are critical to maintaining their continued interest in using technological resources outside the classroom for learning. This is because learning with technology is often associated with unstructured or uncertain learning events, and the use of technological resources beyond the classroom often involves interacting with authentic learning materials and real-life scenarios that are usually cognitively challenging and more or less push learners out of their comfort zone. Furthermore, autonomous language learning with technology beyond the classroom is emotionally demanding and involves learners' regulation of various affective needs, such as dealing with their anxieties in interacting with technology and managing and learning from successes and failures in their experimentation with technological resources. Thus, learners' emotional management skills are critical to their continued interest in using technology for learning despite the affective challenges. It is equally important to help students perceive the availability of psychological and cognitive counselling and support that facilitate their technology-enhanced learning experience beyond the classroom.

The resource aspect

Van Dijk (2005) reasoned that the use of technology for learning depends on the availability of a number of resources, including temporal resources (i.e. time available to spend on the activity) and material resources above and beyond digital resources including monetary resources, mental resources (in terms of relevant knowledge and technical and social skills), social resources (in the sense of social networking and relationships), and cultural and discursive resources. Thus, to engage in autonomous language learning with technology, learners need to have access not only to a set of digital resources but also to the social, cultural and discursive resources that support their utilization of the digital resources.

A lack of access to useful digital resources or lack of awareness of the potentials of digital resources for learning is an oft-reported challenge to autonomous learning with technology (Bailly, 2010; Lai et al., 2015; Li, 2013). The HK university foreign-language learners interviewed in Lai, Yeung and Hu's (2015) study listed recommendations concerning technological resources as the no. 1 support they needed for self-directed learning with technology due to the challenges they had encountered in locating and selecting appropriate, trustworthy and proficiency-level-compatible online resources. Furthermore, they did not want the controlled learning resources created and delivered by their instructors; rather, they expected their instructors to provide them with tips and guiding criteria on how to locate and select quality online learning resources. A similar preference for self-selecting digital resources for learning has been reported in quite a few studies (Conole, 2008; Saadatmand and Kumpulainen, 2012; Steel and Levy, 2013). Thus, it is important to generate a better understanding of quality out-of-class learning experiences and provide learners with a set of selection criteria for locating and evaluating individual technological resources and guiding principles for selecting and generating learning ecologies with technological resources. Moreover, learners need not only to have access to appropriate technological resources, but also to be equipped with an understanding of the 'potential forms of assistance which make up the resource elements' and the interactive relationships between the technological resources (Beckman, Bennett and Lockyer, 2013; Luckin, 2010, p. 111; Stolk et al., 2010).

Social, cultural and discursive resources are important learning aids that mediate learners' interaction with technological resources. Research studies have found that teachers and peers are major forces that influence university students' decision-making regarding whether and how often to use technology to support their language learning beyond the classroom (Lai and Gu, 2011; Lai, 2013; Margaryan and Littlejohn, 2008). Learners perceive that feedback and guidance from teachers on what technology-enhanced materials they could utilize for learning and how to use these materials are critical to enhancing their self-directed use of technology for language learning (Castellano, Mynard and Rubesch, 2011; Lai and Gu, 2011; Deepwell and Malik, 2008; Lai, 2013). Furthermore, resources available in learners' peer networks have also been found to affect the frequency of language learners' technology use for learning (Lai, 2015a). Thus, learners need to be supported in actively locating various online and offline social networks and capitalizing on the discursive, social and cognitive capitals from such networks.

The capacity aspect

Littlewood (1996) conceptualized three types of autonomy that need to be fostered: autonomy as a communicator, autonomy as a learner and autonomy as a person. He further elaborated that autonomy as a communicator refers to learners' ability to use language creatively and their grasp of situation-appropriate communication strategies; autonomy as a learner involves the ability to select and utilize appropriate learning strategies to solve learning problems and to conduct independent work; and autonomy as a person refers to learners' ability to construct their personal learning contexts and to express personal meanings. Thus, the essential capacity for autonomous learning with technology is multidimensional.

To enhance learners' autonomy as communicators, educators need to support learners to engage in socioculturally appropriate online interactions and in benefiting from them. To enhance learners' ability to engage in online communication, they need to be guided in different cultural expectations and norms of communication, social relations and communicative use of technology in order to avoid potential misunderstandings and reinforcements of cultural stereotypes and feelings of difference (Kramsch and Thorne, 2002; Lawrence, 2013; O'Dowd, 2007). Learners need support in developing an understanding of how culture shapes one's interactions, behaviours and expectations. They also need a critical perspective towards their own culturally shaped behaviours and expectations and the multiple ways of interpretations of events/topics. Familiarity with the online communication conventions and strategies used to initiate and sustain online communication are also critical (Chamberlin-Quinlisk, 2013). Furthermore, training in some basic communication and compensation strategies might also be necessary, especially for learners with relatively limited language proficiency, who usually lack the confidence and motivation to use the target language actively to communicate with others (Shih and Yang, 2008).

Autonomy as a learner entails both generic self-regulation skills and the specific skills of using technology for language learning (Lai, 2013). The skills to use technology for language learning include not only technical skills in operating digital platforms and resources but also critical digital literacies that keep learners informed of their choices and actions concerning digital technologies and help them develop a full range of creative abilities to utilize technologies to solve learning problems (Selwyn, 2011). Critical digital literacy skills include a good grasp of the affordances of individual technological resources for language learning, the ability to evaluate and map different technological resources for different learning and pedagogical purposes, and the ability to use the technological resources in socially and culturally appropriate ways (Benson, 2013; Healey et al., 2011; Lai, 2013; Lai, Shum and Tian, 2016). Critical digital literacy skills also include the ability to seize language-learning opportunities from technological experience, to use technological resources in pedagogically appropriate ways to assist language comprehension and production and to enhance language-learning competence (Healey et al., 2011). Such competence includes selective attention to and noticing of linguistic features, inductive and deductive inferencing and the ability to generate rules from patterns, the productive use of the features embedded in the resources in ways that benefit language learning, and the strategic viewing and interaction of behaviours with the resources that could optimize learners' incidental language acquisition from access to media (Hubbard, 2013; Kuppens, 2010; Oxford, 2008; Reinders and White, 2010; Toffoli and Sockett, 2010). For instance, Kim, Park and Baek (2009) trained 117 ninth-graders on three metacognitive strategies specific to game playing (self-recording; modelling and thinking aloud) to support their interaction with *Gersang*, a massively multiplayer online role-playing game (MMORPG), and found that training students in the three metacognitive strategies contributed to both students' achievement in learning and game performance. Furthermore, since autonomous learning with technology beyond the classroom is social and contextual in nature and involves the transition from co-regulation and shared regulation to self-regulation (Crabbe, Elgort and Gu,

2013), social-learning skills such as collaboration and reciprocity also need to be fostered and supported (Lewis, 2013).

Autonomy as a person accentuates the development of learners' ability to generate their personal learning ecologies. In this dimension, learners need guidance in developing a critical awareness of their own needs and preferences, and a high level of critical analysis of resources and the interactive relationships that accompany these resources. They also need help in utilizing the cognitive, affective, metacognitive, material and epistemic resources in their environments in order to generate quality learning experience, and balance and coordinate the experience temporally and spatially to meet individualized learning goals, needs and preferences (Kop and Fournier, 2011; Luckin, 2010). Additionally, they need to develop personal knowledge-management skills, 'ranging from creating, organizing and sharing digital content and information, to higher order more complex PKM skills such as connectedness, the ability to balance formal and informal contexts, critical ability and creativity' (Dabbagh and Kitsantas, 2012, p. 5).

How to support?

Various models and frameworks have been proposed to support the affective, resource and capacity aspects of autonomy development. One influential model is the socio-cognitive model of self-regulation, the fundamental component of which is a cyclical feedback loop, which functions in a temporal sequence (before, during and after dimensions) (Cleary and Zimmerman, 2012). This model addresses the cognitive and metacognitive dimensions of self-regulation and is a viable model in self-regulation skill and strategy development. The model highlights planning and motivation belief before task performance, attention focusing and strategy implementation during task performance and reflection on the effectiveness of strategy implementation after task performance (Zimmerman and Campillo, 2003).

Several self-regulation intervention programmes have been developed to induce cyclical phase changes in students' cognitive and metacognitive engagement during specific task performances. One such programme was conceptualized by Graham and Harris (2005) – the self-regulated strategy development intervention programme (SRSD). In the before-task stage, tutors elicit students' prior knowledge and current strategies in performing the task, engage them in analysing the essential components of the task, and guide them in setting process goals. In the during-task stage, tutors explain, model and prompt students to use strategies in structured, guided practice sessions, and guide students in analysing their strategy implementation and making adaptive plans. In the after-task stage, tutors prompt students to evaluate their performance and attribute success or failure to strategy use. Another more recent invention programme developed by Cleary and colleagues (Cleary et al., 2008; Cleary and Zimmerman, 2004) involves the use of evidence-based learning tactics or strategies to cultivate adaptive cognition throughout the cyclical loop. The programme highlights the use of a self-regulation graph that prompts students to self-record the strategies they employed during studying. In the before-task stage, students are guided in plotting their outcome goal and recording the strategic plan to accomplish it. In the during-task stage, students are encouraged to add, modify or adjust their strategic plans. In the after-task stage, students are prompted through a series of reflection questions and activities to self-evaluate their performance against their goals and to make causal attributions and adaptive inferences in reference to their strategy plans on the self-regulation graph. The self-regulation graph can be used across a series of development sessions to enhance learners' ability to implement and adjust strategies to achieve success.

Focusing specifically on the development of autonomous language learning, Reinders (2000) developed a pedagogical framework in line with the cyclical feedback loop of the socio-cognitive model of self-regulation but expanded the focus beyond the performance of a specific cognitive task. This framework starts by identifying a learning need, then continues by setting goals and planning learning, selecting relevant resources and learning strategies, practising the strategies in specific tasks, monitoring the implementation of the strategies through teacher and peer feedback, and ends with assessment and revision. More importantly, the framework highlights the engagement of students in constant reflection throughout the whole cycle, in pairs or group work and sharing sessions so that students can provide one another with the cognitive and affective support needed in order to engage successfully in the sometimes-frustrating process.

Hubbard (2004) devised an intervention framework to develop learners' ability to use computer applications for language learning. The framework consists of five practice-based principles that align with the cyclical model. According to the framework, before learners start practising the CALL activities, trainers are advised to adopt a learner perspective, eliciting learners' current understanding and inducing the attitudinal and cognitive preparation learners need to engage in the these activities. Trainers may give learners the pedagogical training on matching the CALL activities with their learning needs, and guide them to plan the CALL activities based on their enhanced pedagogical knowledge. Then when learners progress to the during-activity stage, a progressive, cyclical approach is advised. Trainers are advised to construct the training in small junctures of training content each time, with the contents building on one another to give learners a comprehensive view of the various issues and processes involved in the CALL activities. The training session of each content needs to start with engaging students in first experiencing the CALL activities themselves without assistance. As learners build up some initial understanding from the experience, trainers then direct their attention to the strategic use of the activity for language-learning purposes. Then the training programme approaches the last stage: the after-practice stage. At this stage, the framework accentuates the importance of collaborative debriefings. Trainers are advised to hold collaborative debriefing sessions among the learners to share their learning experience and the knowledge and strategies they have picked up through the experience. These sessions will help trainers to monitor and reinforce the training effects, and create social-learning opportunities. Trainers can then come up with follow-up activities to help learners to exploit the CALL experience further for additional language-learning opportunities.

These frameworks conceptualize the application of the cyclical feedback loop to support strategy training in autonomous language learning with technology, highlighting issues to attend to at different stages of the cyclical process. Rubin, Chamot, Harris and Anderson (2007) went beyond the process of strategy training to discuss the content of the training task. They argued that it is important to integrate strategy training into the regular language curriculum, and thus, the training tasks need to originate from the regular language curriculum. They proposed strategy-based instruction as an effective approach to the development of learner autonomy. The researchers underscored four core steps in the strategy-based instruction model: 1) raising learners' awareness of their existing strategies in handling a curricular task; 2) explaining and modelling new strategies that could enhance the performance of the curricular task; 3) providing ample practice opportunities to employ trained strategies to complete the curricular task, receptive or productive, in the target language; and 4) evaluating the effectiveness of employing the strategies and transferring them to new tasks. In this framework, the development of individual strategies is embedded in and serves the regular language curriculum.

The intervention frameworks reviewed above illustrate the cyclical process in training tasks to develop learners' metacognitive and cognitive strategies to engage in autonomous learning with technology. Metacognitive and cognitive strategies are just part of the support that learners need in order to engage in autonomous language learning with technology. Other researchers have proposed more comprehensive models to support learners' holistic development of autonomous learning beyond the classroom, which go beyond metacognitive and cognitive strategy training. Nunan (1997) proposed a five-level model of learner autonomy development, which conceptualized five stages of the development: awareness, involvement, intervention, creation and transcendence. In the first stage of the development model, learners develop an enhanced awareness of their beliefs of and approaches to learning and alternative approaches. In the second stage, learners are encouraged to move towards active experimentation with different options. With the knowledge and skills developed during the involvement stage, learners then progress towards the intervention stage, in which they are supported in improving their current learning process by making small modifications to their learning goals or contents. In the creation stage, learners move towards taking up more responsibility to create their own personalized learning goals, learning content and tasks. Finally, in the transcendence stage, learners make connections between their learning experience across different formal and informal contexts. Nunan's five-level developmental model highlights the different stages educators can move learners through towards becoming autonomous language learners, and each stage involves relevant affective, metacognitive and cognitive strategy training in which the before–during–after cyclical intervention programmes proposed by Zimmerman and others could play a role.

Holec (2009) focused further on scaffolding in autonomy development. She highlighted autonomy development as a scaffolding process, delineating two stages of autonomy development with gradual withdrawal of teacher control and support. Stage one involves the development of co-directed learning within a teacher-designed curricular structure, with the primary focus on language-learning objectives, whereby learners progress from minimal control and management of their learning towards assuming increasing responsibility and involvement in defining learning objectives, selecting resources, selecting learning scenarios, evaluating learning effectiveness and adjusting learning plans. Stage two integrates the learning-to-learn objectives into the pedagogical design and focuses on developing self-directed learning, whereby learners are prepared and supported to be affectively, cognitively and socioculturally ready to assume the responsibility for self-directing their own learning beyond the classroom and constructing their personalized learning ecologies. The scaffolding process applies equally to different stages of autonomy development at the macro level and to strategy training concerning task performance at the micro level.

Dabbagh and Kitsantas (2012) further accentuated the collaborative aspect of learner autonomy development. They discussed a pedagogical approach that emphasizes the development of self-regulation skills through collaborative learning, using the construction of personalized learning environments with social media tools as an example. The pedagogical cycle starts with learners' setting up a learning goal and selecting and using social media tools to generate, collate and organize contents to create their personalized learning environments. They then use the commenting, co-editing and sharing features of social media to share their personalized learning environments with each other and give peer comments and share strategies. After this collaborative stage, learners engage in refining their personal learning spaces in response to peer feedback and by incorporating the resources shared by their peers. They are also guided in reflecting on the effectiveness of their personalized learning environments in achieving their learning objectives and in devising new strategies to enrich their personal learning environments further. Thus, collaborative learning can be utilized to elevate individuals' development of autonomous language learning with technology beyond the classroom.

These development models, despite their different orientations, all underscore two critical components of autonomous learning support – reflectivity and collaboration – in scaffolding learners to move gradually from enhanced awareness towards boosted capabilities. Kumaravadivelu (2006) emphasized these two components in his discussion of autonomy development: 1) the importance of engaging learners in assuming the role of mini-ethnographers and reflecting on their developing identities through diary writing; and 2) the importance of helping learners to form learning communities and mutually supportive groups, and of providing them with opportunities to bring their out-of-class learning experience and materials into classroom discussions. Blaschke (2012) further argued that the ultimate goal of learner autonomy development is heutagogy, whereby learners possess not only the necessary knowledge and skills but also confidence in their capacity for self-organized adaptation in response to both familiar and unfamiliar and changing situations – that is to say, when a knowledge gap occurs, they can locate, evaluate and select the appropriate venues to seek relevant and trustworthy information to fill the gap (Hase, 2009). Moreover, the core of a heutagogical approach to learning consists of reflective practices and collaborative learning (Blaschke, 2012; Hase, 2009).

Enhancing reflectivity

'Reflection-in-action' is essential for self-directed learning to take place (Fischer, 2014) because the essence of the development of autonomy is internal transformation with regard to locus of control and pedagogical roles and knowledge, and reflection is a key factor in driving the process of transformation (Chateau and Zumbihl, 2012; Mozzon-McPherson, 2007). Various approaches have been devised to support the reflection component. Thanasoulas (2000) emphasized the development of learner autonomy by engaging students in self-report – both introspective self-report to become aware of their own strategies and retrospective self-report to evaluate and think back on their learning – and the use of diaries and evaluation sheets to confront them with evidence and convincing information to induce changes in their learning behaviours. Blaschke (2012) and Hase (2009) elucidated that design elements, such as learning journals and action learning, that engages students in experimenting with real-life scenarios, and ongoing personalized assessment with feedback support could be incorporated into intervention programmes to support reflective practices. Previous studies have examined intervention programmes that used experiential learning experience to strengthen reflective practices. One such intervention programme was reported by Carter (2005), where the researcher preceded reflective activities with action research or experiential learning. The programme consisted of two stages: the first stage comprised abundant reflection activities to raise learners' awareness of themselves as learners and of learning. The reflection was based on learners' responses to learning history questionnaires, learning style inventories and information sessions on metacognitive planning. The second phase consisted of a grammar-based project, in which students were asked to identify five grammatical structures that they needed to work on, collect a corpus of written French that contained those structures from the press and magazines, analyse the structures against the corpus, explain the structures to classmates and create short exercises and answer keys for the structures. Carter observed that the reflection paved the way for the epiphanic effects of the grammar project that led students to a clear understanding of what it meant to be an autonomous learner. Karlsson and Kjisik (2011) also reported a study that combined reflection with experiential learning. However, in this case, reflective interludes in the form of autobiographical texts were used concurrently with experiential learning to support and enhance experiential learning. In this project, students were encouraged to experiment with different types of technological resources on their own. At the same time, they were required to write down autobiographical texts to document the cognitive and emotional processes they went through. The authors argued that such autobiographical texts could help encourage self-reflexivity by facilitating learners to actively engage their past learning experience, their present skills and motivation, and their future plans and wishes. These autobiographical texts could also elicit emotional and metacognitive responses to strengthen experiential learning. Previous studies have also reported intervention programmes that supported reflective practices by tracking learning records and providing ongoing assessment and feedback. For instance, Kim (2014) reported on a study where language learners were engaged in weekly voice recordings and received guidance on how to monitor their own speech production. The researcher found that leaving a voice track to engage students in constant assessment of their own oral proficiency helped learners' to develop their personal speech-monitoring skills. Moreover, learners were found to develop speech-improvement strategies by using self-study resources and instructor feedback. King (2011) reported another study that featured enhanced reflectivity in the form of portfolios. The portfolio programme started with guided reflection on learning needs and perceptions of learning beyond the classroom. This was followed by learners' experiential learning through language-learning tasks with out-of-class resources, with the tasks starting off highly structured with designated resources and gradually becoming learner directed. Students engaged in evaluative reflection upon completion of each task. The researcher found that the enhanced reflectivity increased the frequency of learners' self-directed learning beyond the classroom over time. Acknowledging that reflection (metacognition and metalinguistics) is the essence of the European Language Portfolio, Little (2010) also advocated the use of the portfolio – which consists of a language passport (a reflection on linguistic identity, language-learning history and language progress against a self-assessment grid), a language biography (a reflection on the language-learning process and evolving identity) and a dossier (record keeping of work in progress) – as a tool for autonomy development.

Strengthening collaboration

As autonomy development involves the transition from co-regulation and shared regulation to self-regulation (Crabbe, Elgort and Gu, 2013), creating opportunities for developing autonomy through co-regulation and shared regulation is featured in several support-intervention programmes as well. Blaschke (2012) proposed the construction of collaborative spaces for learning, such as communities of practices, which focus primarily on the learning process and how learners learn (Hase, 2009), and communities of knowledge sharing, where learners are encouraged to share resources and information (Ashton and Newman, 2006). Arguing that supporting self-directed learning involves helping learners to frame and solve personally meaningful problems, Fischer (2013) proposed the establishment of cultures of participation, where people could co-learn in communities in which they could contribute actively to and work together on personally meaningful problems, and in which they could share their expertise with each other. Goh, Seet and Chen (2012) used persuasive SMS messages to move students from co-regulation to self-regulation. Tailored weekly SMSes were sent to the students to provide emotional support, metacognitive assistance and cognitive strategies. The researchers found that the SMS intervention helped maintain, improve and enhance students' self-regulation strategies. Reinders (2011) conceptualized the supporting of collaborative learning by building a close connection between in-class learning and out-of-class learning. The three-phase implementation model he proposed was aimed at enhancing collaboration through connecting in-class learning with out-of-class learning and preparing students for self-directed learning beyond the classroom through targeted co-regulation inside the class. In this model, the first phase is for teachers to build an inventory of all the activities they employ in class that incorporate technological resources and materials. The second phase is to organize these activities in ways that can help learners to develop a range of essential skills for engagement with out-of-class technological resources, and make explicit links between what students do in the classroom and what they do outside the classroom while engaging them with these activities in class. The third phase is to engage students in dialogues with peers about their experiences outside the classroom through sharing sessions or via learning diaries with their teacher. These intervention programmes showcase some approaches educators are taking to scaffold learners' autonomy development through social support and interaction.

Figure 5.1 illustrates the key factors in the development of learners' autonomous language learning with technology beyond the classroom. At the core is the cyclical feedback loop for autonomy development, which elucidates the fundamental process of learner development: affective, cognitive and metacognitive preparation → practice → evaluation and reflection that triggers the next cycle of learner development. This cyclical process helps to support the development of the three core components of autonomous language learning with technology beyond the classroom: the affective aspect, the capacity aspect and the resource aspect.

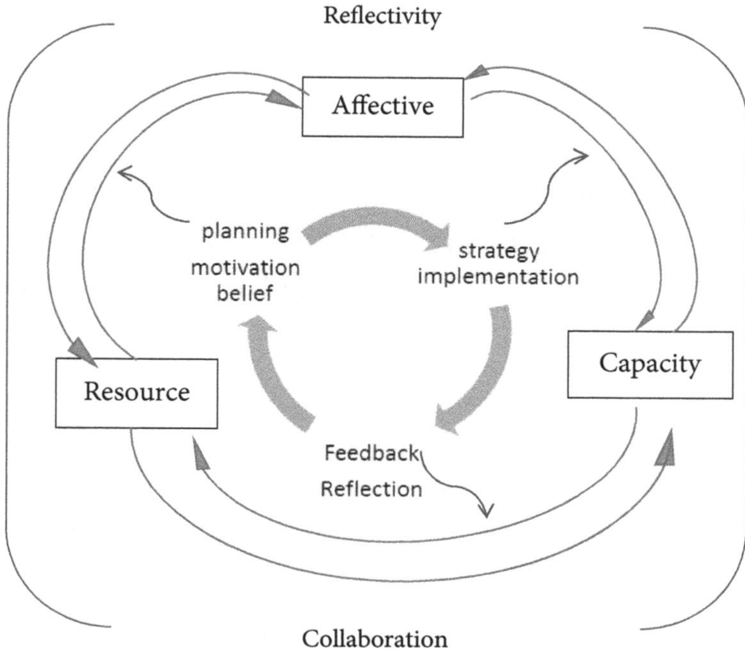

Figure 5.1 Essential components and processes in learner preparation.

The bi-directional arrows between the three components suggest that the three aspects are interdependent of each other: A belief in autonomous learning with technology will trigger learners' interest in utilizing their capacity to engage in such activities, and an enhanced capacity for doing so will in turn strengthen their belief in and willingness to engage in such activities. Learners' capacity for autonomous learning with technology will enhance the likelihood of their perceiving the relevance of resources for language learning, and the availability of cultural and discursive resources will in turn enhance learners' capacity. The availability of resources will strengthen learners' willingness to engage in autonomous learning with technology, and learners' interest in autonomous learning with technology will open learners' eyes to and enhance their likelihood of perceiving the relevance of resources for such activities. The interdependency of the three core components shows that efforts to foster learners' autonomous language learning with technology beyond the classroom need to address all three components. The two components in the outer circle represent the two major characteristics that intervention programmes need to possess in order to make optimal impact on autonomy development.

6

Promoting Out-of-Class Autonomous Language Learning with Technology: Teachers' Role

To foster autonomous language learning with technology beyond the classroom, we need to not only understand learners' needs for and expectations of support, but also to conceptualize how teachers, important players in learners' academic life, could provide that support. Teachers are important social agents who influence the nature and quality of students' learning experiences, including intellectual and social experiences (Davis, 2003). The pedagogical and interpersonal relationships that teachers develop with students shape their affective, cognitive, and social-learning behaviours (Davis, 2003; Farmer, Lines and Hamm, 2011). Teachers' influence could be exerted explicitly through their instructional arrangements and implicitly through their role modelling (Katyal and Evers, 2004). As a result, both students' intellectual and social engagements at school and their learning beliefs and approaches to learning could change in response to teacher influence (Davis, 2003). Thus, a discussion about learners' learning behaviours outside the classroom needs to include an examination of the role of the teacher.

Learner autonomy is socially mediated by more capable others (Hardwin and Oshige, 2011; Little, 2004), and teachers are the significant ones in the school life of learners. Learners' autonomous learning behaviours both inside and outside the classroom may be influenced, intentionally and/or unintentionally, by teachers' beliefs, attitudes and instructional practices (Lamb, 2008). Research evidence has suggested that teachers play important roles in shaping the quantity and quality of students' autonomous use of technology outside the classroom for learning (Lai et al., 2012; Margaryan and Littlejohn, 2008), and teachers' expectancies and instructional arrangements (Selwyn, 2008), their recommendations of possible technology-enhanced materials for learning and their guidance on effective selection and use technological resources (Castellano, Mynard and Rubesch, 2011; Lai and Gu, 2011; Lai et al., 2014; Deepwell and Malik, 2008) are all potential influential factors. As various facets of teacher instructional arrangements and practices are closely related to students' out-of-class autonomous learning behaviours, it is critical to illuminate the various direct and indirect routes through which teachers influence students' autonomous use of technology for language learning beyond the classroom. A clear identification of teachers' roles will allow a better understanding of what teachers can do to help language learners to become autonomous users of technology for language learning. This chapter conceptualizes a framework of teacher influence on students' out-of-class autonomous use of technology for language learning, and discusses teachers' perceptions of their responsibilities and roles and how teachers and educators can develop their awareness and abilities to foster students' out-of-class, self-directed use of technology for language learning.

Conceptualizing teachers' roles in promoting out-of-class autonomous use of technology for language learning – the component view

Discussions about teachers' roles in promoting learners' out-of-class autonomous use of technology for language learning need to revolve around the different dimensions of learner autonomy. Benson (2008) pointed out that learner autonomy entails both learners' capacities for exerting autonomy and the situational freedom that learners utilize in the learning process. In other words, learners need to possess the skills necessary to self-regulate their learning and be willing and able to self-direct their learning processes across settings and contexts. As scholars have pointed out, autonomous learning encompasses both the self-regulation skills needed in managing the cognitive, metacognitive, motivational, behavioural and contextual factors in the process of learning and the willingness and capacity to make use of the learning opportunities in one's surroundings (Candy, 1991; Knowles, 1989; Stolk et al., 2010). As discussed in Chapter 5, learners expect to be supported in their autonomous language learning with technology beyond the classroom along three dimensions: affective support, resource support and capacity support. Accordingly, teachers can exert their influence along these three dimensions. Voller (1997) categorized teacher influence on autonomous learning into two major aspects: psychosocial support and technical support. Psychosocial support involves raising students' awareness of the importance of autonomous learning and of the benefits of various resources, and motivating students through the process. Technical support involves supporting students in setting objectives, planning, organizing, monitoring and evaluating the independent learning experience, and helping them develop the related skills. Thus, in conceptualizing teachers' roles in promoting autonomous out-of-class learning, we discuss both the dimension of promoting self-regulation skills and the dimension of promoting learner selection and utilization of learning experience in different contexts.

Teacher influence on students' autonomous use of technology for language learning can manifest itself at two levels: within the classroom and at the interface between in-class and out-of-class learning. Teachers can help students to develop self-regulation skills and build positive dispositions towards autonomous learning by manipulating the instructional and environment arrangements within classrooms. Teachers can play an essential role in bridging in-class and out-of-class learning contexts to boost students' willingness and capacity to engage in self-directed out-of-class learning. They can also build support mechanisms both inside and outside the classroom to support students' experimentation with self-directed out-of-class learning with technology.

Fostering autonomous learning skills through in-class instructional arrangements and discourse

To facilitate the development of self-regulation skills, teachers may need to shift their classroom roles away from being controlling authoritarian figures to being facilitators, counsellors, resource providers, and so on (Benson, 2001). Scholars conceptualize that, in order to help students become autonomous, teachers can prepare them methodologically, psychologically and sociopolitically (Benson, 2001; Dickinson, 1992; Holec, 1981; Little, 1991). For instance, Zimmerman and Risemberg (1997) highlighted three types of support that teachers could provide in promoting self-regulated learning: 1) affective support by motivating students towards self-regulation of learning, 2) cognitive and methodological support by teaching self-regulated learning strategies and developing self-regulation skills, and 3) resource support by helping students utilize various social and material resources. Stefanou et al. (2004) elaborated further on the various kinds of support that teachers could provide inside the classroom: 1) organizational autonomy support, whereby teachers encourage and support students to take the initiative to organize their learning environments, including seating arrangements, student grouping, the evaluation process, class rules and so on; 2) procedural autonomy support, whereby teachers encourage and support students to make decisions about the learning materials, learning activities and forms of learning products; and 3) cognitive autonomy support, whereby teachers encourage and support students to lead the learning process and become independent problem solvers who actively plan, monitor and evaluate the learning process. Thus, to promote autonomous learning, teachers need to involve, coordinate and support students in managerial and instructional decision-making (Stefanou et al., 2004; Reeve, 2006). Kistner et al. (2010) argued that teachers could promote self-regulation skills both directly by teaching self-regulation strategies and indirectly by creating a supportive learning environment that enables students to practise and fine-tune their self-regulation skills. The following section discusses how teachers can develop students' self-regulation skills through in-class arrangements.

First, teachers could incorporate explicit training in self-regulation strategies and skills into the curriculum and instruction. Self-regulation strategies and skills include self-management strategies, self-advocacy and self-monitoring skills, and self-evaluation and self-realization skills (Nguyen and Gu, 2013; Wehmeyer, Agran and Hughes, 2000). Moreover, the training of self-regulation skills could be achieved both explicitly and implicitly (Kistner et al., 2010). Teachers could implicitly help students develop these skills by modelling and verbalizing strategies and behaviours, such as think-alouds. Teachers could also explicitly train students by emphasizing the importance of the strategies and behaviours and elaborating on when and how to use and monitor them. Researchers have found that modelling and the use of worked examples help enhance students' self-regulatory cognitive and metacognitive skills (Kostons et al., 2012; Zimmerman and Kitsantas, 2002). For instance, Kostons et al. (2012) found that explicit modelling of metacognitive skills like self-assessment and task selection helped secondary school students achieve greater self-assessment accuracy and develop a greater ability to select learning tasks. At the same time, however, scholars point out that, although teacher modelling may enhance students' use of a particular strategy, explicit training of strategies leads to better maintenance and transfer of strategies and behaviours (Kistner et al., 2010). Certain strategies, such as metacognitive knowledge and skills, and certain students, such as weaker students, have been found to benefit more from explicit training (Veenman, 2007). Furthermore, scholars argue that explicit training might be more effective if it were integrated seamlessly into the curriculum. Veenman, van Hout-Wolters and Afflerbach (2006) summarized the critical principles of a successful training programme: 1) the training needs to be embedded in a content-based learning context; 2) the training needs to enhance students' willingness to employ the strategies; and 3) the training needs to engage students in extensive practice of the strategies in a variety of contexts.

Second, teachers could develop students' mentalities for self-regulated learning and fine-tune their self-regulation skills through autonomy-supportive instructional arrangements. Autonomy-supportive instructional environments are argued to be those in which teachers engage students in the active construction of knowledge in authentic learning situations, incorporate 'communal, collaborative ... and reflective' class procedures, utilize 'exploratory, interpretative and participatory' pedagogical procedures and provide students with opportunities for self-exploration and research (De Corte et al., 2004; Ebner et al., 2010; Little, 2007, p. 20; Siemens, 2003). Teachers should provide students with opportunities to make choices, coordinate the set-up of choices in consultation with students' preferences, interests and values, and advise and help students in making choices that align with their personal goals (Elgort, 2011; Patall et al., 2013). Research studies have shown that constructivist-oriented pedagogies that engage students in active problem-solving and decision-making in authentic learning situations can shape students' dispositions towards autonomous learning and help them internalize self-regulation strategies (Haerle and Bendixen, 2008; Kistner et al., 2010). For instance, Kek and Huijser (2011) found that when teachers employed a student-centred teaching approach and engaged students to question, explain, justify and evaluate their own and their classmates' ideas, they were more likely to engage in self-directed learning. Little (2007) summarized three principles of supporting autonomy in language classrooms: 1) learner involvement (identifying the areas where students could be involved to make decisions from day one and then gradually involving students in decision-making in more areas); 2) learner reflection (arranging 'reflective intervention' that engages students in 'explicit detached reflection' on the content and process of learning (p. 24)); and 3) intensive use of the target language (to scaffold students in the use of the target language during autonomy-supportive instructional practices).

Third, teachers' classroom discourse is critical in supporting or suppressing the development of learner autonomy. Autonomy-supportive class discourse needs to help create non-controlling, inviting, facilitative and student-responsive learning environments (Elgort, 2011; Patall et al., 2013). Teachers' positive and non-controlling classroom discourse needs to respect student perspectives, accept errors, engage students in seeking answers themselves, and avoid directive language (Ebner et al., 2010; Patall et al., 2013). Such classroom discourse could help strengthen students' feelings of autonomy (Patall et al., 2013). Teachers should also encourage, invite and support student-initiated critical inquiry discourse such as questioning, hypothesis making and testing, and the taking of multiple perspectives, which is much needed in student-centred explorative and inquiry-based learning environments. In the language classroom, teachers need to perform an extra role, namely, to skilfully scaffold students' understanding and production of autonomy-supportive classroom discourse in the target language (Little, 2007).

Fostering a willingness and a capacity to engage in self-directed out-of-class learning through interfacing in-class and out-of-class learning

To boost students' willingness and capacity to engage in self-directed learning outside the classroom, it is essential to help them perceive the connection between in-class learning and out-of-class learning. In this respect, teachers play an important role in helping students to bridge in-class learning and out-of-class learning experiences (Henry, 2013).

First of all, the nature of the course aims, curriculum and academic work influences students' willingness to engage in, and capacity for, self-directed learning outside the classroom. For one thing, making one's class motivating could enhance learners' likelihood of engaging in extra learning beyond the classroom. Hagger and Chatzisarantis's (2012) trans-contextual model of motivation theorizes that the motivation for educational activities in a formal instructional context could be transferred into motivation towards related activities in an extracurricular or informal learning context as long as teachers structure learning activities, processes and environments that support perceived autonomy support and learners' autonomous motivation towards the educational activities. The enhanced perceived autonomy support could be achieved by helping students to perceive the personal relevance of the tasks, boosting their goal setting and task engagement, using autonomy-supportive class discourses, such as the use of empathic statements that acknowledge their perspectives and so on. For another, teachers could also influence students' out-of-class use of technological resources for language learning by making the technological component salient in course aims and structures. For instance, Selwyn (2008) found that if students did not perceive the necessity of using technology to learn from the curriculum and the assessment regimes, they would not make the effort to use it on their own. Scholars have argued that when teachers align the nature of the course aims, curriculum and academic work closely with the students' lives outside the classroom, students are more likely to engage in autonomous learning behaviours (Fukuda and Yoshida, 2013; Kuh et al., 1994). Kuh et al. (1994) argued that assignments that involve students in applying what they have acquired in class in other aspects of life would help boost out-of-class learning. When the curriculum and coursework is connected to students' lives, the learning contents and activities are more likely to be connected to their interests, which are the major driving forces behind their agentive and sustained efforts to learn in informal contexts (Barron, 2006). The nature of class assessments also affects the quantity and quality of students' self-directed learning outside the classroom (Zhan and Andrews, 2014). Saad, Yunus and Embi (2013) found that formative assessments where students were required to prepare for and complete outside the classroom often opened up opportunities for self-directed out-of-class learning. Furthermore, it is advisable to explain to students the parts of the curriculum that connect to out-of-class learning. Läzaro and Reinders (2009) pointed out that it is important for teachers to identify in-class activities and materials that could help encourage out-of-class learning, and also help students perceive the links between what they do inside the classroom and what they do outside the classroom.

Second, teachers' attitudes towards incorporating student-generated materials from outside the classroom into classroom activities also affect students' self-directed out-of-class learning. Reinders (2010) regarded teachers' incorporation of student-prepared materials from outside the school into classroom learning as an important step towards promoting autonomous learning. For one thing, student-centred interactive approaches that involve their contribution of content and resources to instruction in the classroom could increase their out-of-class study time (Fukuda and Yoshida, 2013). For another, when teachers show their appreciation of student-prepared materials and use the language samples that students have produced and collected from outside the class, students will be motivated to maintain their out-of-class learning behaviours and will see more value in such activities. Guo (2011) found that when teachers asked students to collect examples of English on the street and the products that they used every day and bring them into the class for a group discussion of the language features and use, students became more aware of and attentive to the out-of-class English-learning opportunities in their surroundings.

Third, the variety of in-class topics, activities and resources could potentially enrich the out-of-class learning repertoire of students. When the topics covered in the class and the class resources and activities used are more varied, students are more likely to find things that interest them and hence, are more likely to exert agency to explore related materials further on their own. For instance, Lai (2014) noticed that when students found that the topics in the class appealed to them and aroused their interest, they often built on what they had learned in class to explore the topics further on their own outside the classroom. The students talked about searching for video or audio resources that teachers used in class, after class, which often led them to a large amount of related resources that they habitually visited afterwards. Green-Vänttinen, Korkman and Lehti-Eklund (2010) examined Finnish secondary school students' out-of-class language-learning behaviours and found that the students reported being motivated towards language learning beyond the classroom because of the varying methods and materials used by their Swedish-language teacher and the opportunities the teacher provided to use Swedish beyond the classroom. Fagerlund (2012) further found that when teachers invited guest speakers into their classes, students were encouraged to go online to follow the lives of these visitors.

Fourth, the amount and variety of technological resources that teachers use in class directly affects students' out-of-class learning with technology. Tang (2014) examined the effects of teachers' attitudes and use of technology in class on students' technology use outside the classroom. Two teachers who showed different attitudes and in-class use of technologies were identified: Teacher A encouraged students to use technology both inside and outside the language classroom and used different technologies for a large variety of instructional purposes in her Chinese-language class; whereas Teacher B was cautious about student use of technology outside the language classroom and only used a limited set of technologies to serve a narrow set of instructional purposes. Tang found that students in Teacher A's class reported using technologies to serve a wider variety of language-learning needs than did students in Teacher B's class. The author thus concluded that teachers' technology use inside the classroom influenced the nature of students' out-of-class self-directed technology use for language learning. Students have often been found to utilize the technological resources that they were exposed to or engaged with inside the class for self-directed learning purposes outside the class (Lai, 2014; Lai and Gu, 2011). Lai and Gu (2011) found that when teachers used a certain technology in class, it was more likely to be adopted by the students. Thus, Wong and Looi (2012) argued that it is important for teachers to model seamless learning by incorporating out-of-class learning activities into the formal curriculum and by encouraging students to extend their in-class learning into informal contexts. Furthermore, scholars suggest that the technologies that students frequently use in their daily lives should be included in the curriculum so that students can realize the pedagogical value of these technologies and develop their ability to use these daily-life technologies for language learning (Opettaja, 2011). This in-class experience can help students become aware of the pedagogical values of the technologies that they frequently use in their daily lives for entertainment, thereby helping them to transform their use of the technologies. Lai and Gu (2011) examined university language learners' self-directed use of technology outside the classroom and found that blogs and wikis were among the least used technologies incorporated in students' out-of-class learning repertoires. However, the few students who did report blog writing as part of their out-of-class learning-technology repertoires attributed it largely to the influence of teachers. One participant's foreign-language teacher asked her and her classmates to keep a blog for a semester, which made her develop a daily routine of blog writing in the target language even beyond the course. Teachers' utilization of in-class technological activities that could be continued by learners in informal learning contexts, such as listening to songs and watching videos, are also found to boost students' learning beyond the classroom (Fagerlund, 2012).

Last but not least, teachers have an important mediating role to play in preparing students for the 'intimidating and overwhelming' learning experiences they will encounter outside the language classroom (Davis, 2013, p. 93). Lund (2006) pointed out that communication in the in-class and out-of-class contexts demand different kinds of competences, and the different communication patterns and routines in out-of-class contexts, a technology-mediated environment in particular, threaten students' enjoyment of and learning from the experience. Scholars have also pointed out the importance of scaffolding students' interaction with various technological resources outside the language classroom (Neville et al., 2009; Sykes et al., 2010). Lund (2006) referred to this as the 'need to "didacticize" zones that currently are beyond the socio-historically co-located classroom practices' (p. 188). In other words, teachers need to help students develop 'polycontextual awareness and competence' (Lund, 2006, p. 197) and facilitate the use of communication strategies and techniques across different social worlds. Toffoli and Sockett (2015) argued that this mediating role is a new and crucial teacher role in the twenty-first century. Scholars have suggested that teachers could help to prevent students from feeling overwhelmed or lost as a result of the freedom of action in most online platforms by providing lists of objectives at different stages (Davis, 2013; Neville et al., 2009) and by helping students to familiarize themselves with the unique culture and conventions of social behaviours and interactions and come up with strategies to deal with the unique conversational patterns and discourse features in many online social networking environments (Örngren Berglund, 2006; Sykes et al., 2010). Thorne and Reinhardt (2008) proposed the 'bridging activities' model, whereby the digital texts and practices generated during out-of-class interactions are brought into class discussions to raise students' critical awareness of the social practices and the language used in a particular digital context and to encourage the application of this critical awareness vis-à-vis language socialization in different communication contexts.

Fostering self-directed use of technology for out-of-class learning through teacher counselling and support mechanisms

Teacher encouragement and guidance influence students' willingness to engage in self-directed out-of-class learning and the nature of the activities they engage in beyond the classroom (Fagerlund, 2012). Research studies have found that a teacher's advice on what and how to use technology for learning often serves as the primary source of learning and invigorate students' out-of-class language learning (Deepwell and Malik, 2008; Inozu, Sahinkarakas and Yumru, 2010). In modelling how various factors interact with one another to affect undergraduate learners' out-of-class self-directed use of technology for language learning, Lai (2013) found that sharing and encouragement from teachers and peers in using technology to support learning was a critical determinant of students' self-directed use of technology for learning. And teachers affected learners' autonomous technology use by orienting them to assume more responsibility for their learning process and helping them perceive the benefits of technology for language learning. Lai (2014) also found that the university foreign-language learners in her study reported frequently utilizing the learning resources and activities shared and recommended by their teachers in the out-of-class learning contexts. The participants felt that their teachers' introduction of different resources and approaches played an extremely important guiding role in shaping their out-of-class learning behaviours. And the same teacher effect was found for middle school students, where teachers' encouragement influenced the range of students' out-of-class learning experiences (Lai et al., 2014). The participants not only frequently reported incorporating the out-of-class learning activities that were recommended by teachers but they also reported that teacher guidance on how to use different out-of-class learning activities shaped their approaches to learning from such activities. For instance, one participant reported listening to songs to understand how words are pronounced because her teacher had advised her to do so. The researchers also found that teachers influenced the types of resources that these middle school students used for out-of-class learning indirectly through their parents. The participants reported that teachers' acknowledgement of the value of and recommendations of a certain learning venue or activity directly influenced their parents into encouraging them to use that learning venue or activity outside the language classroom.

Teachers also have a critical role to play in enhancing students' capacities and skills for self-directed out-of-class technology use for learning. Selwyn (2011) pointed out that teachers have a heightened role to play in helping students develop 'critical digital literacy', whereby students are aware of the technological choices around them and how they could make best use of the technological resources. Luckin (2010), in her ecology of resources model, conceptualized the role of teachers as one that helps students to get a clear sense of their own learning needs, introduces the affordances of the available resources and assists students in selecting the resources that fit their learning needs. Castellano, Mynard and Rubesch (2011) examined students' use of technological resources in a self-access centre and found that students requested explicit training in how to use technological resources effectively for language learning. The author concluded that teachers need to give students explicit instruction on how to select appropriate technological resources that match their learning needs and purposes and how to use them effectively for language learning.

Incorporating pedagogical mechanisms that support students' use of technology for learning outside the classroom is equally critical. These pedagogical mechanisms include teacher advice and structures that support students' experimentation with self-directed learning with technology. Carson and Mynard (2012) pointed out that effective pedagogical mechanisms supporting students' self-directed learning outside the classroom need to: 1) enhance students' conceptual understanding of key metalinguistic and metacognitive concepts, and of what language learning involves, and raise students' awareness of their own language-learning approaches and processes; 2) provide students with methodological information about resources and strategies that they could utilize for out-of-class learning and provide opportunities for students to experiment with these resources and strategies and discover what works for them and what does not; and 3) provide students with affective support throughout the process. The pedagogical mechanisms could be in the form of tools that support self-regulation, such as logbooks or portfolios, or teacher advice that helps connect students with out-of-class learning materials. Dam (2009) described how student logbooks could be used to engage students in active planning, evaluation and reflection. She reasoned that when logbooks were used to engage students in dialogues and cooperation with teachers in the learning process, they helped develop students' awareness of the learning process and enhance their ability to organize their learning. King (2011) reported a research study where a self-access portfolio was used to accompany a sixteen-week English-language course. Students were given a self-access portfolio to be completed on a voluntary basis. The portfolio included ten one-page worksheets on which students were asked to reflect on their learning activities during the week. A set of guiding questions was provided on the cover of the portfolio to prompt them to reflect on their learning outside the classroom. The students were first given specific out-of-class learning activities to do and asked to reflect on the experience. Then, they were gradually asked to select their own personalized English-learning activities that fitted their learning needs. King found that students demonstrated an enhanced awareness of English use outside the classroom. Lázaro and Reinders (2009) discussed how teachers could play an active advisory role in connecting students to learning resources and venues outside the language classroom and support their interactions with those resources and venues. The tips the authors provided included advising students on the link between specific resources and venues in a self-access centre and their class learning, engaging students in teacher-guided learning activities that involved the use of the materials in the self-access centre, and giving students credits for their use of the self-access centre and for the development of learner autonomy. More importantly, the researchers pointed out that what matters more is not the physical set-up of a self-access centre, but rather the pedagogical principles underlying it. Thus, their suggested pedagogical mechanisms to support self-directed language learning could be employed by any language teacher, with or without access to a self-access centre, to encourage and support students to utilize the resources available, online or offline, to engage in self-directed learning outside the classroom.

In all, the roles teachers could play in facilitating the autonomous use of technology for language learning outside the classroom are multifaceted. In this section, we have discussed the components that make up teacher roles. Figure 6.1 lists the set of roles that teachers could play. These roles target the development of students' ability to engage in self-regulated language learning in general, and enhance students' willingness and capacity for self-directed use of technology for out-of-class learning. These roles target both the capacity and situational freedom aspects of autonomy, and provide affective, resource and capacity support that learners need for autonomous language learning with technology.

For the convenience of organization, different teacher roles are categorized either under the capacity or the situational freedom aspects according to

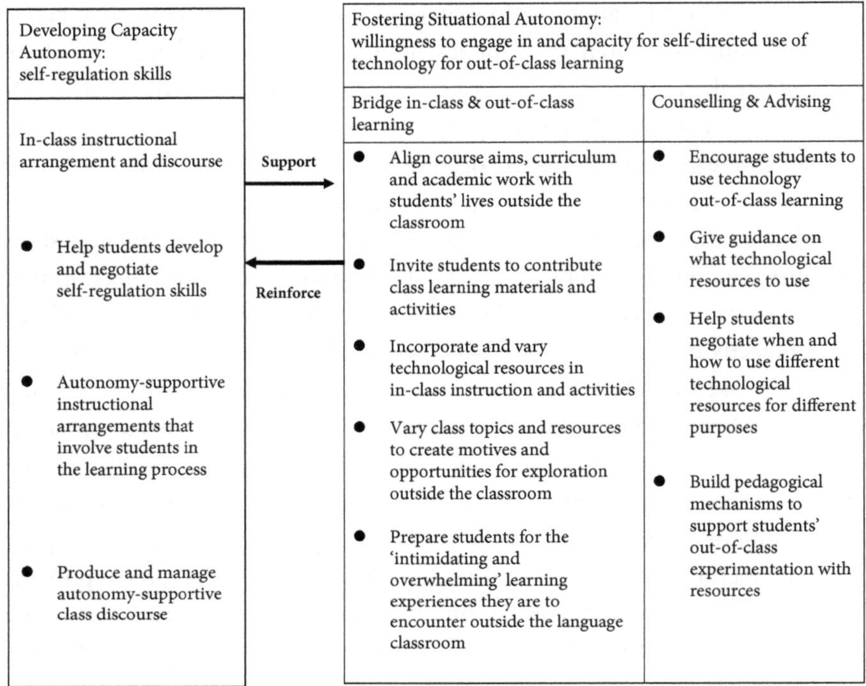

Figure 6.1 Teachers' roles in supporting students' autonomous use of technology for out-of-class learning – component view.

their main functions. The categorization is not mutually exclusive, but only to emphasize that different teacher roles may have differential effects on learners' autonomous language learning with technology beyond the classroom, and need to be employed concurrently. For instance, Lai (2015) found that teacher affective support (i.e. teacher encouragement and advice) enhanced learners' perception of the usefulness of technological resources for learning, and teacher capacity support and behaviour support strengthened their perceptions of support available and boosted their self-efficacy in using technology for language learning.

Conceptualizing teachers' role in promoting out-of-class self-directed use of technology for language learning – the process

Given the increasing emphasis on the social aspects of learner autonomy and a process approach to learner autonomy in the current literature, it makes sense to apply a process view as well when discussing the teacher's role in promoting autonomous language learning outside the classroom. Heron (1989) advocated three modes of teacher facilitation of learner autonomy: the hierarchical mode, whereby teachers make the major decisions; the cooperative mode, which is characterized by teachers sharing control and decision-making with the students; and the autonomous mode, which involves teachers relinquishing all the control and decision-making to the students. Heron argued that different combinations of the three modes are needed in response to students' readiness and objectives. Although Heron was talking about varying the configurations of teacher facilitation in response to student diversity, if we apply the argument to individual student development, it does suggest a developmental view of gradually withdrawing teacher support as students' learning autonomy develops. McCaslin and Hickey (2001) argued for a process view of the development of self-regulation skills. According to them, the development of self-regulated learning starts with shared practices and emergent interaction within a zone of proximal development (co-regulation) and is a transitioning process from co-regulated learning to self-regulated learning. In Hadwin and Oshige's (2011) words, 'Co-regulation is the temporary sharing or distributing of self-regulatory processes and thinking between a learner and a more capable other' (p. 249). Thus, interaction with more capable others and co-regulation are the processes through which students achieve self-regulation. Similarly, Little (2004) argued for a social-interactive view of learner autonomy. He highlighted the fact that the development of learner autonomy is a continuous process through which teachers adjust the support they provide to help students negotiate and renegotiate areas of responsibility and the self-regulatory processes and behaviours in response to their developing language proficiency and learning skills. The above propositions on the socialization process of learner autonomy highlight the view that scaffolding is an important option that teachers need to provide in order to facilitate learner autonomy, and that it is through scaffolding that teachers can evaluate the appropriate amount and types of support students need at different stages before gradually withdrawing support to help students internalize and automatize self-regulatory cognitive and metacognitive processes.

Zimmerman (2000) further pointed out that self-regulatory skills span different developmental levels and go through different phases. He conceptualized four developmental levels of regulatory skills: level 1 is observing the performance of a more capable agent; level 2 is emulating with social assistance the skills demonstrated by the more capable agent; level 3 is independently performing the skill under structured conditions; and level 4 is self-regulated and adaptive use of the skill across different conditions. Progressing from one level to the next draws heavily on social resources. In the school context, teachers play an essential role in creating favourable conditions for each level of development and in ensuring support is gradually withdrawn to help students progress without faltering. Zimmerman (2000) further proposed a social-cognitive approach to learner autonomy, which argues that the development of self-regulation is a cyclical process based on feedback on previous performance. Zimmerman proposed a cyclical self-regulatory process of three phases through which self-regulation develops. The first phase is the forethought phase, where learners analyse tasks and motivate themselves towards self-regulatory behaviours. In this phase, teachers' roles focus on facilitating needs analysis, providing psychosocial support, raising students' awareness of the affordance of various technological resources and scaffolding the planning of personalized learning experience. The second phase is the performance or volitional control phase, where learners use self-control strategies to focus on the task and optimize learning efforts, and actively observe and monitor their own performance. In this phase, teachers need to focus on providing relevant technical support and building pedagogical mechanisms to scaffold student self-exploration. The last phase is the self-reflection phase, where learners evaluate their own performance and make adjustments based on their evaluation. Teachers' roles at this phase focus on facilitating reflection, building collaborative learning opportunities and scaffolding students' understanding of the affordance of different technological resources and how to utilize them more effectively. Thus, the developmental approach to learner autonomy defines different aspects of learning that teachers could scaffold at different phases and levels of autonomy development.

Hereby, the social and developmental approaches to learner autonomy demand a process view when conceptualizing teachers' role in fomenting autonomous language learning with technology outside the classroom. The process view highlights the important teacher role of scaffolding the autonomy development process and identifies the foci of scaffolding at different stages of development. Figure 6.2 combines the component view reflected in Figure 6.1 and the process view to represent a more comprehensive picture of the teacher's role.

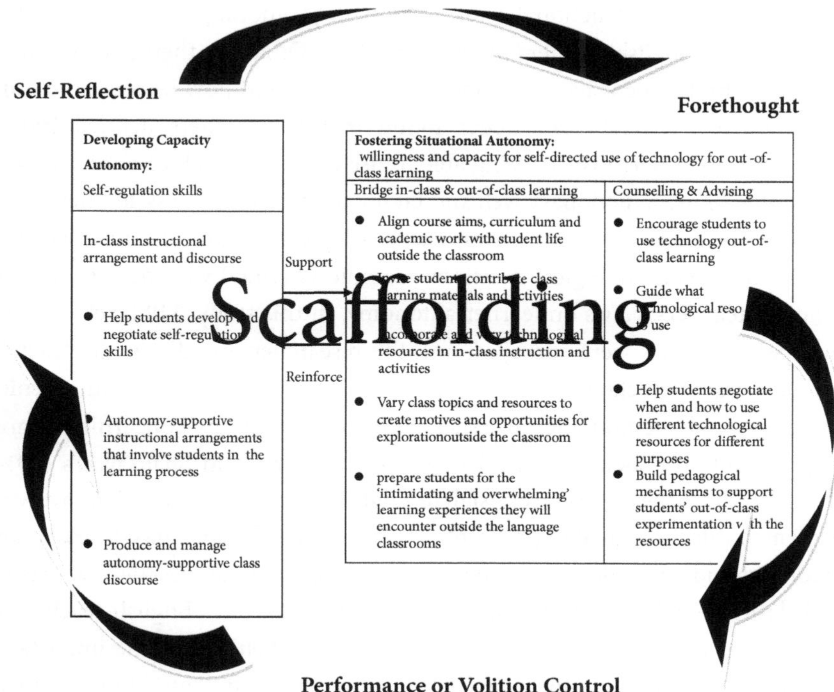

Figure 6.2 Teachers' roles in supporting autonomous use of technology for out-of-class learning – component and process view.

Teachers' perceptions of teachers' role

Despite thirty years of research efforts on autonomous learning, limited attention has been paid to understanding teachers' perceptions of learner autonomy and their roles in fomenting it (Borg and Al-Busaidi, 2012). Recent years have seen an accumulation of research studies that focus on teachers' views of learner autonomy both inside and outside the language classroom. The current research suggests that teachers generally believe in the importance of learner autonomy and that they, as teachers, have the responsibility to help learners develop learner autonomy (Al Asmari, 2013; Chan, 2003; Shahsavari, 2014; Nguyen Thanh, 2011). However, their understanding and actual implementation of learner autonomy is limited.

Research evidence has shown that teachers have a narrow view of learner autonomy and of their roles in fomenting learner autonomy, and that they are selective in their instructional arrangements in promoting it. Al-Shaqsi (2009) surveyed 120 English teachers in state schools in Oman on their perceptions of students' ability to engage in autonomous learning and how learner autonomy could be fostered. The researcher found that the teachers defined learner autonomy quite narrowly as being able to use computers to locate information, being able to use a dictionary well and taking the initiative to ask teachers when they do not understand. Moreover, teachers were reluctant to relinquish their control over methodological decisions. Camilleri's (1999) was the first study to examine teachers' views on learner autonomy. In this study, 328 teachers in six European contexts were surveyed, and the researcher found that the teachers were generally reluctant to involve learners in making decisions about learning objectives and methodological issues. Similar reservations concerning shared responsibility for methodological issues were observed in Shahsavari's (2014) study, in which the experienced Isfahan English teachers reported that involving students in decision-making on topics was the most feasible and desirable and involving students in decision-making on teaching methods was the least feasible and desirable. Chan's (2003) survey study with university English teachers in Hong Kong also found that, although the teachers believed in the importance of fostering learner autonomy and felt positive about students' ability to make methodological decisions on materials and activities in the classroom, they still believed that setting up learning objectives and making the instructional decisions in the learning process were their primary responsibilities. Similar findings of teachers discouraging student involvement in decision-making on the content and process of learning were reported in Al Asmari (2013) survey results of sixty English teachers in Saudi Arabia. Furthermore, studies have identified a gap between teachers' beliefs and their actual practice. Nakata (2011) surveyed seventy-four high school English teachers in Japan on their readiness to promote learner autonomy. The author found that, although the teachers felt it was important to employ various strategies to promote learner autonomy, their actual utilization of the strategies was quite low. In particular, strategies such as helping students to discover answers themselves, involving them in making decisions about the content of learning and helping them to learn from peers were least utilized by the teachers. Ürün, Demir and Akar (2014) surveyed 118 high school English-language teachers in Turkey and identified four types of strategies teachers had used to promote learner autonomy: 1) 'activity-based practices', such as utilizing autonomy-supportive activities and offering choices of activities; 2) 'material-based practices', such as using ICT in class or encouraging students to use ICT outside the class; 3) 'student-centered practices', such as involving students in analysing their learning needs and setting personal learning objectives; and 4) 'objective-based practices', such as informing students of the general objectives of the classes and the curriculum implementation process. However, the author found that the teachers in the study utilized the objective-based practices significantly more frequently than the other practices.

Research on teachers' perceptions of learner autonomy in out-of-class contexts suggests that teachers perceive themselves to be playing a limited role in students' autonomous learning outside the language classroom, and that they did not perceive any link between learners' autonomous learning outside the language classrooms and in-class instruction. Chan (2003) surveyed forty-one English teachers of different cultural backgrounds teaching at a university in Hong Kong on their perceptions of their responsibility for student learning both inside and outside the classroom. The researcher found that the teachers did not feel responsible for students' learning activities and processes outside the classroom, and they perceived that students had the ability and should take the responsibility to plan their learning and choose learning materials and activities outside the classroom. Similar findings were reported in Thanh Van's (2011) survey study with fifty-seven university English teachers, in which the majority of the teachers felt that the responsibilities of organizing the learning experience outside the language classroom should be left in the hands of the students. Toffoli and Sockett (2013) surveyed thirty English-language teachers in French universities on their perceptions of students' out-of-class language learning and found that teachers tended to underestimate the amount of out-of-class learning their learners engaged in. More importantly, quite a few teachers did not perceive any effects of student-initiated out-of-class learning on their in-class teaching and did not realize their mediating role in helping students to bridge their learning experiences in different contexts. Focusing specifically on teachers' views of learner autonomous language learning with technology, Lai, Yeung and Hu (2015) found that teachers tended to overestimate learners' competencies of locating and utilizing technology for language learning, and thus downplay their roles in recommending technological resources to learners and relegate their supportive role to a passive one.

Thus, the current literature suggests that teachers play a limited role in promoting students' autonomous learning both inside and outside the language classroom despite their belief in the importance of learner autonomy. Although they are aware of the instructional practices that are important in promoting students' self-regulation skills, they are reluctant to relinquish instructional control to the students. They do not realize the responsibilities and roles they need to take in guiding and supporting autonomous learning outside the language classroom. Neither are they aware of the important roles they need to play in bridging learning inside and outside the language classroom.

Helping teachers achieve their roles

Scholars stress the symbolic relationship between teacher autonomy and learner autonomy, and highlight the fact that teacher autonomy is a necessary condition for teachers to foster learner autonomy (Benson, 2001; Lamb, 2008; Little, 2007; Nakata, 2011). Thus, to help teachers better fulfil their roles in promoting students' autonomous use of technology for language learning, fostering teacher autonomy is a must.

Little (2007) defined teacher autonomy as including three dimensions: 1) autonomy in professional practices and self-learning; 2) teaching practices that engage students with the same autonomy process; and 3) the ability to manage the new set of classroom discourses in the target language that are associated with an autonomous classroom and the related exploratory and interpretive pedagogies. Nakata (2011) further categorized teacher autonomy into two major components: teaching autonomy, which refers to teachers' readiness and ability to develop learner autonomy; and professional autonomy, which refers to teachers' personal attributes of feeling and acting as autonomous professionals.

The current literature suggests various directions and approaches to support teachers' development of professional autonomy and teaching autonomy in school contexts. To enhance teachers' professional autonomy, they need to be supported in developing critical analyses and independent judgements about others' decisions on syllabus, curriculum, examinations and textbooks (McGrath, 2000), and in negotiating the boundaries of their institutional constraints and forming autonomous reactions to these decisions (Benson, 2001). To raise teachers' awareness of their roles in fomenting learner autonomous learning with technology beyond the classroom, it is important to present student voices to them and confront them with the divergences in student expectancies and their own views (Lai et al., 2015). To promote teachers' readiness to support learner autonomy, teachers and educators need to focus on three dimensions according to Nakata (2011): behaviour readiness (whether teachers are able to employ strategies to support the development of learner autonomy), situational readiness (whether teachers can employ the most appropriate strategies for specific groups of learners), and psychological readiness (whether teachers are committed to promoting learner autonomy and grasping the relevant strategies). To promote autonomy-supportive pedagogies in the school contexts, critical reflective approaches that engage teachers in collaborative 'action-based inquiry into the development of pedagogy for autonomy in schools' has been proposed as an effective approach (Lamb, 2008; Vieira et al., 2008, p. 219). Holec (2009) further pointed out that teacher training towards supporting learning autonomy needs to prepare teachers with the professional knowledge and skills in assuming new roles in autonomous learning contexts: learner educator and material provider. Learner educator is a regular role that teachers play, but to support autonomous language learning with technology beyond the classroom, the preparation needs to include not only an enhanced understanding of the existent and alternative understanding of language learning and teaching, and of the knowledge and skills in developing learners' self-direction, but also their abilities to assume the counselling functions in assisting learners' self-directed learning with technology (Lai, 2015). The material provider role demands equipping teachers with the knowledge and skills in constantly updating information in relation not only to the language-learning potentials of existent and emerging technological platforms/tools but also to the knowledge and skills in matching the affordances of technological platforms/tools with pedagogical/learning purposes. Holec also highlighted an additional pedagogical leadership role that teachers need to assume, manager of change, whereby teachers need to have the ability to coordinate the various stakeholders, including learners, parents, colleagues, resource centres, etc., in supporting their endeavours in promoting learners' autonomous use of technology for language learning.

Supporting self-directed learning outside the classroom and bridging in-class learning and out-of-class learning are also important components of teaching autonomy. To help teachers heighten their awareness of the self-directed learning process and the uncertainties surrounding it, it would be viable to engage teachers in experiencing the same autonomous learning experience as that of autonomous learners (Little, 1995). Experiential learning could help teachers better perceive what their students might experience in self-directed learning and identify the supports that students need in autonomous learning. Hafner and Young (2007) reported a study on enhancing teachers' awareness of self-directed learning. The teachers in their study were provided with an online on-demand professional development system, whereby they were required to engage in self-regulated learning with the online system. The authors found that the teachers' hands-on experience enhanced their awareness of the key issues involved in self-directed learning. Helping teachers to perceive the link between in-class instruction and out-of-class use of technology for learning is critical for boosting their awareness of the importance of out-of-class learning and enhancing their conscious integration of in-class instruction with out-of-class learning, including learning in a self-access centre (Lázaro and Reinders, 2009). It is equally important to raise teachers' awareness that out-of-class learning is not the sole responsibility of learners; rather, their encouragement and support play a critical role in enhancing the quantity and quality of students' out-of-class learning experience.

7

Promoting Out-of-Class Autonomous Language Learning with Technology: The Resource and Environment Design

Autonomous language learning with technology beyond the classroom depends on learners' willingness and capacity to engage in such learning, a favourable sociocultural and discursive environment and the availability and accessibility of learning resources to support such an engagement. The previous two chapters discussed the fostering of a positive interaction between learner agency and learning contexts from the perspectives of learner development and teacher roles. This chapter explores the issue from the perspective of resource and environment design, which includes learning material design, tool selection and design, and the construction of learning environments and experience (Levy and Kennedy, 2010; Reinders and Pegrum, 2015). The design and selection of self-access learning materials and tools need to take into consideration not only the quality of the materials in terms of their learning potentials but also the affordances and constraints of self-directed learning and learning beyond the classroom. As Tomlinson (2010) put it, the design principles for self-access materials need to refer to universal principles (i.e. principles of language acquisition and development), delivery-specific principles (i.e. the particularities of self-access) and local principles (i.e. the characteristics and learning expectancies of the target learners). The affordances of technological resources also need to be taken into consideration in creating technology-enhanced learning experiences (Reinders and Pegrum, 2015). The discussion of the construction of out-of-class autonomous language-learning environments and experiences cannot do without taking into consideration in-class learning. This chapter discusses how these factors shape the design of out-of-class technological resources for language learning.

Design Principle 1: To maximize the learning potentials of the experience design principles in relation to the language-learning potentials

Chapelle (2001) devised a framework with a set of criteria to evaluate CALL materials. This framework includes a few key second-language learning principles such as the proximity of the language-learning materials to language used outside the classroom, primary attention given to meaning and opportunities to focus on language forms. It also highlights the importance of materials catering for different learning styles and stages of development. In addition, it stresses that materials should have a positive impact on learners' attitudes to language learning and should provide them with opportunities to learn about sound pedagogical practices and strategies. In a similar vein, Tomlinson (2010) proposed that the design of self-access materials needs to satisfy a few key principles of language acquisition, such as offering rich, meaningful and comprehensible language in use and opportunities to use language for communicative purposes, stimulating learner affective and cognitive engagement in the learning experience, cuing students to notice salient features of the input and imposing positive affect impact beyond the language per se, such as positive attitudes towards the learning experience, confidence in learning the language and so on. Thus, both Chapelle (2001) and Tomlinson (2010) highlighted the following key characteristics of quality language-learning materials: 1) diversity of language exposure and use, 2) authenticity of language exposure and use, 3) potential for affective and cognitive engagement, 4) mechanisms for inducing noticing, and 5) providing broader learning benefits beyond language gains.

Language exposure and use

Varied language exposure and use have been regarded as vital to language acquisition. Fagerlund (2012) found that learners who engaged in both receptive and productive activities in the target language perceived their out-of-class learning experience as more positive and empowering than did those who engaged in receptive activities only. Consequently, it is necessary to include both types of activities in out-of-class learning. Lai, Zhu and Gong (2015) further found that it was learners' focus of attention when dealing with receptive and productive technological resources that really mattered. In particular, learners who achieved a greater balance of form-focused and meaning-focused activities in their out-of-class learning experience were found to have greater language gains. In terms of the content of the language exposure, varied target-language sources are much valued. Tomlinson (2010) argued that self-access language-learning materials should include a variety of text types and genres in relation to topics, themes, contexts. Researchers have also emphasized varying the form of language use. Crook (2008) categorized four types of learner interaction with Web 2.0: 'The playful, the expressive, the reflective, and the exploratory' (p. 9). Playful use refers to socialization by playing games or through virtual worlds. Expressive use involves expressing feelings and opinions by producing and sharing media files. Reflective use refers to a deeper understanding or reflecting on the significance of a feeling or an experience in developing personal identity and building sophisticated knowledge. Exploratory use manifests itself mainly in the exploration and aggregation of information on the internet to keep abreast of new materials. Correspondingly, Crook (2008) advocated using Web 2.0 to support four principal dimensions of learner experience: collaboration, publication, new modes of representation and expression through digital artefacts, and inquiry. Laurillard (2002) focused on media forms and advocated its varied use in engaging learners in learning with technological resources: narrative media (i.e. non-interactive materials), interactive media (i.e. hyper- and multimedia resources that lend themselves to user control and interaction), adaptive media (i.e. computer-based media that respond to users' actions, such as simulations and virtual environments), communicative media (which support the exchange of ideas and discussion), and productive media (which allow learners to generate their own products). Thus ensuring the diversity of language exposure and use is a critical consideration in resource development and selection.

Authenticity of language exposure and use

Liang (2013) pointed out that the current discussion of authenticity in language learning is mostly concerned with the authenticity of texts (i.e. the origin of the materials) and tasks (i.e. reflecting the real use of language and activities in a target society), and argues for a broader view of authenticity. Gilmore's (2007) eight dimensions of authenticity provide lenses through which resource designers might achieve the advocated broader view of authenticity. These eight dimensions include language interlocutor, language receiver, context, interaction, task, social situation, assessment and culture. In addition to defining authenticity with respect to the characteristics of artefacts, interlocutors, situation and environment, researchers have also highlighted the importance of learners' reactions and responses in defining authenticity (Widdowson, 1979). For instance, Henry (2013) emphasized the need to go beyond the narrow focus of the authenticity of artefacts, texts and learning materials to consider learners' perceptions of authenticity when engaging with the language, which he argued was closely related to 'the aesthetic pleasure associated with creation, innovation and discovery' (Vannini and Burgess, 2009, p. 111) and the opportunities for personal expression and creativity. Rule (2006) emphasized learners' engagement in student-centred, collaborative and empowering learning experiences – such as learning through inquiry and thinking strategies, learning via discourse among a community of learners and learning with a focus on learner empowerment – in order to achieve authentic learning experiences. Thus, the construing of authentic resources and experiences rests not only on the superficial levels of what, who and where but also on the degree of affective, social and cognitive engagement in the learning experience.

Mechanisms for inducing noticing

The noticing of linguistic features can be realized by presenting input in ways that enhance the saliency of linguistic features and by engaging learners in various experiential and discovery activities. Textual enhancement and input flood are two features that can induce the noticing of linguistic features in language input (Han, Park and Combs, 2008; Lee and Huang, 2008). For instance, with respect to the former, researchers have manipulated typographical cues such as underlining, boldfacing, italicization, capitalization, colour coding or using different font sizes or types to enhance target linguistic features to make them perceptually more salient in language input. Visual input enhancement has been found to have beneficial effects on learners' acquisition of grammatical structures (Lee and Huang, 2008). Researchers have suggested enhancing audio input by increasing the volume of target grammatical structures, slowing down the speed of the target items or including short pauses before and after the target items to help make the target grammatical features stand out (Cho and Reinders, 2013). Sagarra and Abbuhl (2013) further examined the efficacy of enhancement in computer-delivered written and oral feedback, and found that oral, not typological, recast enhancement through volume and intonation stress helped enhance the effectiveness of computer-delivered recasts. Input flood, the artificial increase of the frequency of target linguistic features in a written or oral text, has also been found to be beneficial to inducing the noticing of linguistic features (Han, Park and Combs, 2008; Lee and Huang, 2008). For instance,

Bahrani and Sim (2012) examined learners' use of audiovisual materials and their language gains, and found that learners benefited more from audiovisual news than from cartoons. They concluded that audiovisual mass-media news lent itself more to language development because of the greater vocabulary recycling in this type of media. However, at the same time, researchers point out that the efficacy of input enhancement through both input flood and textual enhancement resides only in promoting noticing, which would not have much impact unless followed up with explicit instruction and inquiry activities (Winke, 2013). Various inquiry and discovery activities have been proposed to enhance learners' noticing of linguistic forms. For instance, Tomlinson (2010) proposed accompanying starter materials with targeted analytic activities that engage students in searching for extra authentic materials and discovering the usage of specific linguistic features in these materials. Written and spoken language corpora have also been proposed to enhance learners' noticing of linguistic features and communication strategies (Caines, McCarthy and O'Keeffe, 2016; Chambers, 2016).

Potential for affective and cognitive engagement

To stimulate learners' affective and cognitive engagement in the learning experience, Tomlinson (2010) suggested the following strategies: 1) creating and selecting texts and tasks – such as using controversial texts or engaging students with problem-solving tasks – that could elicit learners' emotional responses and cognitive investment; 2) engaging learners in thinking and feeling before, during and after engaging with the resources; and 3) giving learners suggestions on possible activities and directions that they could take using the materials and activities they select from a pool of materials or find on their own. Similarly, Reinders and Pegrum (2015) listed affective principles as an important criterion in the design of self-access learning materials and highlighted the importance of structuring resources in ways that lower learners' affective filters, such as reducing their anxiety levels. Reeve (2016) concurred with Reinders and Pegrum on the importance of stimulating emotional engagement by supporting task-facilitating emotions (e.g. interest and curiosity) and reducing task-withdrawing emotions (e.g. distress, anxiety and fear). He further proposed enhancing cognitive engagement by eliciting active self-regulation and the use of personalized and deep learning strategies, and by directing learners' attention to seeking conceptual understanding rather than surface knowledge. In addition to affective and cognitive engagement, Reeve added two more levels of engagement that designers need to attend to, namely, behavioural engagement (high level of concentration and persistence) and agentic engagement (proactive and constructive contribution to the learning experience rather than passively receiving it as given). More importantly, the sources of these various forms of engagement are learners' inner motivational resources – both inherent and acquired sources of motivation. In order to spark and sustain learners' inherent sources of motivation, materials and learning experience need to satisfy their psychological need for autonomy (perceived choice of action and psychological freedom), competence (effectiveness of pursuing and interacting with the environment) and relatedness (close emotional bonds and responsive relationships with others). Furthermore, a certain level of congruence between the resources and learners' self-endorsed values, intrinsic goals and personal aspirations needs to be achieved in order to bring about acquired sources of motivation to support high-quality learner engagement. All these different aspects of issues need to be taken into consideration in order to enhance learners' affective and cognitive engagement in the learning experience.

Broader learning benefits beyond language gains

Learning benefits need to extend beyond language proficiency to include cognitive, metacognitive and affective gains. Researchers have highlighted the value of self-access materials in exerting a positive influence on learners' attitudes to language learning and in boosting their confidence and self-esteem in language learning and use (Chapelle, 2001; Tomlinson, 2010). In addition to these affective outcomes, researchers also argue for the need to achieve cognitive and metacognitive gains by structuring the learning experience in ways that could enhance learners' understanding of the learning processes and approaches to learning (Tomlinson, 2010) and by guiding learners to interact with and process authentic language materials with a primary focus on meaning first before moving on to focus on the language forms (Levy and Kennedy, 2010; Tomlinson, 2010). It has also been suggested that components of learner strategy training need to be incorporated into the design either as a coherent piece or as parallel modules to go with the self-access learning materials (Cooker, 2010).

In order to maximize the language-learning potentials of out-of-class learning resources, the design of these resources needs to take these various aspects into consideration to meet the critical conditions for second-language learners. In addition to this, since these resources are used in an autonomous manner, the characteristics of self-directed learning need to be taken into consideration as well to ensure that these well-designed materials from the second-language acquisition perspective will be selected and used by learners.

Design principles in relation to the characteristics of self-directed learning

Personalization

Given that learner control is the essence of self-directed learning (Stubbé and Theunissen, 2008), the extent to which learners can readapt learning resources to meet their personal needs is a key factor in determining the likelihood of learners incorporating self-access materials into their learning repertoires. In a report on language learners' preferences for digital learning materials, Conole (2008) found that ownership, personalization and appropriation of technologies are key factors that shape learners' selective engagement with technological resources. Thus, learning materials in autonomous set-ups need to be easily accessible and flexible and lend themselves to personalization and customization. To meet this expectation, Holec (2009) elucidated that language-learning materials for self-directed learning – whether individual or collective – need to possess two basic characteristics: adaptability and open access. Holec argued that the materials should first and foremost be adaptable so that individual learners can selectively make use of them to fit their learning goals and methods. Consequently, the materials need to be diversified and not pre-defined according to specific learning objectives and thematic contents, specific proficiency levels, specific learning styles or pace of learning. Nor should they be constraining in terms of processing time, infrastructural resource and progression requirements. Open access, the second characteristic highlighted by Holec, refers to the materials being easily accessible when needed. Holec suggested organizing existent commercial sources and authentic materials in loose categories (such as language competency and language functions) that are accompanied by activities and exercises or instructions for suggested use. Another option that Holec suggested is to make a collection of varied authentic materials available to students with a list of suggested activities and tips concerning learning objectives (such as 'how to learn vocabulary' or learning techniques such as 'games for learning vocabulary') to support learners' selective use of a particular collection of materials. Levy and Kennedy (2010) concurred with Holec and argued that the key to designing self-directed learning materials is to move away from the one-size-fits-all approach that characterizes in-class learning. They hence advocated approaching design from a learner-centric perspective, whereby the content is structured not as a set of prescribed and pre-sequenced materials but as segments that can be retrieved and sequenced in response to learners' requests, and that are offered as possible materials for learners to choose from, accompanied by hints and suitable support that they can rely on to empower themselves to choose and learn on their own (Chiu, 2015). Idros et al. (2010) constructed an online learning system along this line of thinking wherein their Malaysian learners were given a resource pool and online diagnostic tests that they could access at any time. The diagnostic tests indicated to the learners their competency levels and suggested remedial and enrichment materials and tasks that they could select from the resource pool to improve their areas of weakness. In addition, students could also choose to join some project-based modules targeting different language areas to learn together with their peers. Thus, the content of the materials needs to be loosely structured so as to enable personalized use.

The degree of personalization also relies heavily on the nature of the learner control that the materials provide. Buchem, Tur and Hölterhof (2013) analysed learner control in personalized learning environments in detail and concluded that learner control in such learning environments needs to go beyond the superficial instructional-design levels of control that are most common in computer-delivered instructional environments. The instructional-design-level of control often takes the form of choice over topic, task sequencing and difficulty level, control over the speed of presentation, control of the content display and control over whether to use the learning materials recommended by the system. Buchem, Tur and Hölterhof (2014) argued that learner control in personalized learning environments needs to manifest in multiple aspects: 1) instruction-design levels of control; 2) control over learning goals, outcomes and associated tasks, resources and support; 3) control over whom to communicate and collaborate with and who to initiate the social interaction and collaboration; and 4) control over the aggregation of and selection from a wide range of proffered and self-added tools. Consequently, with respect to the critical need for personalization in self-directed learning, the design of self-access materials needs to consider not only the form and presentation of contents but also the nature and level of learner control that they afford.

Support

Another key characteristic of self-directed learning is the absence of immediate teacher support, which influences learners' selective use of resources. In Lai's (2015a) study, the university foreign-language learners reported preferring out-of-class learning resources containing learning support that facilitated their use of the resources. The participants said that they chose to watch videos because of the availability of subtitles to help bridge the gap between their limited proficiency levels and the potential of the resource. They reported not incorporating into self-directed learning the resources that were perceived to lack structure and supporting mechanisms. Thus, learners expect self-access learning materials to contain support for learning, and the need for support is multilayered.

First of all, learners need general support in navigating the complex information world with its vast amount of information, in dealing with the abundance of information and resources and building connections between various pieces of information (Huang et al., 2013; Saadatmand and Kumpulainen, 2012). Thus, mechanisms need to be built into self-directed learning resources to help students select, make sense of and organize the information and resources. These mechanisms could take the form of peer support through collaborative work and strategy sharing, and of cognitive scaffolding packages with strategies and tools that students could access while selecting and interacting with resources. For instance, Tomlinson (2010) recommended that students should be informed of what is available to them so that they would have a clear idea of the affordances of the various resources around them and what is required of them in order to benefit from these resources. She further suggested that such information could be delivered through poster promotion, text messages and so on. Huang et al. (2013) reported on an intervention study in which information graphics methods were adopted to reduce learners' cognitive overload when interacting with online resources. Such methods involve the use of tags to visualize verbal information and the relationships between the tags and the associated multimedia materials. The researchers used information graphic maps of the relationships to present a set of rich and varied self-directed learning materials, and found that the visualization of relationships was associated with reduced intrinsic cognitive load of the materials, which in turn influenced learner-perceived learning effectiveness. The support learners need at this information level pertains not only to their retrieval and organization of online authentic language materials but also to their selection and organization of the vast amount of online resources sites and tools for language learning.

In addition to support at the general information retrieval and organizational level, language learners also need support in order to exploit language-learning opportunities more effectively while interacting with authentic materials. Some support functions could be built within the resources to facilitate learners' interaction with the authentic materials. Choi (2015) studied students' selective use of video sources and found that they preferred sources with help/support functions such as the provision of subtitles, vocabulary support and speech-rate adjustment. The researcher suggested that support mechanisms should be added to video viewing, whereby students would be given the transcripts of the audio files and guided to infer the meanings of new and difficult words prior to viewing the video sources and would be led through some language-extension activities after completing the video-viewing tasks. Plug-ins could be included in the system to provide emergent language and cultural support to facilitate learners' interaction in the online system. For instance, Rankin et al. (2008) embedded chat prompts into online games with references to relevant expressions and explanations concerning conversation conventions in order to assist students' social interactions during gameplay. This kind of support could also be achieved through selectively including and recommending technological resources in the resource pool. For example, Lin and Siyanova-Chanturia (2015) suggested selecting internet or TV programmes in the factual, drama and comedy categories rather than the music, learning and religion categories, arguing that video resources in the former categories contain more everyday language use. They further recommended proceeding from narrow viewing to random viewing – that is, learners select from a variety of video sources of a similar nature before moving on to watching random, unrelated video sources. Similarly, Hanf (2015) also suggested that learners watch movie series before proceeding to watch independent movies. She further recommended differentiated use of captions or subtitles for learners of different proficiency levels – subtitles in the native language for beginners and captions in the foreign language for intermediate and advanced learners.

Potential for self-direction

Related to lack of teacher support is the view that learning environments and experiences should contain support mechanisms not only to enhance students' learning from the resources but also to boost learners' potential for self-direction and lifelong learning in general. Tomlinson (2010) argued that the ultimate aim of self-access materials should be to support learner development so that learners become truly independent learners. This aim can be achieved by structuring self-access materials in ways that would lead learners to seek additional relevant authentic texts for further exploration, and by providing feedback that recognizes their achievement and facilitates further improvement and consequently boosts their self-esteem in self-directed learning. This aim could also be achieved by building in mechanisms within the experience or environment that support learners' development of related skills. Reinders

(2013) argued that the construction of learning environment needs to focus on supporting learners' learning process rather than on the mere provision of resources: 'Materials for autonomy need to be integrated into the teaching context through learner training and ongoing support and it is not sufficient simply to provide learners with access to resources, no matter how good those resources are in themselves, if learners are to have any chance of success in their out-of-class learning' (Reinders, 2011, p. 176). This point was confirmed in an action-research study conducted by Chen (2013), in which a group of university English majors in China were given the latest tablets to use on their own. Learners' daily usage reports suggested that the participants spent only a small portion of tablet time on learning English and failed to take advantage of the connectivity of tablets for interactive and collaborative activities. Hence, the researcher concluded that simply providing learners with the latest mobile tools alone did not automatically lead to effective use of the tools for language learning, and it was important to enhance their ability to use tablets for language learning. In the second round of the action research, the researcher engaged students in exploring the potential of tablets for language learning in groups, reviewing different apps for language learning and designing learning activities around the apps. As expected, this awareness-raising activity was found to boost the proportion of tablet time that the participants spent on English learning. In addition to raising learners' awareness of the usefulness of technological resources for language learning through activity design, Reinders (2011; 2013) argued that it is equally important to raise learners' awareness of the language-learning process and their roles therein. For this purpose, needs analysis in the form of self or institutional assessments, awareness-raising activities such as checklists or questionnaires, and learning records in the form of learning diaries and portfolios are often utilized to support the learning process. In addition, strategy instruction and language-advising sessions are employed to enhance learners' development of autonomous learning skills. Levy and Kennedy (2010) took yet another approach to supporting learners' self-directed learning. They sent SMSes with vocabulary-learning strategies to students to support learners' interaction with authentic language materials. These vocabulary-learning strategies included determination strategies that would help learners discover the meanings of new words and memory and cognitive strategies that would help them consolidate their understanding of words. To sustain learners' motivation in accessing and using these messages, the researchers varied the format in which the messages were sent, such as making suggestions, asking questions and setting problem-solving tasks. They also included other information in the messages that was of interest to the students, such as course deadlines, and information about popular out-of-class learning resources such as TV programmes or target-language community events.

In addition to using parallel learner development modules that accompany learners' engagement with self-access learning materials, Blaschke and Hase (2016) also argued for the design of learning environments to support self-determined learning. According to them, in order to develop learners' capacities to function effectively in novel and constantly changing environments, heutagogic learning environments need to be constructed, where emphasis is given to 'developing capability, self-reflection and metacognition (an understanding of one's own learning process)' (Blaschke and Hase, 2016, p. 27). The researchers elaborated further on a few design elements of heutagogic learning environments: 1) opportunities and support for learners to explore, whereby teachers provide possible resources for students to engage in self-directed inquiry-based learning and venues and tools for learners to organize their discoveries and information resources; 2) opportunities for learners to engage in individual and collaborative creative work; 3) venues for learners to collaborate and share information and experiences; 4) venues for learners to share their learning and learning processes with each other using various information-sharing tools and applications; and 5) opportunities for constant reflection for learners to consolidate their understanding, critically examine their learning processes and approaches and re-examine their value systems and beliefs about learning.

Design principles in relation to the characteristics of out-of-class learning

Fragmented and brief

Out-of-class learning is episodic and is constrained by the fragmented nature of after-school hours consisting of segments of short duration (Reinders, 2011; Ucko and Ellenbogen, 2008). Thus, self-access learning resources need to possess certain features to be perceived as affording possibilities for actions. Olemdo (2015) found that secondary school students tended to avoid activities that demanded a great deal of time; for instance, they preferred watching online videos to watching films. Jones (2015) also found that students used mobile devices to fill in the small gaps in their schedule such as daily commutes, lunchtime or time in between activities for language learning. Similarly, Lai (2015a) found that her university foreign-language learner participants preferred flexible resources that would take shorter periods of time. Consequently, they preferred watching TV series because they were short (with each episode only taking around twenty minutes), and engaging in interaction on Facebook because it was convenient and people could quit at any time. They also regarded activities like reading long paragraphs or passages as more suited to in-class learning. Thus, to enhance the likelihood of self-access language-learning materials being utilized, it is important to make them flexibly structured and, preferably, to design them in such a way that they can stand alone in small segments so that learners do not need to devote long periods of time to completing them.

Interest driven

Out-of-class learning is largely interest driven (Barron, 2006); consequently, learners' selective use of out-of-class learning resources is closely related to their interests (Beckman, Bennett and Lockyer, 2014). Among the studies that examined learners' preferences for out-of-class learning activities, personal enjoyment is an oft-cited criterion for selection. For instance, Doyle and Parris (2012) reported that students would not engage with a learning resource if they did not find it enjoyable. Barbee (2013) further found that learners prioritized enjoyability over effectiveness when deciding whether to use a certain resource for learning beyond the classroom. Specifically, Cabot (2014) found that secondary school students preferred playful and expressive types of activities, with males predominantly choosing the former and females selecting the latter. Moreover, it has been found that the activities learners engage in are strongly connected with their personal interests and social life, with the most extensively and frequently used materials and activities being those related to pop culture and leisure entertainment, such as games, chatting, music and videos (Bailly, 2010). Choi (2015) asked forty-eight students to evaluate a set of video sources in the target language and found that the videos that were chosen by students as useful and interesting were those that were related to their daily lives and inspirations. In response, Cooker (2010) proposed a major principle for designing and selecting self-access learning materials: they should be fun, entertaining and related to everyday activity.

Attrition-resistant design

Out-of-class learning is voluntary and lacks support and guidance, and hence, is characterized by a high attrition rate (Lin, Warschauer and Blake, 2016). It is often found that learners' enthusiasm for and actual use of self-study materials dwindle over time, and learners have a hard time maintaining their engagement with the materials over long periods (Jones, 2001; Nielson, 2011). Lin et al. (2016) pointed out that teacher and peer drive are important factors in such learning contexts, and that it is important that the materials are of high quality, contain advice and training components, and support interaction and a sense of community (Blake, 2008; Sockett and Toffoli, 2012). Henry (2013) also suggested incorporating the affinity-space features of the gaming society to enhance learners' motivational autonomy in self-directed learning. In particular, he recommended grouping students to work on self-generated or other-generated problem-solving tasks, or cases related to language learning, in order to foreground learners' voices and sense of community and enhance the perceived meaningfulness of self-directed learning. In addition, guiding learners to develop strategies to boost interactions in their communities could also help, such as formulating specific questions about their submissions to enhance the possibilities of interaction concerning their postings (Kozar, 2016).

Design principles in relation to technological affordances

Information and communication technologies that language learners normally use are characterized by high levels of connectivity, ubiquity and interactivity, and thus lend themselves well to constructivist pedagogies such as inquiry-based learning, task-based learning, situated learning and embodied learning, all of which support their development of creativity, critical thinking, collaboration and autonomy (Reinders and Pegrum, 2015). Reinders and Pegrum (2015) used mobile devices as an example and argued that the key affordances of mobile devices are interaction, connection with both local and global environments, episodic learning, personal learning and social learning. The researchers thus advocated that in constructing mobile-assisted language-learning environments, it is important to use mobile devices to support constructivist approaches so as to maximize these educational affordances. This point was supported by Kukulska-Hulme et al. (2015), who argued that the design of technology-enhanced learning experiences should ensure that the learning activities will actively exploit teachers' expertise (experience and strategies), the affordances of digital devices (such as multimodality, seamlessness, authenticity and collaboration), and the abundance and diversity of circumstances, resources and mobility afforded by the digital devices (places, times, contexts, cultures, learner goals, etc.). Similarly, they recommended the use of digital devices such as mobile devices to engage students in creative language production and sharing, capturing authentic language samples and connecting with language users anywhere.

At the same time, Hamilton (2013) reminded researchers and educators that the affordances of technologies should be not viewed narrowly in terms of the pedagogical values that the technological features support; rather, they should be considered in terms of the 'totality of relationships' of learners' interaction with others in the learning environment with the presence of the technological platforms. Consequently, the construction of out-of-class resources should take into account the provision of well-designed pedagogical tasks mediated by technologies. What is equally, if not more, important is to construct out-of-class resources with a clear understanding of how the introduction of technologies

Table 7.1 Design Principle 1 and the key issues

Principle 1: To enhance the learning potentials	Maximize language-learning potentials • Varied language exposure and use not only in language but also in media forms • Authenticity of learning experience in terms of not only learning contents and tasks but also learning experience that could strengthen the degree of learners' affective, social and cognitive engagement • Affective and cognitive engagement by using materials that could incite emotional responses, reduce emotions that impede learning and stimulate and maintain learners' motivational resources • Induce noticing of linguistic features through input enhancement and flood • Learner growth beyond language to include enhancement of learner confidence, strategy and learning-skill gains Facilitate self-directed learning • Support personalization via loosely structured content and various levels of learner control • Provide information-organization support and language-learning support by embedding functional tools and through selective structuring of learning materials • Promote self-directed learning skills through parallel external learner development arrangements and inherent design components Satisfy the features of out-of-class learning • Make the materials flexible and of short duration • Include fun and entertaining materials • Use collaborative learning to reduce potential learner attrition

into the learning environment might reconfigure the social relationships in the environment and whether learners are willing and able to take advantage of the pedagogical potentials of the technologies to engage in autonomous behaviours in such a social milieu.

Design Principle 1 focuses on maximizing the possibility of the designed resources being perceived as useful and being incorporated into learners' out-of-class learning repertoires through enhancing the learning potentials of the resources. Table 7.1 summarizes the various issues educators need to take into consideration in relation to this design principle.

Design Principle 2: To achieve an optimal relationship between in-class and out-of-class learning

As long ago as the 1990s, Pusack (1999) had already proposed that the ultimate goal of software design is to strive for the optimal mix of in-class and out-of-class learning. He stated: 'My concept for the design of foreign language instructional software derived from the need to achieve an optimal mix between in-class and out-of-class learning' (p. 26). This goal is increasingly relevant in today's world, with out-of-class language learning being normalized with the abundance of online resources and tools. One of the keys to reaching an optimal relationship between in-class and out-of-class learning is to take advantage of and complement the respective strengths of each context. Levy and Kennedy (2010) argued that in order to construct quality out-of-class learning experiences, one should search for a reciprocal relationship between in-class and out-of-class learning, whereby the learning experience could extend teachers' influence on learners' out-of-class learning agenda and magnify the learning potentials of such experience while providing a different kind of environment from that of the classroom.

For one thing, out-of-class learning experiences should not involve simply repeating what goes on inside the classroom. Taking the use of podcasting as an example, Middleton (2011) argued that when podcasting was used as knowledge transmission that repeated what was normally done in the classroom, it was often not well received by the learners. He suggested focusing on using mobile audio to mediate knowledge construction, and promote learner knowledge production and sharing as suggested by Ciussi, Rosner and Augier (2009). He also suggested using mobile audio to address learners' desire for a social, active, and interactive experience of learning, and to support their enquiry and reflection in knowledge construction. For Middleton, the construction of learning experience with mobile audio involves extending the in-class learning experience rather than repeating it.

For another thing, in-class learning should support and extend learning from out-of-class learning experiences. Wong et al. (in press) proposed a seamless language-learning framework to make use of both in-class and out-of-class learning experiences to help learners continually recontextualize their previously constructed knowledge to achieve increasingly sophisticated understanding. Their framework emphasizes the interweaving of teacher- and student-initiated tasks across different learning settings to provide opportunities for authentic activities. The framework also underscores incorporating and connecting language-input and language-output activities, and meaning-focused and form-focused activities. The framework further accentuates connecting in-class and out-of-class learning to support non-linear learning of linguistic knowledge, application and reflection, and facilitate learner co-construction of linguistic knowledge. The researchers reported on the design of a seamless Chinese idiom learning experience where teachers first help learners to develop a basic understanding of new idioms in-class (in-class learning engagement), followed by learners actively recording their daily encounters with the idioms outside the classroom and applying their initial understanding of the idioms to episodes in their daily lives (personalized contextual learning). Learners then strengthen their understanding of the idioms through the online sharing of and commenting on one another's language artefacts produced during personalized contextual learning (online peer learning). Their understanding is then further refined and consolidated through a teacher-facilitated in-class discussion session (in-class consolidation). Flipped learning is an example of attempts to integrate learning across in-class and out-of-class spaces to achieve optimal effects. Hwang, Lai and Wang (2015) illustrated how teachers could anchor students' learning across different contexts through issue-quest learning, problem-based learning or project-based learning. They illustrated flipped learning through an example of the nutrition unit of a health course. Group problem-based learning on the causes of obesity, for example, could be carried out before class, whereby students are required to collect information from various online and offline physical and human sources they could resort to. They then upload the information they collected into an online site where they share and categorize the information collaboratively in groups before coming to the class. In class, students were guided in critiquing one another's peer sites and learning from in-class discussions of the information assembled on these sites.

Although the example does not relate to language learning per se, the design could easily be implemented in language learning. Both these pedagogical arrangements aim to utilize and interweave the pedagogical strengths of the in-class learning (metalinguistic and metacognitive functions [Cabot, 2014]), and out-of-class learning contexts (authenticity, situatedness and ubiquity) to support the continuity of learning efforts across time, space and technologies, and facilitate learners' spiral knowledge construction. In order to achieve an optimal relationship between in-class and out-of-class learning experience, in-class learning could be structured in a way that prepares learners for out-of-class learning, supports learners' out-of-class experience and strengthens the learning outcome. To prepare learners for out-of-class learning, in-class learning may involve teachers utilizing their meta-knowledge about language learning to guide the learners to construct appropriate out-of-class learning experiences, which in turn influence what materials and activities are to be used in class to prepare students for their out-of-class learning experience. To support learners' out-of-class learning experience, in-class learning may focus on equipping them with the necessary metacognitive knowledge, skills and strategies that enable their successful interaction with authentic language resources and with peer learners via digital tools outside the classroom, thereby helping them learn from the experience. To strengthen the learning outcomes from learners' out-of-class learning experience, in-class learning may engage them in metalinguistic, metacultural and metacognitive discussions concerning their out-of-class language-use experience and the language use and cultural issues that occurred during the experience.

Such an approach argues against connecting learners' in-class and out-of-class worlds in the technical sense, that is, bringing learners' out-of-class technological tools into the classroom for the sake of making in-class learning more entertaining and relevant. Henry (2013) pointed out that 'saturating classrooms with the forms of popular culture students are accustomed to in their leisure time' (p. 58) runs the risk of being greeted with learner resistance as an intrusion on their personal lives (Sharples, 2009a) and leads to rather different experiences, which may be counterproductive to achieving learning goals (Crook, 2012). Similarly, Beckman, Bennett and Lockyer (2014) adopted Bourdieu's key concepts – field, capital and habitus – to elucidate that learners' different technology practices inside and outside the classroom may be incongruent and do not lend to smooth transfer across contexts. Examining the interview responses of a group of secondary school students on their perceptions of the use of Web 2.0 tools at school, Crook (2012) identified various aspects of incompatibility and tensions between features of school culture and the inquiry, collaboration, publication and multimedia literacy opportunities that Web 2.0 affords in out-of-school contexts. Crook concluded that, because of the differences in the 'operating characteristics' of in-class and out-of-class settings, it is not an easy task to appropriate technology use outside the classroom to transform educational practices inside the classroom (p. 79). Therefore, instead of striving for full integration of out-of-class technological resources to make in-class teaching more interesting, researchers and educators may think of utilizing these resources and experiences in ways that help learners to utilize similar resources and experiences to construct their personalized out-of-class learning environments.

These two approaches represent different ways to integrate technology into classroom instruction: integrating technological resources to enrich in-class instruction versus integrating technological resources inside the class to support learners' use of these resources outside the classroom. These two approaches prioritize different goals and may bring about different outcomes: the former aims primarily at the development of learners' language competency and cultural understanding, whereas, the latter focuses more on developing learners' strategic skills and sociocultural understanding to interact more effectively and on developing their ability to select appropriate technological resources and use them effectively for language learning. Language and cultural development would come along as a natural product of the experience. The former is technocentric and underscores the flow of technological practices from out-of-class contexts to in-class instruction. In contrast, the latter approach is skill-centric and accentuates supporting the transfer of technological resources from in-class fields to out-of-class fields. To facilitate the successful transfer from in-class to out-of-class contexts, it is important to enhance the congruence of habitus and capital around the use of technological resources across the fields and strengthen learners' ability to utilize and gain capital in a particular field (Beckman et al., 2014). For instance, watching videos is often adopted as a useful out-of-class resource because it is frequently used in language classes, and students have already developed the skills to utilize the capital. Thus, it is important for in-class activities to equip students with the appropriate social and cultural capital so that they are capable of learning with authentic materials mediated by technological platforms in the out-of-class contexts. As Beckman et al. (2014) argued, 'Without the skills and knowledge or training required to effectively (to utilize and possibly gain capital) use the internet, or the support networks to provide assistance, one would not have the capital to benefit from connectivity' (p. 16). To achieve this goal, Thorne and Reindhardt (2008) proposed the development of 'bridging activities', whereby the digital texts and practices generated in informal learning experiences are brought to class discussions to raise learners' critical awareness of the social practices and language used in a particular digital context and encourage their application of this critical awareness vis-à-vis language socialization in different communication contexts. Similarly, Henry (2013) also recommended adopting an inclusive approach that explicitly recognizes the values of non-standard language forms and celebrates different types of language use. Henry further suggested that students be helped in matching their out-of-class learning experiences with specific language-learning objectives. For instance, teachers can guide students to search for and identify argumentative, descriptive, contrastive and narrative texts that they might encounter in digital gaming and the affinity spaces to enhance their awareness of the language learning potentials of different technological experience. Sockett and Toffoli (2012) proposed yet another solution whereby, instead of incorporating Facebook into classroom activities, teachers are recommended to use thematic forums, which are of a less personal nature and lend themselves more to instructional use but which require similar sets of skills for participation in exchanges on Facebook (such as providing comments on one another's posts). In this way, learners could be helped to develop relevant communication skills needed for Facebook interaction by expanding the focus to developing learning and communication strategies while using existing virtual instructional communities.

Design Principle 2 focuses on facilitating the incorporation of technological resources in the out-of-class learning contexts by building optimal connections between in-class and out-of-class learning. Table 7.2 summarizes the key issues related to this design principle.

Table 7.2 Design Principle 2 and the key issues

Principle 2: Achieve an optimal relationship between in-class and out-of-class	• Out-of-class should not repeat but should provide a different learning experience from in-class learning • Structure in-class learning to support and elevate the learning from out-of-class learning experience • Incorporate pop culture resources inside the classroom to enhance learners' abilities to utilize and maximize the language-learning potentials of out-of-class learning

Design Principle 3: To make learners an integrative part of the design process

Out-of-class learning with technology is by nature learner centred. Hamilton (2013) pointed out that learners respond selectively to different elements of technological environments according to what they perceive to be of value. Thus, it is important for learners to assume an integral role in selecting and designing out-of-class learning resources and in promoting and supporting peer learners' use of out-of-class learning resources (Cooker, 2010). Luckin (2010) introduced the ecology of resources model to elucidate important considerations in designing a learner-centred, technology-enhanced learning experience and environment. The model emphasizes educators working together with learners to identify and organize resources of learning that learners could potentially utilize, and developing the scaffolds and creating the ecology of resources that learners could actually use for learning. This creation process involves a close negotiation between the design team and the learners in order to reach a clear understanding of the focus of the design, which addresses learner needs and identifies potential resources and enablers. The potential resources include possible resource elements (such as knowledge, skills, tools, people and the environment), potential resource filters (which could constrain learners' access to the resources) and the inner resources (competence, awareness and dispositions) that learners bring with them. The possible enablers are the potential partners that could mediate and facilitate learners' interaction with the resources. The design aims to make use of the partners to scaffold learners' use and orchestration of the potential resources, reducing the constraining filters and capitalizing on learners' inner resources, to construct personalized ecologies of resources outside the classroom. Underwood, Luckin and Winters (2012) elaborated on how Luckin's (2010) ecology of resources design framework could be utilized to assist in the design of a vocabulary-learning environment. Experienced and successful independent language learners were involved at the beginning of the design process to work together with the designers in identifying potential resources available in their particular settings and the support they needed in making use of the resources. The environment design supported learner-centred personal and collaborative inquiry, whereby learners identified language items to study themselves. Resource and reference banks were made available in the environment to assist learners to make sense of the language items and to learn collaboratively with other learners who were also interested in the language items. Learners could also add their personal favourite language resources to the

Table 7.3 Design Principle 3 and the key issues

Principle 3: Learner-centric design	• Involve learners throughout the whole design process • Use knowledge not only of potential resources that learners have access to but also of learners' habitual time and space for using the resources to inform the design

resource and reference banks and could share their resource collections and use with other learners to keep themselves updated with the rapidly growing range of resources available to them. In addition, the environment would prompt learners to reflect on their use of resources to enhance their abilities to construct their own personalized language-learning environments. Although the system that Underwood et al. (2012) reported specifically targeted the construction of a vocabulary-learning environment, the same learner-centred collaborative process could be applied to support language learners' construction of language-learning environments in general. In addition to the resources, Kukulska-Hulme (2012) further argued that the construction of learning experiences also needs to take into consideration the time and spaces where learners habitually or spontaneously use relevant technological sources.

Design Principle 3 stresses maximizing the likelihood of technological resources being utilized by learners by adopting a learner-centric approach to design. Table 7.3 summarizes the key issues related to this design principle.

This chapter has discussed some major principles that need to be taken into consideration in the matter of design of out-of-class, technology-enhanced language-learning resources. It illustrates various dimensions suggested by the current literature as critical to enhancing the possibility of the designed resources being perceived as useful and being incorporated into learners' out-of-class learning repertoires.

Part Three

Researching Out-of-Class Autonomous Language Learning with Technology

8

Towards a Research Agenda of Out-of-Class Autonomous Language Learning with Technology

Language-education research has long focused predominantly on language learning inside the classroom, with the exception of a small body of literature on self-access language centres and language-learning strategies that is dedicated to student learning outside the classroom. The technological and educational landscapes in the 1990s and 2000s, however, have brought out-of-class learning to the forefront: technological advancement and the accessibility of PCs and mobile devices now provide resources and venues for students to engage in learning beyond the formal classroom (Cox, 2013), and propositions for lifelong and life-wide learning permeate educational discourses (Field, 2000). Correspondingly, the literature on out-of-class autonomous language learning with technology has been expanding rapidly since 2000. This chapter analyses current research on out-of-class autonomous language learning with technology and identifies future areas of research.

Key areas of research

Current research on out-of-class autonomous language learning with technology has focused primarily on describing learners' autonomous learning behaviours, unravelling the effects of such learning behaviours, and exploring different approaches to enhancing these learning behaviours. This section reviews and discusses in detail some of the key research activities and showcases studies that have been conducted in each key area of research.

Key Area 1: Profiling out-of-class autonomous language learning with technology

A large number of research studies have reported on language learners' self-initiated use of technology beyond the classroom. This body of literature has studied language learners from different regions of the world, with European and Asian countries being the most studied regions. Although a wide range of foreign languages have been explored, the majority of studies have focused on the learning of English as a foreign or second language. Studies have examined both K–12 students and university students, and a few have also investigated adult learners who are self-studying the language. Thus, the current literature represents a wide range of research contexts, although the research samples are somewhat biased towards certain regions and the learning of English.

Sub-Area 1: Nature of autonomous language learning with technology

The highest proportion of studies on out-of-class autonomous language learning with technology has focused on describing the nature of learners' out-of-class autonomous language learning with technology. This body of literature has yielded research findings on how frequently language learners use technology for language learning beyond the classroom, what technological resources they use most frequently and what language-learning and autonomous-learning contexts they use technology to support. Information on the nature of learners' use of different technological resources helps identify the resources that learners often use and how they use them, which could suggest areas that educators may focus on to enhance the quality of learners' interaction with these resources. At the same time, such information stimulates discussions about and investigations into the resources that learners seldom use and the dimensions of use they rarely focus on so that educators can understand the reasons behind the selective use of resources and devise potential support and interventions. Thus, research findings concerning the 'whats' of learners' autonomous use of technology for learning offer useful foundational knowledge for in-depth exploration into the 'whys' and 'hows' of their autonomous use of technology for learning so that educators can target the aspects for which learners need the most support.

Current research has analysed the nature of technology use from the technical perspective (i.e. specific technological tools and resources), the pedagogical perspective (e.g. receptive vs. productive use), the language perspective (e.g. different language skills and knowledge), and the autonomous learning perspective (e.g. dimensions of self-regulated learning). See Table 8.1 for the example of a study on the nature of out-of-class language learning with technology

Table 8.1 A study on the nature of out-of-class language learning with technology

Lai and Gu (2011)
This study examined the nature of learners' out-of-class language learning with technology.
Adopting the key dimensions of self-regulated learning identified in influential socio-cognitive models of self-regulated learning, the study surveyed a group of HK university foreign-language learners on their use of technological resources to self-regulate various aspects of language learning. The survey responses were followed up with semi-structured interviews to elicit learners' rationale behind their selective use of technology for language learning.
The study found that learners reported positive perceptions of and engagement in the use of technology for goal commitment regulation, learning resource regulation, cultural learning regulation and affective regulation. They reported the least positively on the use of technology to connect with native speakers and to seek language support from peer learners around the world. The authors further found that learners' hesitancy to interact with unfamiliar people online due to unease in interacting with strangers and a lack of similar cultural backgrounds, their language proficiency, their language-learning beliefs and dispositions, and their learning history and habits all contributed to the variation in their selective use of technology to self-regulate their language-learning process.
Commentary: This study used a self-regulation framework to tap into the nature of language learners' autonomous use of technology for learning beyond the classroom. It identified the aspects of learning that learners did not actively use technology to support and revealed the reasons behind the limited use of technology. The findings could inform designers on what features need to be built in so as to stimulate and support the dimensions of self-initiated technology use that learners seldom engage in. The findings could also inform teachers on the support they need to provide to learners to facilitate such learning behaviours outside the classroom.

from the autonomous learning perspective. Diversified as these perspectives are, quite a number of them lie at the surface level (e.g. specific technological tools; different language skills) and fall short of providing useful insights into possible interventions. However, there are many other more fine-tuned, informative perspectives that could be referred to when analysing the nature of technology use. Examples of such perspectives include 1) different affordances of technologies for language learning (e.g. the three dimensions of affordance of mobile devices for learning proposed by Kearney et al. [2012] – the use of mobile devices to enable personalization such as personal agency and learning customization, supporting collaboration such as conversation and data sharing, and enhancing authenticity in terms of situatedness and contextualization of the learning experience); 2) different types of learner interaction with technology (e.g. the four types of learner interaction with Web 2.0 as proposed by Crook [2008] – the playful, the expressive, the reflective and the exploratory); 3) other-autonomous learning dimensions (e.g. the three aspects of autonomous learning highlighted by scholars like Littlewood [1996] and Benson [2012] – autonomy as learner, autonomy as language user and autonomy as person), and 4) learners' attention foci when interacting with technological resources (e.g. focus on language form vs. focus on meaning as discussed in Lai, Gong and Zhu [2015]). Future research may consider adopting these more in-depth, fine-grained perspectives to delve deeper into the nature of technology use beyond the classroom.

Furthermore, current research on the nature of out-of-class technology use has often been conducted at a single point in time. Although a few studies have captured snapshots of technology-use profiles from language learners of different proficiency levels and different ages, these cross-sectional studies are indicative at most and are inadequate at best to reveal the minute changes in individual learners' technology selection and use as they progress along the learning trajectory. It would be interesting to take a dynamic approach to documenting in detail the types of technologies learners use and the nature of their technology use at different stages of learning and language development.

Sub-Area 2: Learner interaction with technological resources

The use of technologies outside the classroom does not necessarily lead to enhanced learning. What is more critical is how learners interact with these technological resources and whether they use them in beneficial ways. Thus, research into learners' learning process and learning strategies with technological resources is much needed. A small body of literature has begun to explore the issue, focusing on the tempo-spatial contexts of the activities and learners' attentional resource allocation during the activities. The research findings revealed when and where language learners reported using the technological resources for learning and whether they focused on meaning and/or on the language forms when interacting with the resources. A few studies have also examined the language-learning strategies that learners employ when interacting with technological resources and revealed some new learning strategies that students utilize to enhance learning in technological learning environments. Findings from these research studies could inform the design of technological resources and optimal pedagogical arrangements concerning them. They could also inform educators on how they could support language learners to achieve more effective interaction with the technological resources.

Unfortunately, only a small proportion of research studies has been devoted to this research area. Henry (2013) observed that, in contrast to the relatively better understanding of what technological resources learners use in their free time, researchers know very little about the learning process involved in the use of technological resources and the language use associated with it. Henry further argued that the lack of nuanced and in-depth knowledge of this aspect often leads to devaluation of the communicative practices and competencies that are unique in the context of out-of-class autonomous language learning with technology, and makes it difficult for educators to create opportunities to bridge in-class and out-of-class learning. In line with Henry's observations, Steel and Levy (2013) called for greater research efforts focusing on technologies that learners frequently use in out-of-class contexts and seeking a deeper and more precise understanding of the conditions and circumstances of learners' use of these technologies (see Table 8.2 for the example of a study that examined

Table 8.2 A study on learners' interaction with technological resources

Levy and Steel (2015)
This study examined language learners' perception and use of dictionary-type resources for learning outside the classroom.
This study was part of a large-scale research project that surveyed Australian undergraduate foreign-language learners on the technologies they used inside and outside the language classroom. In that research project, it was found that the use of online dictionaries stood out in the survey as the most frequently used resource both inside and outside the classroom and as the resource that learners perceived as most beneficial. This particular study focused especially on learners' interaction with online dictionary-type resources, analysing participants' questionnaire responses to the open-ended question related to their use of online dictionaries. Participants' responses were coded and categorized into two major categories: functionality and usability from the learner perspective.
The study found that look-up time, ease of use and portability across time and location were fundamental considerations in determining the 'usability' (p. 184) of electronic dictionaries from the learners' perspective. The participants used dictionaries mainly to expand vocabulary and seek information on 'word choice and appropriate contexts of use' (p. 188). They appreciated the updated content in online dictionaries and perceived the variety of search and input functions as critical. They also valued the expanded multimodal functionalities and complementary tools such as creating flash cards and quizzes. A small portion of them mentioned discussion forums concerning word use as a useful function.
Commentary: This study started from the learner perspective and examined learners' perceptions of and interaction with a technological resource that they used most often. By focusing on a technological resource that learners are already using outside the classroom, the research findings are likely to make a bigger practical impact. Furthermore, the study reported on learners' naturalistic interaction with the technological resource, which is a better representation of learner behaviours outside the classroom than studies conducted in the lab setting, and hence more informative for the design of resources for out-of-class use.

learners' perception and use of dictionary-type resources). Consequently, more research studies are needed that focus on learners' interactions with different technological resources and platforms. It is even more important to investigate how their interactions with the same technological resources might vary across different settings in response to differences in the sociocultural realities of the settings (Beckman et al., 2014).

Even fewer studies have delved deeply into the quality of learners' experiences with different technological resources. What is quality interaction with technological resources? What should learners do to enhance the quality of their interaction with them? As informal learning contexts are characterized by limited or little teacher presence, learners are unavoidably confronted with the task of judging the trustworthiness of the information retrieved online, discriminating valuable and useful resources from misleading and unbeneficial ones and scaffolding their learning experiences to build more sophisticated understanding (Cox, 2013). Now, in facing all these challenges, what strategies do learners adopt to enhance the quality of their interaction with the technological resources? What strategies do they employ to select materials from these technological resources? What scaffolding sources, procedures and techniques do they utilize to enhance the effectiveness of the experience? All these are worthwhile and important questions, the answers to which could yield a better understanding of the quality of learners' interaction with technological resources. Therefore, studies are needed that associate different patterns of learner-technology interaction with learning outcomes so as to identify the quality indicators of learning experience with technology beyond the classroom. Studies are also needed to reveal learner strategies in interacting with technological resources.

It is equally important to examine the interplay between the design of technological resources and learners' interaction with these resources. Although quite a few CALL studies have revealed the relationship between design and learner experience, they were primarily conducted in formal educational contexts. Levy (2015) questioned how far findings from a contrived lab set-up could apply to real-world technology use and interaction behaviour, as technology use in informal contexts brings with it a whole new suite of questions relating to learner motivation and intention. Thus, the interaction between design and learner experience needs to be examined anew in informal learning contexts, where teacher intervention is missing.

Furthermore, as learners' language proficiency and experiences of informal learning with technological resources increase, their interaction with technological resources and strategies utilized during interaction may change, and the criteria for judging the quality of the interaction may change as well. Thus, for all these research directions, a longitudinal perspective is critical to revealing these potential changes and to informing the development of more responsive support and intervention programmes.

Sub-Area 3: Variations in autonomous language learning with technology

Research studies exploring the nature of out-of-class autonomous language learning with technology have often reported variation across learner internal and external factors including gender, language proficiency, learning beliefs and dispositions, social influence and support, institutional culture and the characteristics of the technological resources. With these dimensions identified, other studies have begun to conceptualize and test explanatory models of how these various variables interact with each other to influence learners' autonomous language learning with technology. Some progress has been made in this line of inquiry, and research findings thereof help identify the direct and indirect determinants of learners' engagement in out-of-class autonomous language learning with technology. These findings could help inform the development of intervention strategies to enhance learners' engagement in out-of-class autonomous language learning with technology.

However, most studies so far have focused on the variation in the types of technologies used and the frequencies thereof, and only a limited number have examined the variations in the ways learners interact with technological resources. A refined understanding of the variations in learners' interactions with technological resources could offer more useful information since it is learners' interactions with technological resources that really matter in terms of learning. Similar limitations exist in studies intended to identify the factors influencing these variations. Current studies that conceptualize and test explanatory models of autonomous language learning with technology have predominantly used frequency of technology use as the sole outcome. It would be useful to identify explanatory models of direct and indirect variables that predict the variation in learners' interactions with technological resources.

In addition, few studies have compared the variations and the influencing factors across different levels of education, and different languages and sociocultural contexts. Table 8.3 gives the example of a study that examined the variation of autonomous language learning with technology across sociocultural contexts. It is quite likely that explanatory models of autonomous out-of-class language learning with technology may vary between K–12 students

Table 8.3 A study on variation in autonomous language learning with technology

Viberg and Grönlund (2013)
This study examined cultural differences in language learners' attitudes towards using mobile devices for language learning.
The study adopted the pedagogical framework of mobile learning from a sociocultural perspective generated by Kearney et al. (2012) to examine learners' attitudes towards different dimensions of mobile learning. The study also adopted Hofstede's framework of national cultural values to measure individual-espoused cultural values. Foreign-language students from universities in China and Sweden were surveyed on their attitudes towards different aspects of mobile language learning and on their cultural values. Correlation analyses were conducted on the relationship between cultural values and age and mobile-learning attitudes, and Mann-Whitney U tests were conducted to assess the relationship between other personal actors such as gender.
The study found that learners perceived the use of mobile devices for personalized language learning most positively, followed by the use of mobile devices for collaboration and for enhancing the authenticity of language learning. The study further found that female learners were more positive towards the use of mobile devices in language learning across all three dimensions. However, the correlation between cultural values and attitudes to mobile language learning was very weak.
Commentary: This study examined the variation in language learners' attitudes towards different aspects of mobile language learning across several individual variables. The study adopted a fine-tuned framework to measure the nature of out-of-class learning with technology, and contributed to a more nuanced understanding of the influence of various factors on the variation in learners' attitudes and use of technologies in different aspects.

and university students, between advanced-level learners and beginner or intermediate learners, and between learners who have just begun to explore the use of technology for language learning and those who have already incorporated some technological resources into their language learning. In addition, even fewer studies have traced the relative influence of these variables over time as learners progress through different stages of autonomous language learning with technology and different stages of language development.

Sub-Area 4: Learner construction of language-learning ecology

Learners' construction of a language-learning ecology with technology is the least explored research area. Only a few studies have examined how language learners coordinate the technological, physical and human resources inside and outside the classroom to construct their language-learning ecologies, and how language learners construct and reconstruct their ecologies over time and in response to changes in educational settings. Research findings from these studies could inform educators of learners' perceptions of the affordances of different resources, of their agentic actions in taking advantage of these affordances, and of the enablers and inhibitors of their perceptions of the affordances and agentic actions. An understanding of learners' construction of language-learning ecologies helps educators better conceptualize the roles of teachers and in-class instruction in learners' overall learning experiences, which is critical to the development of optimal pedagogical arrangements that capitalize on the strength of both in-class and out-of-class learning. An understanding of the enablers and inhibitors of learners' ecology construction also has the potential to guide educators in better supporting learners in constructing quality language-learning ecologies.

Previous research in this area has mainly examined the ecology-construction process of university language learners, and, coincidentally, the few available studies were conducted mainly in the Asian context. Thus, there is a need to expand the educational and cultural contexts of this line of research. Furthermore, existing research has focused mainly on describing learners' perceptions of the use of technological resources outside the classroom and their use of the resources in different contexts and over time, without probing deeper into the nature and affordances of the different contexts that learners navigate and the forms of knowledge that they acquire in these different contexts (Barron, 2010; Bennett and Maton, 2010; Leander, Phillips and Taylor, 2010). For instance, Bennett and Maton (2010) suggested using Bourdieu's 'field' theory to examine the different structures, social practices, capitals and status hierarchies in different educational and everyday contexts, and the embodied dispositions that learners carry with them to these contexts, so as to reach a deeper understanding of the different contexts in which learners use technology. They also suggested using Berstein's concepts of 'horizontal discourse' and 'vertical discourse' to understand the nature of knowledge that they acquire in different contexts (Berstein, 1999, p. 161). Also, learner practices in one setting need to be interpreted in relation to learner practices in other settings (Benson, 2009b; Leander, Phillips and Taylor, 2010).

Understanding the nature of learning in different spaces and how learners build qualitatively distinct relations with different spaces is only the first step. What is more important is to examine the quality of the holistic learning ecology that learners construct. What factors do learners consider when constructing their learning ecologies? What criteria do learners use to judge the quality of their learning ecology? Do these criteria align with what is suggested by the current research literature? What are the indicators of a quality learning ecology? All these are important questions that await exploration. In this respect, 'metrics that gauge the diversity and quality of a learning ecology' is useful for learners and designers (Barron, Martin and Roberts, 2007, p. 100).

Moreover, existing studies have mainly studied ecology construction from the 'geographies of learning' perspective (Leander, Phillips and Taylor, 2010, p. 331) in terms of how learners traverse various settings inside and outside the language classroom. Future studies may also examine the issue from the technological perspective as well as the perspective of the interaction between technology and geography – that is, how learners make decisions about when to rely on technological resources and when to rely on physical resources; how they perceive the affordances of different technological resources; how their perceptions of the affordances of technological resources interact with their perceptions of the nexus

Table 8.4 A study on learner construction of language-learning ecologies

Cabot (2014)
This study examined learners' construction of English-learning ecologies in and out of school over time.
The study was a case study of six upper-secondary English-language learners at a secondary school in Norway, three male and three female. Exploratory focus interviews and follow-up in-depth individual interviews were conducted to understand the technological artefacts and the pedagogical and content orientations in their English-learning ecologies at different times – the past, present and future.
The study found differences in learners' construction of learning ecologies both at different times and across genders. In particular, the study found that the learners made use of both digital and non-digital artefacts in constructing their English-learning ecologies in the past, but the ecologies of the present and the future were mostly influenced by digital artefacts. The introduction of certain rules for digital artefact use, and the content and new functionalities in digital artefacts all served as 'triggers' (p. 14) for agencies in ecology construction with technologies. 'Playful artefacts' were prevalent in the ecologies of the male students, whereas 'expressive artefacts' (p. 73) were prevalent in the ecologies of the female students. Furthermore, the ecologies of the male students seemed to go through an evolution from expressive artefacts in the past to playful artefacts at the present, whereas the pattern of evolution was reversed for the female students. The learners generally valued the metalinguistic functions of the school settings and the input functions of the out-of-school contexts.
Commentary: The study reveals the nature of language learners' learning ecologies across settings and over time. It provides information on the types of technological resources that students utilize at different stages of learning and how they use these technological resources. It also identifies triggers for learners' agentic actions in learning ecology construction with technology. The study also offers a nuanced understanding of gender difference in both the configuration of current ecologies and the evolution of ecologies over time. The findings of the study suggest a dynamic view of learning ecology construction and inform researchers/educators of learners' considerations in their agentic actions in constructing learning ecologies.

of relationships in different places to shape their selection and use; and what criteria they use in selecting and coordinating technological resources. In other words, research needs to tap into the questions of why, how, when and where learners construct ecologies of learning for themselves (Cabot, 2014). Table 8.4 gives the example of a study that tapped into the interaction of technology use, geography and time. Insights into these issues can inform both technological resource design and pedagogical design with respect to different technological resources.

In summary, a large proportion of research on out-of-class autonomous language learning has focused on profiling this type of learning. This is understandable given that the research field is relatively new and that learners are the foci of this field. Describing what they do and collecting their voices help educators better understand autonomous technology use in informal language-learning contexts. Table 8.5 summarizes the focus of existing studies

Table 8.5 Existent and recommended research focus for Key Research Area 1

	Current Foci of Research	**Recommendations for Future Foci of Research**
Profiling out-of-class autonomous use of technology for language learning	Nature of technology use • What are technological resources? • How frequently are they used? • Which language-learning needs do they support?	Nature of technology use • Broaden the perspectives from which to analyse the nature of technology use beyond the classroom • Take a developmental approach to examining individual learners' technology use at different stages of language development
	Learner interaction with technological resources • Learning process • Learning strategies	Learner interaction with technological resources • Delve deeper into the language-use practices and competencies involved • Identify indicators of quality interaction with technological resources • Identify learner strategies to enhance the quality of learners' interaction with technological resources • Explore the interaction between the design and learner experience and technological resources in autonomous informal learning contexts • Conduct a longitudinal study on the evolution of learning processes and strategies over time

(Continued)

Table 8.5 (Continued)

	Current Foci of Research	Recommendations for Future Foci of Research
Profiling out-of-class autonomous use of technology for language learning	Variation in technology use • Different learner-internal and -external factors • Explanatory models of the interaction of the factors	Variation in technology use • Explore other variables that might influence out-of-class autonomous learning with technology • Conduct more studies focusing on identifying variation in learners' interaction with technological resources • Conceptualize and test explanatory models that focus not only on the variation in technology adoption but also on the variation in learners' interaction with technological resources • Compare explanatory models across different contexts and populations • Conduct longitudinal studies on the influence of various variables at different stages of development
	Learner construction of language-learning ecology • Construction of a learning ecology across spaces • Reconstruction of a learning ecology over time and in response to setting changes	Learner construction of language-learning ecology • Expand the contexts of the research • Identify indicators of a quality language-learning ecology • Reveal learners' decision-making relating to technological resources in the learning ecology

and presents some recommendations on the possible foci of future research to deepen our understanding of the phenomenon.

Key Area 2: Evaluating the effects of out-of-class autonomous language learning with technology

Quite a few studies have investigated the effects of out-of-class autonomous language learning (Larsson, 2012; Sundqvist, 2011; Sundqvist and Wikström, 2015). These studies have attested to the positive association of out-of-class language learning with various cognitive and affective outcomes. Researchers have normally measured the frequency of students' engagement in out-of-class learning collected through survey responses or diary logs, various cognitive skills (overall language performance or performance on individual skill dimensions) and affective outcomes (confidence in learning, enjoyment of learning, etc.). Correlation studies have then been conducted to check the association between the frequency of out-of-class learning and different learning outcomes (see Table 8.6 for such an example). The research findings from these studies help establish the value of out-of-class learning experience for language learning.

As more and more positive evidence is accumulated attesting to the value of out-of-class language learning with technology, the focus of this area of research needs to shift from providing evidence in support of this learning behaviour towards providing more in-depth information to inform the improvement of related learning behaviours. It is important to delve deeper into the working mechanisms behind out-of-class learning with technology in order to answer questions such as: What motivates students to engage in out-of-class learning with technology? What is the nature of the interpersonal dynamics in out-of-class learning with technology, and how does it affect the learning process? What do various technological environments afford for human–human and human–technology interaction and how do these affordances affect the learning process? Are there

Table 8.6 A study on the effects of out-of-class learning with technology

Sundqvist and Wikström (2015)
This study examined the relationship between out-of-school digital gameplay and learners' in-class L2 English vocabulary outcomes.
The study collected two sets of Swedish secondary school English learners' one-week language diaries recording their out-of-school language-learning activities. Based on the content analysis of the diary entries, students were divided into frequent gamers, moderate gamers and non-gamers. The productive and vocabulary-levels tests were used to measure students' productive and receptive vocabulary. Students' written essays were also collected to examine the vocabulary used in the essays. Their final grades in English from eighth grade and ninth grade were collected as well.
The study found that frequent gamers scored the highest in all vocabulary measures and showed the highest lexical richness in their essays. Furthermore, the correlations between gameplay and vocabulary outcomes and overall grades were statistically significant for the boys.
Commentary: The study focused specifically on the effects of a particular out-of-class activity on various vocabulary outcomes. It provided insights into the relationship between gameplay and language learning, and revealed the differentiated effects of the activity on different genders. The fine-tuned analysis of the differential effects of technology-enhanced activities contributes to an in-depth understanding of the effects of autonomous learning with technology.

fundamental differences between learners' learning behaviours and strategies in out-of-class learning with technology and those in in-class learning, and how do the differences, if any, affect learning? How do we define the success or effectiveness of out-of-class learning with technology? Answers to these fundamental questions will help educators better conceptualize the roles of autonomous language learning with technology and devise strategies to maximize its learning potential (Cohen, 2007; Hamilton, 2013). It is equally important to understand the relative efficacy of different types of learner interactions with individual technological resources so as to compare the learning effects of different approaches to resources and to identify optimal approaches. Future research is also needed on the learning effects of different configurations of language-learning ecology with technology so as to identify the indicators of quality language-learning ecologies.

Moreover, researchers need to broaden the outcomes investigated. Scholars argue that learning beyond the classroom is more conducive to identity development and personal change in the long run (Barron, 2010; Bell, 2008; Block, 2007). Various researchers have argued that there are outcomes of informal learning that go beyond cognitive and affective benefits. For instance, Block (2007) pointed out that learning outside the classroom provides situations that destabilize identity and thus may have a greater impact on identity than in-class learning. Bell et al. (2009) pointed out that learning outcomes from informal learning are manifested in a wide range of aspects, including interest, social competencies, awareness, habits of mind and identities that spur sustained learning, which cannot be captured by conventional academic measures. Thus, future studies are needed to examine the long-term effects of autonomous out-of-class language learning with technology on learner interest and identity development, habits of mind, and personal change (Barron, 2006). Bell et al. (2009) further pointed out that, despite the importance of understanding the effects of informal learning, a more important issue is to show how learning in one setting influences learning in another setting and to identify the synergies and barriers in learning across different settings. Consequently, another promising yet little-explored area is the effect of out-of-class autonomous language learning with technology on in-class teaching and learning (Cox, 2013). For instance, how does learners' out-of-class autonomous language learning with technology affect their expectations regarding the use of technology inside the classroom, in-class curricular and assessment arrangement, autonomy inside the classroom, and teachers' roles in language education? Also, how does teachers' awareness of learners' out-of-class autonomous language learning with technology affect teachers' perceptions of their roles in language education, their teaching styles and their technology

Table 8.7 Existent and recommended research focus for Key Research Area 2

	Current Focus of Research	Recommendations for Future Focus of Research
Evaluating the effects of out-of-class autonomous language learning with technology	• Examine the association between frequency of out-of-class language learning and cognitive and affective outcomes	• Delve into the working mechanisms behind out-of-class learning with technology • Pay greater attention to the learning efficacy of different approaches to technology use (different approaches to interacting with individual technological resources and to constructing language-learning ecologies) • Focus on longitudinal identity development with the use of technology beyond the classroom • Examine the effects of autonomous out-of-class language learning with technology on in-class language instruction

integration? Table 8.7 summarizes the focus of existing studies and presents some recommendations on the possible foci of future research with regard to the effects of out-of-class autonomous language learning with technology.

Key Area 3: Promoting out-of-class autonomous language learning with technology

The literature on self-access language learning has generated quite a few studies on the roles of language-advising sessions in developing and supporting learners' autonomous language-learning skills in general. Recently, several studies have developed and examined integrated or stand-alone intervention programmes specifically targeted at enhancing learners' ability to learn with technology, giving learners relevant technical and pedagogical training and equipping them with the metacognitive and cognitive strategies to interact with individual technological resources. In addition, research studies have begun to reveal the influence of various support factors on learners' use of technology for learning beyond the classroom (see Table 8.8 for an example). The findings from these studies form a good foundation for an understanding of how to enhance learners' effective interaction with individual technological resources: the aspects for which learners need support and the critical conditions for this support to work.

Table 8.8 A study on how teachers could support learners' out-of-class learning with technology

Lai (2015)
This study examined teacher's influence on the frequency of students' out-of-class use of technology for language learning.
The study took place in two phases. In Phase I, individual interviews were conducted with a group of undergraduate foreign-language learners in Hong Kong. The interview study aimed to tap into learners' perceptions of various teacher behaviours that influenced their out-of-class autonomous technology use for language learning, and how these behaviours exerted this influence. Based on the interview responses, the author came up with a conceptual framework with the identified teacher factors and the mediating psychosocial factors as well as the pathways of influence. Then, in Phase II of the study, a group of undergraduate foreign-language learners were surveyed. The conceptual framework was tested against the survey responses using path analysis.
The resultant structure model showed that different teacher behaviours affected students' out-of-class technology use through different routes. The findings suggest that teacher support for learners' out-of-class autonomous technology use is multifaceted. It is not only teachers' incorporation of technological resources into in-class instruction that could influence learners' out-of-class autonomous technology use but also teachers' affective support in terms of encouragement and advice and capacity support in terms of metacognitive, cognitive support and strategies in the selection and use of technological resources.
Commentary: This study generated a model to explain how various teacher behaviours could influence the frequency of language learners' autonomous out-of-class use of technology for learning. The findings suggested the types of support that teachers need to provide when promoting out-of-class autonomous use of technology. The findings could also inform teacher preparation programmes on the capacities that teachers need to be equipped with to support learners' out-of-class technology use more effectively.

However, the majority of learner-training studies are conducted in instructional contexts, and students are tested on their grasp of the strategies upon completion of the training programmes, the results of which are used as evidence for the effectiveness of the training programmes. However, whether learners can easily transfer and apply the strategies acquired and the skills developed in the instructional contexts to informal learning contexts, and whether additional support is needed in these informal learning contexts, need further exploration (Barron, 2006). Furthermore, the current research literature is inadequate to provide information on how to support language learners in constructing language-learning ecologies – that is, information concerning the kinds of resources that support successful learning across settings, and the support learners need to select appropriate technological resources that match

Table 8.9 Existing and recommended research focus for Key Research Area 3

	Current Focus of Research	Recommendations for Future Focus of Research
Promoting out-of-class autonomous language learning with technology	• Evaluate approaches to developing autonomous language learning in general • Evaluate approaches to enhancing learner interaction with individual technological resources	• Assess the transferability of skills acquired in instructional settings to informal learning contexts • Identify the support needed to facilitate learners' construction of language-learning ecologies with technology • Evaluate the efficacy of different approaches and across settings

their learning needs and to coordinate various technological resources in order to construct a language-learning ecology across settings (Barron, 2006). The development of such intervention programmes needs to be based on a clear understanding of how learners' interaction with technological resources might be constrained and shaped by the sociocultural realities of different settings. Thus, research studies are needed not only to examine the transferability of technology use across different settings but also to evaluate different approaches to promoting learners' construction of language-learning ecologies with technology across settings. Table 8.9 summarizes the focus of existing studies and presents some recommendations on the possible foci of future research to delve deeper into the issue of promoting out-of-class autonomous language learning with technology.

Research methods

The previous section reviewed three key areas of research in this research field and suggested some directions to advance knowledge in the field. This section discusses some key methodological considerations and some methodological challenges in capturing the learning process and measuring learning outcomes.

Capturing the process

Methodological considerations

The demand for multilevel, multi-methodological approaches. Sawchuk (2008) reviewed the literature on informal learning and concluded that case study, ethnographic and interview research were the most adopted research approaches. He further pointed out that these forms of inquiry could only reveal part of the picture. In order to gain a more comprehensive understanding of the various issues pertinent to the process of informal learning – such as power/control, cognitive processes and the mediation of sociocultural spheres – a multi-methodological approach that combined different forms of inquiry was needed. Kumpulainen and Sefton-Green (2014) concurred with him on the complexity of learning that is situated across various social spaces and practices, and proposed using the concept of 'connected learning' to capture the complex learning process. They further argued that to capture this complexity, a diversity of approaches with different levels of analysis was very much needed.

Kumpulainen and Sefton-Green (2014) conceptualized three levels of connection that need to be investigated: 1) connections at the temporal level, namely, changes over time within and across spaces; 2) connections at the boundary-crossing level, namely, connections in and movements across boundaries and social spaces; and 3) connections at the 'learning lives' level, namely, individuals' development and change across life-wide and lifelong learning experiences. Concerning connections at the temporal level, Kumpulainen and Sefton-Green (2014) suggested accessing learners' narratives of their experiences at different timescales using Bakhtin's concept of chronotope (1981), namely, the intrinsic connectedness of spatial and temporal relationships in learners' experiences and sense making. They suggested tracing the change of tempo of ongoing activities across time and interpreting them in association with learners' emotions, value systems and identities, and the social, cultural and historical contexts of the action. Researchers can also use the chronotope to examine how learners' agency and identities are negotiated in light of their past experiences, ongoing involvement and future aspirations as they move across different spaces and timescales. With regard to connections at the boundary-crossing level, Kumpulainen and Sefton-Green (2014) suggested examining learners' experiences of applying knowledge from one domain to another – focusing on its complexities, barriers and enablers – through intertextual analysis of written texts, conversational texts, electronic texts and nonverbal texts collected through social-interactional studies and microethnographic studies. They suggested analysing the emergence of intertextuality, cross-referencing and juxtaposition of social practices in different spaces during social interaction and examining whether and how intertextuality is granted social acknowledgement and significance within and across spaces. Sawchuk (2008) further added that situated microanalysis is important in revealing and articulating what is actually going on during the social practices. To understand the third level of connection – connections at learners' 'learning lives' – Kumpulainen and Sefton-Green (2014) suggested using extended case studies, portraiture, ethnographic narrative, life history and biography to explore learners' development of various forms of subjectivity, such as interpersonal and presentational skills, and identity seeking, and to examine the social routes and trajectories of changes within key learning spaces and across key life transitions. Sawchuk (2008) further added that for all three levels of investigation, researchers should not only focus on ongoing practices but also analyse the critical incidents that break the routine.

The need for innovative methodological tools. Cohen (2007) reviewed the research methods used in studies of informal education and found that the most frequently used methodological tools included questionnaires and surveys (27 per cent of the studies reviewed), interviews and written narratives (23 per cent), demographics and comparisons of sub-populations (19 per cent), observation (19 per cent), analysis of materials (17 per cent) and case studies (16 per cent). Tools like focus groups, participatory research and sociometry were rarely used. Cohen concluded that the existing methodological tools adopted in research on informal education are very similar to the ones used to study formal education. There is a need to adopt some methodological tools to capture and display the uniqueness of informal learning, such as tacit outcomes, spatio-temporal frames and so forth, and to deal with the methodological challenges posed by the unique characteristics of informal learning. Kumpulainen and Sefton-Green (2014) highlighted the difficulty and complexity of capturing the learning process in out-of-class contexts at various levels. At the practical level, researchers have difficulty in tracking and physically following learners. At the ethical level, researchers encounter the problem of gaining access to learners' actions in different social domains and of building trust with learners.

Major challenges

Challenge of capturing learning on the move. One of the oft-cited methodological challenges in researching out-of-class autonomous language learning is the difficulty in measuring learning. Out-of-class autonomous learning is characterized as ubiquitous, pervasive, unintentional and tacit (Fagerlund, 2012; Field, 2003). As out-of-class learning is often spontaneous and distributed in different spaces, it is hard to capture learning that takes place on the go (Toh et al., 2013; Sharples, 2009b). Furthermore, as out-of-class learning is part of a holistic experience that takes place in a web of interconnected and interwoven contexts, including in-class instruction, it is difficult to attribute learning gains to out-of-class learning or to any particular resource or space in out-of-class contexts (Lau, 2015; Sharples, 2009b). Also, because out-of-class learning activities are closely tied to daily life and personal interest, learners may not recognize them as learning (Eraut, 2004; Fagerlund, 2012).

To address the practical challenge of recording learning on the move across spaces, Toh et al. (2013) suggested moving beyond technology-centric methods and adopting 'design ethnography'. Design ethnography consists of cooperative inquiry supplemented by participant observation, analysis of learners' artefact repositories, and learner usage and experience data collected through activity-capture tools installed on learners' devices. Cooperative inquiry grants participants an active role in data collection so as to elicit more accurate representations of their stories. To avoid learners experiencing the unease in being closely observed and monitored, that is often the case in traditional observation formats, the researchers suggested using experience clips as one form of cooperative inquiry. Experience clips involve learners capturing their interaction with someone they are familiar with, such as family members or friends, while working together on some deliberately designed tasks related to the use of technology outside the classroom. Toh et al. (2013) also suggested using the photo elicitation method to minimize potential power imbalances between researchers and participants. This method involves learners keeping photographic records of the learning activities they engage in outside the classroom by taking videos or photos, and selecting a few from the photographic records of their learning lives to discuss with the researchers. The participants share the nature of these learning activities with the researchers, using these cultural probes as the visual stimulus. Wallace (2015) argued that such photo-elicitation interviews are powerful in gaining insights into both participants' experiences and attitudes. Stickler and Hampel (2015) also proposed reflexive photography as a promising methodological tool to capture learners' social practices. Schwandt (2000) asked her participants to photograph objects and people that influenced their spoken English development and used these photographs to engage her participants in reflecting on their experience in the field. This tool could be used to capture the distributed social practices that are often not accessible to researchers. Hill (2014) argued that since reflexive photography involves learners thinking about how to capture their ideas and whether the selected photographs could fully represent their ideas, it is likely to generate a deeper level of thought about the issue. Wallace (2015) suggested combining the examination of photos with interview transcripts during data analysis to obtain a richer understanding. Wallace (2015) improved the use of the tool further by incorporating peer discussions. Her participants took photographs of the resources and experiences that benefited or obstructed the development of their spoken English intelligibility over a week. Then, they were instructed to select seven to ten images to share in online focus group discussions. Afterwards, individual interviews were conducted with each participant using the reflexive photographs with reference to issues that arose in the focus group discussions with peers. The photos, the focus group discussions and the individual interview responses were triangulated in the data analysis to shed light on learners' out-of-class learning experience.

Challenge of self-report data. Another methodological challenge in capturing the learning process in out-of-class autonomous learning with technology concerns the issue of self-report data. Out-of-class autonomous language learning with technology is learner initiated and learner directed, and collecting learner voices is a legitimate way to gain insights into the phenomenon (Levy, 2015). The use of interviews has been embraced in the context of informal learning for its potential to elicit life narratives that chart the unfolding of learning activities across time and spaces, revealing learners' decision-making processes and creating techno-biographies – portraits of learning with technology (Barron, 2006; Henwood, Kennedy and Miller, 2001). In effect, Cheung and Hew (2009) found that almost half of the descriptive studies on students' use of mobile handheld devices were based primarily on self-reported data.

One challenge that researchers face is how to make sure that the self-report data collected are thick enough to tell a rich story. To strengthen the depth of learner narratives and reflections, various techniques have been suggested: email interviews or periodical surveys, whereby researchers engage in personal dialogues with learners by email to facilitate their reflection over an extended period of time; structured diaries with daily diary prompts that ask about different dimensions of learners' technological experience to facilitate the recording of their experiences with technological resources on the go; and phoning or texting learners at preset intervals to elicit their recent learning activities (Sharples, 2009b). In order to facilitate learners' reflections during interviews, researchers may use visual cues such as technology cards and ask the participants to rank the cards in the order of importance and, at the same time, verbalize their thinking behind their rankings and the changes in rankings at different time and spaces. Researchers may also ask the participants to draw mind maps of technologies to reveal the relations between these different technologies across time and spaces. For instance, Clark et al. (2009) conducted a study on students' use of technology across different spaces. They used questionnaires to identify the Web 2.0 sites that participants were using and what practices they were using these sites for.

They complemented the questionnaires with a mapping study, whereby the participants were asked to map the technologies they used by responding to prompts that tapped into the relationships between technologies, practices and contexts. Beckman et al. (2014) employed technology diaries to elicit records of technology-use patterns, which were then used as visual stimuli to facilitate interviews. In their study, the researchers asked their participants to record all the technologies they had used over a period of two weeks in a technology diary. The technology diaries provided a stimulus for authentic follow-up interviews that engaged the participants in in-depth discussions of their technology use and the contexts of the use.

More importantly, self-reported data collection runs the risk of being criticized for being subjective (Lau, 2015) and for inducing social desirability responding, that is, the participants adjusting their responses to align with the researchers' expectation (Hakkarainen et al., 2001). At the same time, researchers argue that tapping into learners' accounts of the process of autonomous out-of-class learning with technology alone reveals only part of the picture and cannot shed light on what actually happens during the interaction (Sawchuk, 2008). Benson (2009b) concurred with this observation and pointed out: 'One of the difficulties here is, of course, penetrating beyond observed or self-reported behaviors, into the ways in which people actually learn languages in different settings' (p. 233). To alleviate the potential ethical issue of a power imbalance between researchers and participants, for which self-reported research methods such as interview and survey have most often been criticized, Field (2000) proposed focus group interviews as a possible solution. He argued that the dominating number of participants and the moderator role that researchers typically play in focus group interviews afford participants more power to debate and negotiate the nature, purpose and outcome of the interview as well as to influence the future direction of the research. Field thus proposed the focus group interview as particularly well suited for research on lifelong learning that is learner-centric and at the exploratory stage. Field (2000) further pointed out that using focus group interviews enables the construction of collective narratives that complement the 'methodological individualism' (p. 334) – that is, individual narratives and self-construction of biographies – that has dominated the existing research discourse. In terms of the challenges of revealing what actually goes on in learners' interactions in different social spaces, Sawchuk (2008) suggested conducting situated micro-interaction analysis on learners' actual interactions in situ. Hine (2008) proposed virtual ethnography as a potential tool to collect relevant data. In this respect, Baym (1997) joined a virtual community as an ordinary member and engaged in participant observation over three years. Interactional analysis of the messages posted in the community, and interviews and surveys with group members, together with her participant observation, helped to shed light on the social practices in the virtual community. Virtual ethnography combines different methodological tools and helps add a third-person point of view to the first-person account of learning experience in self-report to build a richer understanding of the phenomena. Blin et al. (2016) advocated employing CALL ergonomics through tracking, gathering and analysing activity data, such as logins, mouse clicks, help requests and so on, to understand learners' actual interaction with technological resources. However, such an approach might be challenged in informal learning contexts. On the one hand, it might be quite difficult for researchers to obtain activity data when learners are accessing commercial or public sites where researchers do not have access to the log data. On the other hand, researchers need to deal with the potential problem that tracking, recording and monitoring learners' interaction with technological resources and behaviours in different spaces may change the very nature of the interaction and behaviour (Lally et al., 2012; Levy, 2015). Levy (2015) argued that capturing learners' dictionary use or look-up behaviours using devices like eye-tracker might not reflect their actual behaviour in real-world settings. Thus, CALL ergonomics collected through PC monitors, despite being useful in allowing researchers to come closer to learners' actual experience with technological resources, need to be complemented with self-report data that reveal important information such as the conditions (in-class or out-of-class) under which learners engage in such behaviours, the challenges they encounter during the interaction and so on.

Challenges with interpreting the data. As research on informal learning with technology often spans time and spaces, descriptions of the complexity of the learning process are often very thick and hence hard to interpret. Researchers have used various graphing techniques to illustrate the process in a more telling manner. For instance, Cabot (2014) adopted a radiograph technique to represent the critical moments in learners' construction of learning ecologies. The radiograph used radio waves to represent the continuous learning experience in three temporal segments – the past, present and future, across out-of-school, semiformal and in-school contexts, with the temporal dimension as the x-axis and the spatial dimension as the y-axis. The emergence of and changes in social practices (i.e. the critical incidents) were marked on its temporal and spatial coordinates and elaborated with textual annotations. The graph clearly communicated to the readers the changes in learners' learning-related social practices at different spaces over time. Hommes et al. (2012) adopted social networking graphs to visualize the invisible social side of student autonomous learning. The participants were asked to identify their informal networks with fellow students by providing the names of friends they received information from and those they provided information to and by rating the intensity of the friendships. The researchers then visualized students' social networks by graphing each learner's connectivity to other learners in the network and indicating the strength of their ties with other learners. Each learner was denoted as a node, and the colour of the nodes differentiated learners' quartile scores on a knowledge test. The social networking graphs presented the relationship between social network and grades in a visually discernible manner, showing that students who learned the most were positioned more in the centre of the informal network and had more ties with other learners.

Challenge of ethics. Last but not the least, research in this field is facing ethical challenges. As informal learning is often associated with learners' personal lives and interests, learners may naturally hesitate to expose their private behaviours and exchanges to research scrutiny (Toffoli and Sockett, 2010). Lally et al. (2012) further pointed out that the spontaneity of out-of-class activities may make it hard for researchers to predict ahead of time the ethical issues that may arise. The uncertainty of the nature of user-generated texts also poses some ethical challenges to research. There is also the issue of how to deal with data – emerging during the research inquiry – that concern people who are not focal participants but that may provide valuable insights into the participants' observed behaviour (Toh et al., 2013). Furthermore, researchers are concerned about the affective attachment effects associated with loaning learners technological devices for a period of time and then withdrawing them at the end of the study. Moreover, there is the ethical issue of logging learners' daily use of technological devices (Sharples, 2009b). To address this challenge of the uncertain and emergent nature of the data and the data-collection process, researchers are calling for treating all consent as 'provisional', that is, subject to ongoing negotiations (Flewitt, 2005; Lally et al., 2012).

Measuring the product

Kumpulainen and Sefton-Green (2014) pointed out that researchers of informal learning are confronted with the theoretical question of what constitutes evidence of learning in such contexts. Hooper-Greenhill (2004) concurred with them that the major challenge that researchers face in measuring learning in informal contexts is not the development of innovative methodological tools; rather it concerns the construction and identification of conceptual generic learning outcomes from experience in the contexts that would enable researchers to measure the impact of learning in such contexts.

Skule (2004) pointed out that informal learning cannot be measured using the same means of indicators traditionally used for formal learning, such as participation rates, enrolments and so forth. Similarly, Hooper-Greenhill (2004) noted that the traditional and mono-dimensional ways of viewing learning as the acquisition of information, knowledge and understanding is not appropriate for informal learning contexts since informal learning 'cannot be separated from the feelings, values, actions and locations associated' and is continuous throughout life, with the development of personal identity as a key outcome (p. 156). In informal learning contexts, learning is not a product to be measured by the amount of knowledge or scholarship acquired but is very much a process that involves not only the development of knowledge but also changes in emotions, feeling, skills and judgement and the formation of attitudes, values and identities. This broader view of learning outcomes has been echoed by various researchers. For instance, Spector (2001), in discussing the assessment of informal learning with technology, argued that learning is manifested in stable 'changes in attitude, beliefs, capabilities, knowledge structures, mental models and/or skills' (Spector, 2001, p. 30). Similarly, Kumpulainen and Sefton-Green (2014) argued that greater research attention should be paid to the linkage between school learning and learners' lives and how learners integrate and translate their interest and knowledge across different spheres of learning. They called for a broadening of the definition of learning beyond academic achievement to include concepts like interest, identity and various dimensions of personal development such as changes in value systems. Hooper-Greenhill (2004) further argued that the learning outcomes of informal learning are often negotiated by learners in response to their own intentions and agendas and are thus hard to predict in advance. He stressed that evaluating learning in informal learning contexts involves systematically recognizing and recording learners' actions as well as their emotional and identity status. Therefore, identifying the generic learning outcomes of out-of-class autonomous learning with technology is critical to assessing the effects of this informal learning context. Focusing on informal learning through museums, archives and libraries, Hooper-Greenhill (2004) identified five generic learning outcomes in this context: 1) an increase in knowledge and understanding; 2) an increase in intellectual skills, learning skills, information management skills, social skills, emotional skills, communication skills and physical skills; 3) changes in attitudes towards or values concerning oneself, others and the organization; 4) enjoyment, inspiration and creativity; and 5) new actions and forms of behaviour and progression towards the use of the resources. These generic learning outcomes could inform our conceptualization of learning outcomes in the context of out-of-class autonomous learning with technology, but the particularities of individual learning contexts demand empirical investigations into the specifications of the generic learning outcomes in particular contexts.

There have been studies with sufficiently sophisticated measures of assessment that could capture some potential generic attitudinal and skill-learning outcomes of autonomous learning unique in the informal learning contexts. For instance, Lau (2015) measured the perceptual changes induced through independent learning as a measure of learning effectiveness. He used word-association questions as a tool to tap into perceptual changes as 'association behavior can reveal information about the development' (Fitzpatrick, 2007, p. 319). Lau collected three words or expressions that learners associated with independent learning both at the beginning of the course and at the end of the course after participating in two rounds of independent learning projects. He sorted the associated words into five categories – physical, mental, actional, personal and compound terms – and also collected learner interview data to elaborate on these word associations. The author found that the participants broadened their view of independent learning and increased their awareness of its various attributes as they progressed through the course. Sharples (2009b) proposed adopting product reaction cards as a more refined method of assessing learner satisfaction since the attitudinal surveys and interviews or observations that are often used to document attitudinal learning cannot provide solid evidence on learning and are often not very informative as students' attitudinal responses to novel technology usually lie within the range of 3.5 and 4.5 on a 5-point Likert scale. For instance, Benedek and Miner (2002) provided their participants with 118 cards containing emotional and appraisal words such as 'flexible' and 'frustrating'. Participants were asked to select the cards that best described their reactions to a technology or to a learning experience, and this was followed by interviews to tap into the reasons behind the attitudinal attribution. Open learning systems have also been constructed to tap into learner choices during informal learning (Schwartz and Arena, 2013). Measurement of learner choices has been achieved through developing open learning environments and capturing and cataloguing learners' choice of resources while solving learning problems (The IMMEX project, Stevens and Thadani, 2007) or by building a system whereby learners can tag and catalogue the informal learning activities in which they engage (Garcia-Peñalvo, Johnson and Alves, 2014).

The initiatives showcased above can shed some light on potential behavioural, perceptual and attitudinal changes associated with out-of-class autonomous learning with technology that are not normally captured in formal education contexts. However, there is still a long way to go in terms of generating a clear conceptual framework for the generic learning outcomes of out-of-class autonomous language learning with technology and developing methodological tools to measure these outcomes.

9

Conclusion and the Way Forward

The review of technological development ... from the 1990s to the present day ... shows a second wave resulting in a blurring of the boundaries between formal and informal settings, traditional curricula/courses and the personalized curriculum, and different levels in education. This second wave of technological developments given below has changed the balance between the control of e-learning from the teacher to the teacher with the learner, from the teacher to the learner, and from formal to informal uses.

– Cox (2013), p. 90

A growing number of researchers from scholarly fields such as education, literacy and media studies, and learning research are pursuing research agendas that involve investigating learning as a series of boundary-crossings in and across social spaces (home, school, and peer cultures; in and out of school) and epistemic practices (formal, informal, authorized, unauthorized).

– Kumpulainen and Sefton-Green (2014), p. 8

Educators today are tasked with developing lifelong learners who can survive and thrive in a global knowledge economy – learners who have the capability to effectively and creatively apply skills and competencies to new situations in an ever-changing, complex world

– Blaschke (2012), p. 56

The above quotes are taken from seminal works in different fields ranging from educational technology to informal learning and adult learning. All these scholars note the emergence of an era in which learning is characterized by learner-centred boundary crossing across various formal and informal learning spaces. Thus, a clear understanding of learners' experiences in different social spaces, both formal and informal, and the interactions in these spaces is of great significance in advancing our understanding of learning. Given that existing research and development work in language learning has been predominantly focused on classroom instruction (Benson, 2009b), there is a pressing need to gain an in-depth understanding of language learners' out-of-class learning and how they traverse in-class and out-of-class learning terrains.

In this book I have reviewed the current research literature on language learners' out-of-class autonomous learning with technology. The review suggests that although the existing literature has only just begun to burgeon, it has yielded some insights into language learners' autonomous use of technology for learning beyond the classroom. First, language learners are, more or less, using technology for learning beyond the classroom, and this use is associated with positive learning gains. Second, there are variations in learners' use of technology for learning, and these variations are subject to the influence of various internal and external factors. Third, learners are aware of the importance of autonomous learning beyond the classroom but need cognitive, metacognitive, behavioural and affective support to enhance the effectiveness of their technology use. Last but not least, both teacher behaviour and resource and environment design can influence the support that students have access to and, in so doing, shape their learning behaviour. Therefore, the existing literature suggests that autonomous language learning with technology beyond the classroom is de facto a common phenomenon in the field of language learning and affects language learners and learning development, hence the need and basis for systematic investigation. Furthermore, this phenomenon is malleable and subject to learner preparation and support, hence the possibilities for interventions. The review of the discussions and research findings in the current literature in this field has led to the following suggestions:

Concerning Learners:

- Given that language learners' use of technological resources beyond the classroom is often narrowly defined, learners need to be encouraged to expand their selection and use of technological resources in more diversified ways so as to reach a balance in both the types of technological resources employed and in the ways they put these technological resources to use
- Considering that various internal and external factors shape learners' use of technology beyond the classroom, it is important to ensure that they receive multidimensional support in making effective use of technology for language learning beyond the classroom

Concerning Teachers:

- Teachers could and should exert a greater influence on learners' out-of-class autonomous learning with technology by providing affective, behavioural and capacity support
- Teacher training needs to prepare teachers in terms of the knowledge and skills they need for their roles as advisers in supporting learners' out-of-class use of technology

Concerning Resources:

- The design of resources needs to pay special attention to the features of out-of-class learning and the affordances of technologies in out-of-class contexts
- The design of resources should be aimed at strengthening learners' willingness and capacity to engage in out-of-class autonomous language learning with technology

These suggestions are based primarily on theoretical discussions in this and related fields. Most of these suggestions apply at a general level, and specific implementation strategies and issues await empirical research. In effect, referring back to the theoretical framework of out-of-class autonomous language learning with technology conceptualized in Chapter 2, existing research has only touched lightly here and there on a few issues in this research terrain, and many issues remain unexplored.

The darkened boxes and arrows in Figure 9.1 stand for the areas that the existing literature has focused on. We can see that existing research in the field represents a piecemeal approach. This piecemeal approach is manifested in the technocentric perspective that characterizes the majority of studies that have examined learner technology use outside the classroom. These studies mainly documented learners' selection and use of technology outside the classroom per se, without taking into consideration their holistic experiences across various non-technological spaces outside the classroom and technological and non-technological spaces inside the classroom. The piecemeal approach is also manifested in the limited set of outcomes that current research studies have focused on in evidencing the effects of out-of-class learning with technology, leaving a wide range of dimensions of potential outcomes from such learning experiences unexplored. The piecemeal approach is further manifested in the snapshot perspective that most research studies and support programmes adopt

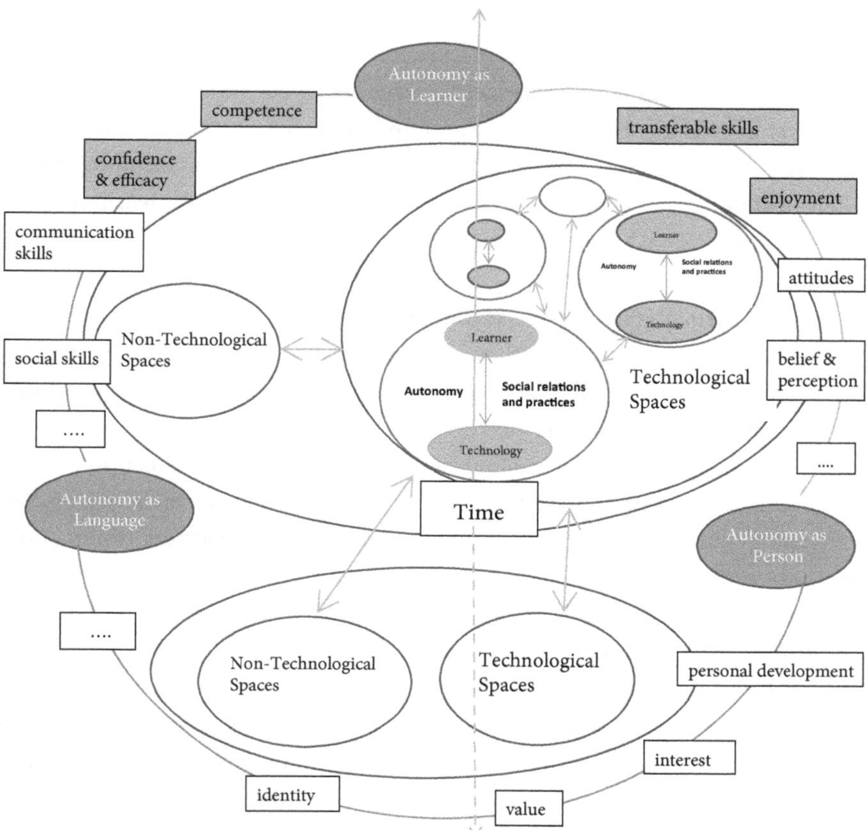

Figure 9.1 Research landscape of out-of-class autonomous language learning with technology.

without considering the past–present–future temporal dimensions. Thus, to advance this field, researchers and educators need to take a more holistic spatio-temporal approach that takes into consideration the interactions of different technological and non-technological spaces inside and outside the classroom as well as learners' sense making and coordination of these spaces, and the changing situations and learning needs over time.

Specifically, in terms of the learning process, research findings from the current literature only concern the interaction between learners and technologies. The existing literature contains rich information on the specific technologies that learners have been using outside the classroom. It also contains information, although quite limited, on the ways in which learners interact with individual technologies in informal learning contexts. There have also been a limited number of studies examining how learners' selection and use of technologies vary across individuals and changes in response to the transit of sociocultural contexts over time. However, a large number of dimensions relevant to the learning process in this framework remain unexplored. For instance, within each technological space, few studies have explored how learners, with the dispositions and capital they bring with them, interact with the social status and relationships within a technological space, how these interactions shape the particular use of the technology, and how these interactions differ across different settings (Hamilton, 2013; Beckman et al., 2014). Within the network of technological spaces in the out-of-school contexts, few studies have examined how learners perceive the interrelationship between and the coordination of different technological spaces and how their perceptions shape their selective use of each technological space to construct their out-of-class technology-enhanced learning ecologies. In addition, learners' interactions in these technological spaces need to be discussed in relation to the other spaces in which they reside concurrently – namely, how learners' interactions in technological spaces beyond the classroom are shaped by their interactions in non-technological spaces beyond, and technological and non-technological spaces inside, the classroom, and how their interactions in technological spaces beyond the classroom in turn influence their interactions in other spaces. Furthermore, a dynamic view needs to be taken in exploring these issues as the sociocultural situation in different spaces inside and outside the classroom might change over time. Learners also experience personal growth over time, which might also influence their interactions in technological spaces beyond the classroom over time.

In respect to learning outcomes, a wider array of outcomes need to be measured and targeted when examining the effects of out-of-class autonomous language learning with technology and when designing intervention programmes to engage students in autonomous language learning with technology. There is, first of all, a great need to generate a list of learning outcomes and specifications of out-of-class autonomous language learning with technology to serve as the frame of reference for design and research work. Design and research work could then explore the learning outcomes of both individual technological spaces and learning ecologies across different individuals and different technological and non-technological spaces.

Consequently, to advance the field, researchers and resource designers may need to adopt the following research and development agenda in developing both learner-training programmes and technology-mediated or technology-enhanced autonomous learning resources and environments:

- Take a holistic spatio-temporal perspective to consider various levels of interaction within and across various technological and non-technological spaces in different contexts
  - To understand learners' interaction with social realities within individual technological spaces and use this understanding to inform the design of resources within individual technological spaces and activities around such spaces
  - To understand learners' interaction across different technological spaces beyond the classroom and use this understanding to design learning environments around multiple technological spaces and support learners' construction of technology-enhanced learning ecologies outside the classroom
  - To understand learners' interaction across non-technological spaces beyond the classroom and various technological and non-technological spaces inside the classroom, and use this understanding to guide the design of learning environments that maximize and complement the strengths of various social spaces of learning and to support learners' construction of language-learning ecologies
  - To understand the temporal changes across spaces and learners' interaction with these spaces and use this understanding to inform the provision of differentiated support for learners' construction of language-learning ecologies at different timescales and stages of learning
- Take a broader view in defining and projecting learning outcomes
  - To construct a framework of learning outcomes in out-of-class autonomous language learning with technology
  - To use this framework as a frame of reference when designing and researching out-of-class autonomous language learning with technology

Developers need to reflect on the following questions when designing learner development programmes or technology-enhanced learning environments:

- Has the design of the technological resources and activities considered the social realities and the knowledge, assumptions and habits of mind that learners bring to the technological spaces?
- Has the design of the technological resources and activities considered the other technological and non-technological spaces that are accessible to learners and the learners' perceptions of these spaces?

- Has the design of the technology-enhanced learning activities and environments maximized and complemented the strengths of in-class and out-of-class learning?
- Has the design of the technology-enhanced learning environments considered the changes in the relationships between social spaces and learners over time?
- Has the support provided for the learners in out-of-class autonomous language learning with technology taken into consideration the various levels of interactions and the potential changes in these interactions over time?
- Does the design and support help learners build the link between different spaces of learning to support their interest-driven learning?

Researchers need to examine the issue of autonomous learning with technology beyond the classroom in relation to the other resources in out-of-class learning contexts and what is going on inside the classroom.

- How could technology enhance out-of-class learning?
  - How do the social realities of various technological spaces interact with the dispositional and capital packages that learners bring with them to the interaction? How do the interactions shape learners' further interactions within and across technological spaces?
  - How do learners coordinate various technological and non-technological resources for out-of-class learning?
  - How can we judge the quality of out-of-class language learning with technology?
- How can technology influence in-class learning?
  - How does learners' technological experience outside the classroom influence their expectations concerning in-class learning and their perceptions of the roles of teachers inside the classroom?
  - How does learners' technological experience outside the classroom influence their assumptions of and expectations for technology use inside the classroom?
- How can in-class learning shape technology use outside the classroom?
  - How can teachers incorporate technology in ways that promote self-initiated, self-directed out-of-class learning with technology?
  - How can in-class technological and non-technological resources and arrangements shape learners' construction of learning ecologies with technology outside the classroom?
- How can technology bridge in-class and out-of-class learning?

- What are some models of technology use that could help achieve an optimal relationship between in-class and out-of-class learning?
- How does out-of-class experience with technological resources bridge or obstruct learners' in-class experience with technological resources?

The field of out-of-class autonomous language learning with technology is a promising but relatively unexplored area that poses more questions than answers. In-depth insights into this field are critical to exploiting the full educational potential of technology and enhancing the quality of language learners' overall learning experience. Kumpulainen and Sefton (2014) envisioned an educational ideality – connected learning – whereby 'the learner is able to pursue a personal interest or passion with the support of friends, caring adults, and/or expert communities and is in turn able to link this learning and interest to academic achievement, career success, or civic engagement' (p. 10). This concept of connected learning sets the overarching goal for out-of-class autonomous language learning with technology. Future research and design work on learners' out-of-class autonomous language learning with technology should strive towards realizing connectedness in language learning.

References

Aguirre-Urreta, M. I., and Marakas, G. M. (2010). Is it really gender? An empirical investigation into gender effects in technology adoption through the examination of individual differences. *Human Technology: An Interdisciplinary Journal on Humans in ICT Environments*, *6*, 155–90.

Ajzen, I. (1985). From intentions to actions: A theory of planned behavior. In I. Ajzen (ed.), *Action Control* (pp. 11–39). Heidelberg, Berlin: Springer.

Ajzen, I. (2005). *Attitudes, Personality, and Behavior*. New York, UK: McGraw-Hill Education.

Alajmi, M. (2011). *Web 2.0 Technologies Adoption in Kuwait*. (Unpublished doctoral dissertation). Texas: University of North Texas.

Ala-Kyyny, J. (2012). *The Role of English-Language Music in Informal Learning of English*. (Unpublished master thesis). Finland: University of Jyväskylä.

Al Asmari, A. (2013). Practices and prospects of learner autonomy: Teachers' perceptions. *English Language Teaching*, *6*, 1–10.

Al-Shaqsi, T. S. (2009). Teachers' beliefs about learner autonomy. In S. Borg (ed.), *Researching English Language Teaching and Teacher Development in Oman* (pp. 157–65). Oman: Ministry of Education.

Arbelaiz, A. M., and Gorospe, J. M. C. (2009). Can the grammar of schooling be changed? *Computers & Education*, *53*, 51–6.

Ashton, J., and Newman, L. (2006). An unfinished symphony: 21st century teacher education using knowledge creating heutagogies. *British Journal of Educational Technology*, *37*, 825–40.

Aviram, A., and Assor, A. (2010). In defence of personal autonomy as a fundamental educational aim in Liberal Democracies: a response to Hand. *Oxford Review of education*, *36*, 111–26.

Bahrani, T., and Sim, T. S. (2012). Audiovisual news, cartoons, and films as sources of authentic language input and language proficiency enhancement. *TOJET: The Turkish Online Journal of Educational Technology*, *11*, 56–64.

Bailly, S. (2011). Teenagers learning language out of school: What, why and how do they learn? How can school help them? In P. Benson and H. Reinders (eds), *Beyond the Language Classroom* (pp. 119–31). Basingstoke: Palgrave Macmillan.

Bakhtin, M. M. (1981). *The Dialogic Imagination: Four Essays by MM Bakhtin*. Texas: University of Texas Press.

Bandura, A. (1997). *Self-Efficacy: The Exercise of Control*. New York: Freeman.

Barbee, M. (2013). Extracurricular L2 input in a Japanese EFL context: Exposure, attitudes, and motivation. *University of Hawaii Second Language Studies Paper*, *32*, 1–58.

Bargh, J. A., and McKenna, K. Y. (2004). The Internet and social life. *Annual Review of Psychology*, *55*, 573–90.

Barnett, R. (2011). Configuring Learning Spaces. In A. Boddington and J. Boys (eds), *Re-Shaping Learning: A Critical Reader* (pp. 167–78). Rotterdam, Netherlands: Sense Publishers.

Barron. B. (2006). Interest and self-sustained learning as catalysts of development: A learning ecologies perspective. *Human Development*, *49*, 193–224.

Barron, B. (2010). Conceptualizing and tracing learning pathways over time and setting. *Learning Research as a Human Science. National Society for the Study of Education Yearbook*, *109*, 113–27.

Barron, B., Martin, C. K. and Roberts, E. (2007). Sparking self-sustained learning: Report on a design experiment to build technological fluency and bridge divides. *International Journal of Technology and Design Education*, *17*, 75–105.

Bäumer, T., Preis, N., Roßbach, H., Stecher, L. and Klieme, E. (2011). Education processes in life-course-specific learning environments. *Z Erziehungswiss*, *14*, 87–101.

Baym, N. K. (1997). Interpreting soap operas and creating community: Inside an electronic fan culture. In S. Kiesler (ed.), *Culture of the Internet* (pp. 103–20). New York: Lawrence Erlbaum Associates.

Beckman, K., Bennett, S. and Lockyer, L. (2008). Understanding students' use and value of technology for learning. *Learning, Media and Technology*, *39*, 346–67.

Bell, L. (2008). Engaging the public in technology policy a new role for science Museums. *Science Communication*, *29*, 386–98.

Bell, P., Lewenstein, B., Shouse, A. W. and Feder, M. A., eds (2009). *Learning Science in Informal Environments: People, Places, and Pursuits*. Washington: National Academies Press.

Benedek, J., and Miner, T. (2002). Measuring desirability: New methods for evaluating desirability in a usability lab setting. *Proceedings of Usability Professionals Association*, *2002*, 8–12.

Bennett, S., and Maton, K. (2010). Beyond the 'digital natives' debate: Towards a more nuanced understanding of students' technology experiences. *Journal of computer assisted learning*, *26*(5), 321–31.

Benson, P. (1997). The philosophy and politics of learner autonomy. In P. Benson and P. Voller (eds), *Autonomy and Independence in Language Learning* (pp. 18–34). London: Addison Wesley Longman.

Benson, P. (2001). *Teaching and Researching Autonomy in Language Learning*. London: Longman.

Benson, P. (2005). Autonomy and information technology in the educational discourse of the information. In Chris Davison (ed.), *Information Technology and Innovation in Language Education* (pp. 173–94). Hong Kong: Hong Kong University Press.

Benson, P. (2007). Autonomy in language teaching and learning. *Language Teaching*, *40*, 21–40.

Benson, P. (2008). Teachers' and learners' perspectives on autonomy. In T. Lamb and H. Reinders (eds), *Learner and Teacher Autonomy: Concepts, Realities, and Responses* (pp. 15–32). Amsterdam, Netherland: John Benjamins Publishing Company.

Benson, P. (2009a). Making sense of autonomy in language learning. In R. Pemberton, S. Toogood and A. Barfield (eds), *Maintaining Control: Autonomy and Language Learning* (pp. 13–26). Hong Kong: Hong Kong University Press.

Benson, P. (2009b). Mapping out the world of language learning beyond the classroom. In F. Kjisik, P. Voller, N. Aoki and Y. Nakata (eds), *Mapping the Terrain of Learner Autonomy: Learning Environments, Learning Communities and Identities* (pp. 217–35). Tampere: Tampere University Press.

Benson, P. (2011a). *Teaching and Researching Autonomy*, 2nd edn. London: Pearson Education.

Benson, P. (2011b). What's new in autonomy? *The Language Teacher*, *35*, 15–18.

Benson, P. (2011c). Language learning and teaching beyond the classroom: An introduction to the field. In P. Benson and H. Reinders (eds), *Beyond the Language Classroom* (pp. 7–16). Basingstoke: Palgrave Macmillan.

Benson, P. (2012). Autonomy in language learning, learning and life. *Synergies France*, *9*, 29–39.

Benson, P. (2013). Learner autonomy. *TESOL Quarterly*, *47*, 839–43.

Benson, P., and Reinders, H. (2011). *Beyond the Language Classroom: The Theory and Practice of Informal Language Learning and Teaching.* Basingstoke: Palgrave Macmillan.

Benson, P., Chik, A. and Lim, H. Y. (2003). Becoming autonomous in an Asian context: Autonomy as a sociocultural process. In D. Palfreyman and R. C. Smith (eds), *Learner Autonomy Across Cultures* (pp. 23–40). Basingstoke, UK: Palgrave Macmillan.

Bernstein, B. (1999). Vertical and horizontal discourse: An essay. *British Journal of Sociology of Education*, *20*, 157–73.

Blake, R. J. (2008). *Brave New Digital Classroom: Technology and Foreign Language Learning.* Washington: Georgetown University Press,

Blaschke, L. M. (2012). Heutagogy and lifelong learning: A review of heutagogical practice and self-determined learning. *The International Review of Research in Open and Distributed Learning*, *13*(1), 56–71.

Blaschke, L. M. and Hase, S. (2016). Heutagogy: A holistic framework for creating twenty-first-century self-determined learners. In B. Gros and M. Maina (eds), *The Future of Ubiquitous Learning* (pp. 25–40). Heidelberg, Berlin: Springer.

Blin, F. (2010). Designing cybertasks for learner autonomy: Towards an activity theoretical pedagogical model. In M. J. Luzón, N. Ruiz-Madrid and M. L. Villanueva (eds), *Digital Genres, New Literacies and Autonomy in Language Learning* (pp. 175–96). Newcastle, UK: Cambridge Scholars Publishing.

Blin, F., Caw, C., Hamel, M. J., Heift, T., Schulze, M. and Smith, B. (2016). Sustainable Interaction-Based Research in CALL. In A. M. G. Sanz, M. Levy, F. Blin and D. Barr (eds), *WorldCALL: Sustainability and Computer-Assisted Language Learning* (pp. 119–131). New York: Bloomsbury Publishing.

Block, D. (2007). *Second Language Identities*. London: Bloomsbury Publishing.

Blyth, D. A., and LaCroix-Dalluhn, L. (2011). Expanded learning time and opportunities: Key principles, driving perspectives, and major challenges. *New Directions for Youth Development*, *131*, 15–27.

Boekaerts, M. (1999). Self-regulated learning: Where we are today. *International journal of educational research*, *31*, 445–57.

Borg, S., and Al-Busaidi, S. (2012). Learner autonomy: English language teachers' beliefs and practices. *ELT Journal*, *12*, 1–45.

Borrero, N. E., and Christine J. Y. (2010). Ecological English language learning among ethnic minority youth. *Educational Researcher*, *39*, 571–81.

Bouchard, P. (2009). Some factors to consider when designing semi-autonomous learning environments. *Electronic Journal of E-Learning*, *7*, 93–100.

Bouchard, P. (2012). Self-directed learning and learner autonomy. In N. M. Seel (ed.), *Encyclopedia of the Sciences of Learning* (pp. 2997–3000). Berlin, US: Springer.

Boud, D. (1988). Moving towards autonomy. In D. Boud (ed.), *Developing Student Autonomy in Learning* (pp. 17–39). London: Taylor and Francis.

Bourdieu, P. (1984). *Distinction: A Social Critique of the Judgement of Taste*. Boston: Harvard University Press.

Bourdieu, P. (1990). *The Logic of Practice*. Stanford, US: Stanford University Press.

Brown, J. S. (2000). Growing up: Digital: How the web changes work, education, and the ways people learn. *Change: The Magazine of Higher Learning*, *32*, 11–20.

Buchem, I., Tur, G. and Hölterhof, T. (2014). Learner control in personal learning environments: A cross-cultural study. *Journal of Literacy and Technology*, *15*, 14–53.

Byrne, J., and Diem, R. (2014). Profiling mobile English language learners. *JALT CALL Journal*, *10*, 3–19.

Cabot, M. (2014). English as a Foreign Language and Technological Artefacts in School and out of School (Unpublished master thesis). Haugesund: University College Stord.

Caines, A., McCarthy, M. and O'Keeffe, A. (2016). Spoken language corpora and pedagogical applications. In F. Farr and L. Murray (eds), *The Routledge Handbook of Language Learning and Technology* (pp. 348–61). London: Routledge.

Callanan, M., Cervantes, C. and Loomis, M. (2011). Informal learning. *Wiley Interdisciplinary Reviews: Cognitive Science*, *2*, 646–55.

Camilleri, G. (1999). *Learner Autonomy: The Teachers' Views*. Strasbourg: Council of Europe.

Candy, P. C. (1991). *Self-Direction for Lifelong Learning*. San Francisco: Jossey-Bass.

Carson, L., and Mynard, J. (2012). Introduction. In J. Mynard and L. Carson (eds), *Advising in Language Learning: Dialogue, Tools and Context* (pp. 3–25). Harlow, UK: Pearson Education Limited.

Carter, B. A. (2005). Reconceptualizing roles and responsibilities in language learning in higher education. *Teaching in Higher Education*, *10*, 461–73.

Castellano, J., Mynard, J. and Rubesch, T. (2011). Student technology use in a self-access center. *Language Learning and Technology, 15*, 12–27.

Castells, M. (2001). Space of flows, space of places: Materials for a theory of urbanism in the information age. In R. T. LeGates and F. Stout (eds), *The city reader* (pp. 572–82). London: Routledge.

Çelik, S., Arkın, E. and Sabriler, D. (2012). EFL learners' use of ICT for self-regulated learning. *Journal of Language and Linguistic Studies, 8*, 98–118.

Chamberlin-Quinlisk, C. (2013). Media, technology, and intercultural education. *Intercultural Education, 24*, 297–302.

Chambers, A. (2006). Written language corpora and pedagogical applications. In F. Farr and L. Murray (eds), *The Routledge Handbook of Language Learning and Technology* (pp. 362–75). London: Routledge.

Chan, V. (2003). Autonomous language learning: The teachers' perspectives. *Teaching in Higher Education, 8*, 33–54.

Chan, V., Spratt, M. and Humphreys, G. (2002). Autonomous language learning: Hong Kong tertiary students' attitudes and behaviours. *Evaluation & Research in Education, 16*, 1–18.

Chang, S. C., and Tung, F. C. (2008). An empirical investigation of students' behavioral intentions to use the online learning course websites. *British Journal of Educational Technology, 39*, 71–83.

Chapelle, C. (2001). *Computer Applications in Second Language Acquisition*. Cambridge: Cambridge University Press.

Chateau, A., and Zumbihl, H. (2012). Learners' perceptions of the pedagogical relations in a flexible language learning system. *Computer Assisted Language Learning, 25*, 165–79.

Chemero, A. (2003). An outline of a theory of affordances. *Ecological Psychology, 15*, 181–95.

Chen, J. L. (2011). The effects of education compatibility and technological expectancy on e-learning acceptance. *Computers and Education, 57*, 1501–11.

Chen, X. B. (2013). Tablets for informal language learning: Student usage and attitudes. *Language Learning and Technology, 17*, 20–36.

Cheung, W. S., and Hew, K. F. (2009). A review of research methodologies used in studies on mobile handheld devices in K-12 and higher education settings. *Australasian Journal of Educational Technology, 25*, 153–83.

Chik, A. (2007). From learner identity to learner autonomy: A biographical study of two Hong Kong learners of English. In P. Benson (ed.), *Teacher and Learner Perspectives* (pp. 41–60). Dublin, Ireland: Authentik Language Learning Resources.

Chik, A. (2014). Digital gaming and language learning: Autonomy and community. *Language Learning & Technology, 18*, 85–100.

Chiu, H. L.W. (2015). Materials design and pedagogy for technology-enhanced language learning. *International Journal of Computer-Assisted Language Learning and Teaching, 5*, 22–34.

Cho, M.Y., and Reinders, R. (2013). The effects of aural input enhancement on L2 acquisition. In J. M. Bergsleithner, S. N. Frota and J. K. Yoshioka (eds), *Noticing and Second Language Acquisition: Studies in Honor of Richard Schmidt* (pp. 133–48). Honolulu, US: University of Hawai'i at Mānoa.

Chusanachoti, R. (2009). *EFL Learning through Language Activities outside the Classroom: A Case Study of English Education Students in Thailand* (Unpublished doctoral dissertation). Michigan: Michigan State University.

Ciussi, M., Rosner, G. and Augier, M. (2009). Engaging students with mobile technologies to support their formal and informal learning. *International Journal of Mobile and Blended Learning (IJMBL), 1*, 84–98.

Clark, W., Logan, K., Luckin, R., Mee, A. and Oliver, M. (2009). Beyond Web 2.0: Mapping the technology landscapes of young learners. *Journal of Computer Assisted Learning, 25*, 56–69.

Cleary, T. J., and Zimmerman, B. J. (2004). Self-regulation empowerment program: A school-based program to enhance self-regulated and self-motivated cycles of student learning. *Psychology in the Schools, 41*, 537–50.

Cleary, T. J., Platten, P. and Nelson, A. (2008). Effectiveness of the self-regulation empowerment program with urban high school students. *Journal of advanced academics, 20*, 70–107.

Cleary, T. J., and Zimmerman, B. J. (2012). A cyclical self-regulatory account of student engagement: Theoretical foundations and applications. In S. L. Christenson, A. L., Reschly and C. Wylie (eds), *Handbook of Research on Student Engagement* (pp. 237–57). Berlin, US: Springer.

Coffin, R. J., and MacIntyre, P. D. (1999). Motivational influences on computer-related affective states. *Computers in Human Behavior, 15*, 549–69.

Cohen, E. H. (2007). Researching informal education: A preliminary mapping. *Bulletin de Méthodologie Sociologique, 93*, 70–88.

Coleman, J. S. (1988). Social capital in the creation of human capital. *American Journal of Sociology, 94*, S95–S120.

Colley, H., Hodkinson, P. and Malcolm, J. (2003). *Informality and Formality in Learning: A Report for the Learning and Skills Research Centre.* London: Learning and Skills Research Center.

Compton, D. M., Burkett, M. H. and Burkett, G. G. (2003). No sex difference in perceived competence of computer use among male and female college students in 2002. *Psychological Report, 92*, 503–11.

Conole, G. (2008). Listening to the learner voice: The ever changing landscape of technology use for language students. *ReCALL, 20*, 124–40.

Cooker, L. (2010). Some self-access principles. *Studies in Self-Access Learning Journal, 1*, 5–9.

Costa, A. L., and Kallick, B. (2008). *Learning and Leading with Habits of Mind: 16 Essential Characteristics for Success.* Alexandria, VA: Association for Supervision and Curriculum Development.

Cotterall, S. and Reinders, H. (2001). Fortress or bridge? learners' perceptions and practice in self access language learning. *Tesolanz*, *8*, 23–38.

Cox, M. J. (2013). Formal to informal learning with IT: research challenges and issues for e-learning. *Journal of Computer Assisted Learning*, *29*, 85–105.

Crabbe, D. (2003). The quality of language learning opportunities. *TESOL Quarterly*, *37*, 9–34.

Crabbe, D., Elgort, I. and Gu, P. (2013). Autonomy in a networked world. *Innovation in Language Learning and Teaching*, *7*, 193–7.

Cranmer, S. (2006). Children and young people's uses of the Internet for homework. *Learning, Media and Technology*, *31*, 301–15.

Crook, C. (2008). What are web 2.0 technologies, and why do they matter. In N. Selwyn (ed.), *Education 2.0? Designing the Web for Teaching and Learning* (pp. 6–9). London: TLRP.

Crook, C. (2012). The 'digital native' in context: tensions associated with importing Web 2.0 practices into the school setting. *Oxford Review of Education*, *38*, 63–80.

Cutler, A. C. (2005). Gramsci, law, and the culture of global capitalism. *Critical Review of International Social and Political Philosophy*, *8*, 527–42.

Dabbagh, N., and Kitsantas, A. (2012). Personal learning environments, social media, and self-regulated learning: A natural formula for connecting formal and informal learning. *The Internet and Higher Education*, *15*, 3–8.

Dam, L. (1995). *Learner Autonomy 3: From Theory to Classroom Practice*. Dublin, Authentik: Language Learning Resources Ltd.

Dam, L. (2009). The use of logbooks – A tool for developing learner autonomy. In R. Pemberton, S. Toogood and A. Barfield (eds), *Maintaining Control: Autonomy and Language Learning* (pp. 125–44). Hong Kong: Hong Kong University Press.

Dam, L., Eriksson, R., Little, D., Miliander, J. and Trebbi, T. (1990). Towards a definition of autonomy. In T. Trebbi (ed.), *Third Nordic Workshop on Developing Autonomous Learning in FL Classroom* (pp. 96–102). Bergen: University of Bergen.

Dang, T. T. (2012). Learner autonomy: A synthesis of theory and practice. *The Internet Journal of Language, Culture and Society*, *35*, 52–67.

Davis, F. D. (1989). Perceived usefulness, perceived ease of use, and user acceptance of information technology. *MIS Quarterly*, *13*, 319–40.

Davis, H. A. (2003). Conceptualizing the role and influence of student-teacher relationships on children's social and cognitive development. *Educational Psychologist*, *38*, 207–34.

Davis, M. (2013). Beyond the classroom: The role of self-guided learning in second language listening and speaking practice. *Studies in Self-Access Learning Journal*, *4*, 85–95.

Davis, K., and James, C. (2013). Tweens' conceptions of privacy online: implications for educators. *Learning, Media and Technology*, *38*, 4–25.

De Corte, E., Verschaffel, L. and Masui, C. (2004). The CLIA-model: A framework for designing powerful learning environments for thinking and problem solving. *European Journal of Psychology of Education*, *XIX*, 365–84.

Deci, E. L., and Ryan, R. M. (1985). The general causality orientations scale: Self-determination in personality. *Journal of research in personality*, *19*, 109–34.

Deci, E. L., and Flaste, R. (1996). *Why we do what we do: Understanding Self-Motivation*. London: Penguin books.

Deepwell, F., and Malik, S. (2008). On campus, but out of class: An investigation into students' experiences of learning technologies in their self- directed study. *ALT-J, Research in Learning Technology*, *16*, 5–14.

Demouy, V., Jones, A., Kan, Q., Kukulska-Hulme, A. and Eardley, A. (2016).Why and how do distance learners use mobile devices for language learning? *The EuroCALL Review*, *24*, 10–24.

Dewey, J. (1966). *Lectures in the Philosophy of Education, 1899*. Ran: New York.

Dickinson, L. (1977). Autonomy, self-directed learning and individualized instruction. In E. M. Harding-Esch (ed.), *Self-Directed Learning and Autonomy* (pp. 12–34). Cambridge: Department of Linguistics and CRAPEL.

Dickinson, L. (1987). *Self-Instruction in Language Learning*. Cambridge: Cambridge University Press.

Dickinson, L. (1992). *Learner Training for Language Learning*. Dublin: Authentik.

Dickson, L. (1995). Autonomy and motivation: A literature review. *System*, *23*, 165–74.

Doughty, C., and Long, M. (2003). Optimal psycholinguistic environments for distance foreign language learning. *Language Learning* & *Technology*, *7*, 50–80.

Doyle, H., and Parrish, M. (2012). Investigating students' ways to learn English outside of class: A researchers' narrative. *Studies in Self-Access Learning Journal*, *3*, 196–203.

Ebner, M., Lienhardt, C., Rohs, M. and Meyer, I. (2010). Microblogs in higher education – A change to faciltite informal and process-oriented learning? *Computers in Education*, *55*, 92–100.

Ekşi, G., and Aydın, H. (2013). What are the students doing 'out' there? An Investigation of out-of-class language learning activities. *Abant İzzet Baysal Üniversitesi Sosyal Bilimler Enstitüsü Dergisi*, *13*, 191–210.

Elgort, I. (2011). Dealing with complexity through course design. *On the Horizon*, *19*, 97–108.

Ellis, R. (2005). Principles of instructed language learning. *System*, *33*, 209–24.

Emirbayer, M., and Mische, A. (1998). What is agency? *American Journal of Sociology*, *103*, 962–1023.

Ertmer, P. A., and Ottenbreit-Leftwich, A. T. (2010). Teacher technology change: How knowledge, confidence, beliefs, and culture intersect. *Journal of Research on Technology in Education*, *42*, 255–84.

Fagerlund, T. (2012). Learning and using English and Swedish Beyond the Classroom: Activity Systems of Six Upper Secondary School Students (Unpublished master thesis). Finland: University of Jyväskylä.

Farahani, M. (2014). From spoon feeding to self-feeding: Are Iranian EFL learners ready to take charge of their own learning? *Electronic Journal of Foreign Language Teaching*, *11*, 98–115.

Farmer, T. W., Lines, M. M. and Hamm, J. V. (2011). Revealing the invisible hand: The role of teachers in children's peer experiences. *Journal of Applied Developmental Psychology*, *32*, 247–56.

Ferede, T. (2010). Major hindrance to the development of autonomy among grade nine students in learning English: Baso general secondary school in Debreberhan in focus. *Ethiopian Journal of Education and Sciences*, *6*, 1–28.

Field, J. (2000). Researching lifelong learning through focus groups. *Journal of Further and Higher Education*, *24*, 323–35.

Field, J. (2003). Researching lifelong learning: Trends and prospects in the English-speaking world. *Teraznjejszosc Czlowjek Edukacja*, *21*, 63–81.

Fischer, G. (2013). Supporting self-directed learning with cultures of participation in collaborative learning environments. In E. Christiansen, L. Kuure, A. Morch and B. Lindström (eds), *Problem-based Learning for the 21st Century* (pp. 15–50). Denmark: Aalborg University Press.

Fishbein, M., and Ajzen, I. (1975). *Belief, Attitude, Intention and Behavior: An Introduction to Theory and Research*. Reading, MA: Addison-Wesley.

Fitzpatrick, T. (2007). Word association patterns: Unpacking the assumptions. *International Journal of Applied Linguistics*, *17*, 319–31.

Fleckenstein, K. S. (2005). Faceless students, virtual places: Emergence and communal accountability in online classrooms. *Computers and Composition*, *22*, 149–76.

Flewitt, R. (2005). Conducting research with young children: Some ethical considerations. *Early Child Development and Care*, *175*, 553–65.

Ford, D. P., Connelly, C. E. and Meister, D. B. (2003). Information systems research and Hofstede's culture's consequences: an uneasy and incomplete partnership. *IEEE Transactions on Engineering Management*, *50*, 8–25.

Fukuda, S. T., and Yoshida, H. (2013). Time is of the essence: Factors encouraging out-of-class study time. *ELT Journal*, *67*, 31–40.

Gamble, C., Aliponga, J., Wilkins, M., Koshiyama, Y., Yoshida, K. and Ando, S. (2012). Examining learner autonomy dimensions: Students' perceptions of their responsibility and ability. In A. Stewart and N. Sonda (eds), *JALT2011 Conference Proceedings* (pp. 263–72). Tokyo: JALT.

Gao, X. (2007). Language learnign experiences and learnign strategy research: Voices of a mainland Chinese student in Hong Kong. *Innovations in Language Learning and Teaching*, *1*, 193–207.

Gao, X. (2010). *Strategic Language Learning: The Roles of Agency and Context*. Bristol: Multilingual Matters.

Gao, X., and Zhang, L. J. (2011). Joining forces for synergy: Agency and metacognition as interrelated theoretical perspectives on learner autonomy. In G. Murray, X. Gao and T. Lamb (eds), *Identity, Motivation and Autonomy in Language Learning* (pp. 25–41). Bristol: Multilingual Matters.

García-Peñalvo, F. J., Johnson, M., Alves, G. R., Minovi, M. and Conde-González, M. A. (2014). Informal learning recognition through a cloud ecosystem. *Future Generation Computer Systems*, *32*, 282–94.

Garrison, D. R. (1997). Self-directed learning: Toward a comprehensive model. *Adult Education Quarterly, 48*, 18–33.

Giddens, A. (1984). *The Constitution of Society: Outline of the Theory of Structuration.* Berkeley, US: University of California Press.

Gieve, S., and Miller, I. K. (2006). What do we mean by 'Quality of Classroom Life'?. In S. Gieve and I. K. Miller (eds), *Understanding the Language Classroom* (pp. 18–46). Basingstoke, UK: Palgrave Macmillan.

Gilmore, A. (2007). Authentic materials and authenticity in foreign language learning. *Language Teaching, 40*, 97–118.

Goh, T. T., Seet, B. C. and Chen, N. S. (2012). The impact of persuasive SMS on students' self-regulated learning. *British Journal of Educational Technology, 43*, 624–40.

Goleman, D. (2006). *Emotional Intelligence.* Bantam.

Goodyear, P., and Ellis, R. A. (2008). University students' approaches to learning: Rethinking the place of technology. *Distance Education, 29*, 141–52.

Graham, S., and Harris, K. R. (2005). Improving the writing performance of young struggling writers theoretical and programmatic research from the center on accelerating student learning. *The Journal of Special Education, 39*, 19–33.

Gray, K., Chang, S. and Kennedy, G. (2010). Use of social web technologies by international and domestic undergraduate students: implications for internationalising learning and teaching in Australian universities. *Technology, Pedagogy and Education, 19*, 31–46.

Green-Vänttinen, M., Korkman C. and Lehti-Eklund, H. (2010). Svenska i finska gymnasier. *Nordica Helsingiensia 22.* Helsingfors: Finska, finskugriska och nordiska institutionen vid Helsingfors universitet.

Greene, J. A., and Azevedo, R. (2007). A theoretical review of Winne and Hadwin's model of self-regulated learning: New perspectives and directions. *Review of Educational Research, 77*, 334–72.

Gremmo, M. J. and Riley, P. (1995). Autonomy, self-direction and self-access in language teaching and learning: The history of an idea. *System, 23*, 151–64.

Griffiths, C. (2008). *Lessons from Good Language Learners.* Cambridge: Cambridge University Press.

Guglielmino, L. M. (2008). Why self-directed learning. *International Journal of Self-Directed Learning, 5*, 1–14.

Guo, S. C. (2011). Impact of an out-of-class activity on students' English awareness, vocabulary, and autonomy. *Language Education in Asia, 2*, 246–56.

Hadwin, A., and Oshige, M. (2011). Self-regulation, coregulation, and socially shared regulation: Exploring perspectives of social in self-regulated learning theory. *Teachers College Record, 113*, 240–64.

Haerle, F. C., and Bendixen, L. D. (2008). Personal epistemology in elementary classrooms: A conceptual comparison of Germany and the United States and a guide for future cross-cultural research. In M. S. Khine (ed.), *Knowing, Knowledge and Beliefs: Epistemological Studies across Diverse Cultures* (pp. 151–76). Dordrecht, The Netherlands: Springer-Verlag.

Hafner, C. A., and Young, J. (2007). From teacher to facilitator: Developing perspective. In L. Miller (ed.), *Learner Autonomy 9: Autonomy in the Classroom* (pp. 103–26). Dublin: Authentik.

Hafner, C. A., Chik, A. and Jones, R. H. (2015). Digital literacies and language learning. *Language Learning & Technology, 19*, 1–7.

Hager, P. J. (2012). Informal learning. In N. M. Seel (ed.), *Encyclopedia of the Sciences of Learning* (pp. 1557–9). Berlin, US: Springer.

Hager, P. and Halliday, J. (2006). The importance of contextuality for learning. In P. Hager and J. Halliday (eds), *Recovering Informal Learning: Wisdom, Judgement and Community* (pp. 159–77). Berlin, Netherlands, Springer.

Hakkarainen, K., Mukkonen, H., Lipponen, L, Ilomäki, L., Rahikainen, M. and Lehtinen, E. (2001). Teachers' information and communication technology (ICT) skills and practices of using ICT and their pedagogical thinking. *Journal of Technology and Teacher Education, 9*, 181–97.

Hall, R. (2009). Towards a fusion of formal and informal learning environments: The impact of the read/write web. *Electronic Journal of e-Learning, 7*, 29–40.

Hamilton, M. (2013). *Autonomy and Foreign Language Learning in a Virtual Learning Environment*. London: Bloomsbury Academic Publishing.

Han, Z. H., Park, E. S. and Combs, C. (2008). Textual enhancement of input: Issues and possibilities. *Applied Linguistics, 29*, 597–618.

Hanf, A. (2015). Resourcing authentic language in television series. In D. Nunan and J. C. Richards (eds), *Language Learning Beyond the Classroom* (pp. 138–48). London: Routledge.

Hase, S. (2009). Heutagogy and e-learning in the workplace: Some challenges and opportunities. *Impact: Journal of Applied Research in Workplace e-Learning, 1*, 43–52.

Healey, D., Hanson-Smith, E., Hubbard, P., Ioannou-Georgiou, S., Kessler, G. and Ware, P. (2011). *TESOL Technology Standards: Description, Implementation, Integration.* Alexandria, VA: TESOL.

Henry, A. (2013). Digital games and ELT: Bridging the authenticity gap. In E. Ushioda (ed.), *International Perspectives on Motivation: Language Learning and Professional Challenges* (pp. 133–55). Basingstoke, UK: Palgrave Macmillan.

Henwood, F., Kennedy, H. and Miller, N. (2001). *Cyborg Lives?: Women's Technobiographies*. York, UK: Raw Nerve Books.

Heron, J. (1989). *The Facilitators' Handbook*. London: Kogan Page.

Hill, L. (2014). Some of it I haven't told anybody else': Using photo elicitation to explore the experiences of secondary school education from the perspective of young people with a diagnosis of Autistic Spectrum Disorder. *Educational and Child Psychology, 31*, 79–89.

Hine, C. (2008). Virtual ethnography: Modes, varieties, affordances. Iin N. G. Fielding, R. M. Lee and G. Blank (eds), *The SAGE Handbook of Online Research Methods* (pp. 257–70). Los Angeles: Sage.

Holden, B., and Usuki, M. (1999). Learner autonomy in language learning: A preliminary investigation. *Bulletin of Hokuriku University, 23*, 191–203.

Holec, H. (1981). *Autonomy is the Ability to Take Charge of one's Own Learning*. Oxford, UK: Pergamon.

Holec, H. (1985). *Autonomy in Foreign Language Learning*. Oxford: Pergamon.

Holec, H. (2009). Autonomy in language learning: A single pedagogical paradigm or two. In F. Kjisik, P. Voller, N. Aoki and Y. Nakata (eds), *Mapping the Terrain of Learner Autonomy: Learning Environments, Learning Communities and Identities* (pp. 21–47). Hong Kong: Hong Kong University Press.

Hommes, J., Rienties, B., De Grave, W., Bos, G., Schuwirth, L. and Scherpbier, A. (2012). Visualising the invisible: a network approach to reveal the informal social side of student learning. *Advances in Health Sciences Education, 17*, 743–57.

Hooper-Greenhill, E. (2004). Measuring learning outcomes in museums, archives and libraries: The Learning Impact Research Project (LIRP). *International Journal of Heritage Studies, 10*, 151–74.

Hsu, M. K., Wang, S. W. and Chiu, K. K. (2009). Computer attitude, statistics anxiety and self-efficacy on statistical software adoption behavior: An empirical study of online MBA learners. *Computers in Human Behavior, 25*, 412–20.

Huang, J. P. (2011). A dynamic account of autonomy, agency and identity in (T) EFL learning. In G. Murray, X. Gao and T. Lamb (eds), *Identity, Motivation and Autonomy in Language Learning* (pp. 229–46). Bristol: Multilingual Matters.

Huang, J. P., and Benson, P. (2013). Autonomy, agency and identity in foreign and second language education. *Chinese Journal of Applied Linguistics, 36*, 7–28.

Huang, Y. M., Huang, Y. M., Liu, C. H. and Tsai, C. C. (2013). Applying social tagging to manage cognitive load in a Web 2.0 self-learning environment. *Interactive Learning Environments, 21*, 273–89.

Hubbard, P. (2004). Learner training for effective use of CALL. In S. Fotos and C. M. Browne (eds), *New Perspectives on CALL for Second Language Classrooms* (pp. 45–68). Mahwah, NJ: Lawrence Erlbaum Associations.

Hubbard, P. (2013). Making a case for learner training in technology enhanced language learning environments. *Calico Journal, 30*, 163–78.

Huffman, A. H., Whetten, J. and Huffman, W. H. (2013). Using technology in higher education: The influence of gender roles on technology self-efficacy. *Computers in Human Behavior, 29*, 1779–86.

Hussein, A. K., and Haron, S. C. (2012). Autonomy in language learning. *Journal of Education and Practice, 3*, 103–11.

Hwang, G. J., Lai, C. L. and Wang, S. Y. (2015). Seamless flipped learning: a mobile technology-enhanced flipped classroom with effective learning strategies. *Journal of Computers in Education, 2*, 449–73.

Hyland, F. (2004). Learning autonomously: Contextualising out-of-class English language learning. *Language Awareness, 13*, 180–202.

Idros, S. N. S., Mohamed, A. R., Esa, N., Samsudin, M. A. and Daud, K. A. M. (2010). Enhancing self-directed learning skills through e-SOLMS for Malaysian learners. *Procedia-Social and Behavioral Sciences, 2*, 698–706.

Inozu, J., Sahinkarakas, S. and Yumru, H. (2010). The nature of language learning experiences beyond the classroom and its learning outcomes. *US-China Foreign Language*, *8*, 14–21.

Johnson, N. F. (2009). Cyber-relations in the Field of Home Computer Use for Leisure: Bourdieu and teenage technological experts. *E-Learning and Digital Media*, *6*, 187–97.

Jones, A. (2015). Mobile informal language learning: Exploring welsh learners' practices. *eLearning Papers*, *45*, 4–14.

Jones, J. F. (2001). CALL and the responsibilities of teachers and administrators. *ELT Journal*, *55*, 360–7.

Kalaja, P., Alanen, R., Palviainen, Å. and Dufva, H. (2011). From milk cartons to English roommates: Context and agency in L2 learning beyond the classroom. In P. Benson and H. Reinders (eds), *Beyond the Language Classroom* (pp. 47–58). Basingstoke: Palgrave Macmillan.

Kanno, Y. (2003). *Negotiating Bilingual and Bicultural Identities: Japanese Returnees Betwixt Two Worlds*. Mahwah, NJ: Lawrence Erlbaum Associates.

Karlsson, L. and Kjisik, F. (2011). Lifewide and lifedeep learning and the autonomous learner. *Out-of-Classroom Language Learning* (pp. 85–106). Helsinki: University of Helsinki Language Centre.

Katyal, K. R. and Evers, C. (2004). Teacher leadership and autonomous student learning: Adjusting to the new realities. *International Journal of Educational Research*, *41*, 367–82.

Kearney, M., Schuck, S., Burden, K. and Aubusson, P. (2012). Viewing mobile learning from a pedagogical perspective. *Research in Learning Technology*, *20*, 14406.

Kek, M., and Huijser, H. (2011). Exploring the combined relationships of student and teacher factors on learning approaches and self-directed learning readiness at a Malaysian university. *Studies in Higher Education*, *36*, 185–208.

Kelly, M. A., and Hager, P. (2015). Informal learning: relevance and application to health care simulation. *Clinical Simulation in Nursing*, *11*, 376–82.

Kennedy, G. E., Judd, T. S., Churchward, A., Gray, K. and Krause, K. L. (2008). First year students' experiences with technology: Are they really digital natives. *Australasian Journal of Educational Technology*, *24*, 108–22.

Kenning, M. M. (1996). IT and autonomy. In B. Elspeth and M. M. Kenning (eds), *Promoting Learner Autonomy in University Language Teaching* (pp. 121–38). France: Association for French Language Studies.

Kessler, G. (2009). Student-initiated attention to form in wiki-based collaborative writing. *Language Learning and Technology*, *13*, 79–95.

Kim, B., Park, H. and Baek, Y. (2009). Not just fun, but serious strategies: Using meta-cognitive strategies in game-based learning. *Computers & Education*, *52*, 800–10.

Kim, S. (2014). Developing autonomous learning for oral proficiency using digital storytelling. *Language Learning and Technology*, *18*, 20–35.

King, C. (2011). Fostering Self-directed Learning through Guided Tasks and Learner Reflection. *Studies in Self-Access Learning Journal*, *2*, 257–67.

Kistner, S., Rakoczy, K. and Otto, B. (2010). Promotion of self-regulated learning in classrooms: Investigating frequency, quality, and consequences for student performance. *Metacognition and Learning*, *5*, 157–71.

Kitsantas, A., and Dabbagh, N. (2011). The role of Web 2.0 technologies in self-regulated learning. *New Directions for Teaching and Learning*, *2011*, 99–106.

Knowles, M. S. (1975). *Self-Directed Learning*. Cambridge: Cambridge Adult Education.

Knowles, M. S. (1989). *The Making of an Adult Educator*. San Francisco: Jossey-Bass.

Kop, R., and Fournier, H. (2011). New dimensions to self-directed learning in an open networked learning environment. *International Journal of Self-Directed Learning*, *7*, 1–18.

Kormos, J., and Csizér, K. (2014). The interaction of motivation, self-regulatory strategies, and autonomous learning behavior in different learner groups. *TESOL Quarterly*, *48*, 275–99.

Kostons, D., van Gog, T. and Paas, F. (2011). Training self-assessment and task-selection skills: A cognitive approach to improving self-regulated learning. *Learning and Instruction*, *22*, 121–32.

Kozar, O. (2016). Text chat during video/audio conferencing lessons: Scaffolding or getting in the way? *CALICO Journal*, *33*, 231–59.

Krackhardt, D., and Hanson, J. R. (1993). Informal networks. *Harvard Business Review*, *71*, 104–11.

Kramsch, C., and Thorne, S. (2002). Foreign language learning as global communicative practice. In D. Block and D. Cameron (eds), *Globalization and Language Teaching* (pp. 83–100). London: Routledge.

Kuh, G., Douglas, K., Lund, J. and Ramin-Gyurnek, J. (1994). Student learning outside the classroom: transcending artificial boundaries. *ASHE-ERIC Higher Education Report No. 8*. Washington: ERIC Clearinghouse on Higher Education. Retrieved from http://files.eric.ed.gov/fulltext/ED394444.pdf.

Kukulska-Hulme, A. (2012). Language learning defined by time and place: A framework for next generation designs. In J. E. Díaz-Vera (ed.), *Left to My Own Devices: Learner Autonomy and Mobile Assisted Language Learning. Innovation and Leadership in English Language Teaching*, 6. (pp. 1–13). Bingley, UK: Emerald Group Publishing Limited.

Kukulska-Hulme, A., and De los Arcos, B. (2011). Researching emergent practice among mobile language learners. In: mLearn2011 Conference Proceedings, 74–7.

Kukulska-Hulme, A., Norris, L. and Donohue, J. (2015). *Mobile Pedagogy for English Language Teaching: A Guide for Teachers*. London: British Council.

Kumaravadivelu, B. (2006). TESOL methods: Changing tracks, challenging trends. *TESOL Quarterly*, *40*, 59–81.

Kumpulainen, K., and Sefton-Green, J. (2014). What is connected learning and how to research it? *International Journal of Learning and Media*, *4*, 7–18.

Kuppens, A. H. (2010). Incidental foreign language acquisition from media exposure. *Learning, Media and Technology*, *35*, 65–85.

Lai, C. (2013). A framework for developing self-directed technology use for language learning. *Language Learning & Technology, 17*, 100–22.

Lai, C. (2015a). Perceiving and traversing in-class and out-of-class learning: accounts from foreign language learners in Hong Kong. *Innovation in Language Learning and Teaching, 9*, 265–84.

Lai, C. (2015b). Modeling teachers' influence on learners' self-directed use of technology for language learning outside the classroom. *Computers & Education, 82*, 74–83.

Lai, C., and Gu, M. Y. (2011). Self-regulated out-of-class language learning with technology. *Computer Assisted Language Learning, 24*, 317–35.

Lai, C., Wang, Q. and Lei, J. (2012). What factors predict undergraduate students' use of technology for learning? A case from Hong Kong. *Computers & Education, 59*, 569–79.

Lai, C., Zhu, W. M. and Gong, G. (2015). Understanding the quality of out-of-class English learning. *TESOL Quarterly, 49*, 278–308.

Lai, C., Yeung, Y. and Hu, J. J. (2016). University student and teacher perceptions of teacher roles in promoting autonomous language learning with technology outside the classroom. *Computer Assisted Language Learning, 29*, 703–23.

Lai, C., Shum, M. and Tian, Y. (2016). Enhancing learners' self-directed use of technology for language learning: the effectiveness of an online training platform. *Computer Assisted Language Learning, 29*, 40–60.

Lai, C., Wang, Q., Li, X. S. and Hu, X. (2016). The influence of individual espoused cultural values on self-directed use of technology for language learning beyond the classroom. *Computers in Human Behavior, 62*, 676–88.

Lally, V., Sharples, M., Tracy, F., Bertram, N. and Masters, S. (2012). Researching the ethical dimensions of mobile, ubiquitous and immersive technology enhanced learning (MUITEL): A thematic review and dialogue. *Interactive Learning Environments, 20*, 217–38.

Lamb, M. (2004). 'It depends on the students themselves': Independent language learning at an Indonesian state school. *Language, Culture and Curriculum, 17*, 229–45.

Lamb, T. (2008). Learner autonomy and teacher autonomy: Synthesising an agenda. In T. Lamb and H. Reinders (eds), *Learner and Teacher Autonomy: Concepts, Realities, and Responses* (pp. 269–83). Amsterdam, Netherland: John Benjamins Publishing Company.

Lamb, T. E., and Reinders, H. (2005). Learner independence in language teaching: A concept of change. In D. Cunningham and A. Hatoss (eds), *An International Perspective on Language Policies, Practices and Proficiencies* (pp. 225–39). Blegrave, Australia: FIPLV.

Lantolf, J. P., Thorne, S. L. and Poehner, M. E. (2015). Sociocultural theory and second language development. In B. VanPatten and J. Williams (eds), *Theories in Second Language Acquisition: An Introduction* (pp. 207–26). London: Routledge.

Larsson, B. (2012). *English Out-of-School Activities-A Way of Integrating Outwards?* (Unpublished master thesis). Gävle: University of Gävle.

Lau, K. (2015). 'The most important thing is to learn the way to learn': Evaluating the effectiveness of independent learning by perceptual changes. *Assessment & Evaluation in Higher Education*, 1–16.

Laurillard, D. (2002). *Rethinking University Teaching: A Conversational Framework for the Effective use of Learning Technologies*. London: Routledge.

Lawrence, G. (2013). A working model for intercultural learning and engagement in collaborative online language learning environments. *Intercultural Education, 24*, 303–14.

Lazaro, N. and Reinders, H. (2009). *Language Learning and Teaching in the Self-Access Centre: A Practical Guide for Teachers*. Sydney, Australia: NCELTR.

Leander, K. M., Phillips, N. C. and Taylor, K. H. (2010). The changing social spaces of learning: Mapping new nobilities. *Review of Research in Education, 34*, 329–94.

Lee, C., Yeung, A. S. and Ip, T. (2016). Use of computer technology for English language learning: do learning styles, gender, and age matter? *Computer Assisted Language Learning, 29*, 1033–49.

Lee, S. K., and Huang, H. T. (2008). Visual input enhancement and grammar learning: A meta-analytic review. *Studies in Second Language Acquisition, 30*, 307–31.

Leidner, D. E., and Kayworth, T. (2006). Review: A review of culture in information systems research: toward a theory of information technology culture conflict. *MIS Quarterly, 30*, 357–99.

Levy, M. (2015). The role of qualitative approaches to research in CALL contexts: Closing in on the learner's experience. *CALICO Journal, 32*, 546–54.

Levy, M., and Kennedy, C. (2010). Materials development in three Italian CALL projects: Seeking an optimal mix between in-class and out-of-class learning. *CALICO Journal, 27*, 529–39.

Levy, M., and Steel, C. (2015). Language learner perspectives on the functionality and use of electronic language dictionaries. *ReCALL, 27*, 177–96.

Lewis, T. (2013). Between the social and the selfish: Learner autonomy in online environments. *Innovation in Language Learning and Teaching, 7*, 198–212.

Lewis, T. (2014). Learner autonomy and the theory of sociality. In G. Murray (ed.), *Social Dimensions of Autonomy in Language Learning* (pp. 37–59). Basingstoke, UK: Palgrave Macmillan.

Li, J., Snow, C. and White, C. (2015). Urban adolescent students and technology: Access, use and interest in learning language and literacy. *Innovation in Language Learning and Teaching, 9*, 143–62.

Li, J., Snow, C., Jiang, J. and Edwards, N. (2015). Technology use and self-perceptions of English language skills among urban adolescents. *Computer Assisted Language Learning, 28*, 450–78.

Li, N., and Kirkup, G. (2007). Gender and cultural differences in Internet use: A study of China and the UK. *Computers & Education, 48*, 301–17.

Li, Y. R. (2013). *Informal Learning in the Web 2.0 Environment: How Chinese Students who are Learning English use Web 2.0 Tools for Informal Learning* (Unpublished master thesis). Texas: The University of Texas at Austin.

Liang, M. Y. (2013). Rethinking authenticity: Voice and feedback in media discourse. *Computers and Composition, 30*, 157–79.

Lin, C. H., Warschauer, M. and Blake, R. (2016). Language learning through social networks: Perceptions and reality. *Language Learning & Technology, 20*, 124–47.

Lin, P. M., and Siyanova-Chanturia, A. (2014). Internet television for L2 vocabulary learning. In D. Nunan and J. C. Richards (eds), *Language Learning Beyond the Classroom* (pp. 149–58). London: Routledge.

Lindgren, E., and Muñoz, C. (2013). The influence of exposure, parents, and linguistic distance on young European learners' foreign language comprehension. *International Journal of Multilingualism, 10*, 105–29.

Little, D. (1991). *Autonomy: Definitions, Issues and Problems.* Dublin: Authentik.

Little, D. (1994). Learner autonomy: A theoretical construct and its practical application. *Die Neuere Sprache, 93*, 430–42.

Little, D. (1995). Learning as dialogue: The dependence of learner autonomy on teacher autonomy. *System, 23*, 175–82.

Little, D. (1996). Freedom to learn and compulsion to interact: promoting learner autonomy through the use of information systems and information technologies. In R. Pemberton, E. S. L. Li, W. W. F. Or and H. D. Pierson (eds), *Taking Control: Autonomy in Language Learning* (pp. 203–18). Hong Kong: Hong Kong University Press.

Little, D. (1999). Developing learner autonomy in the foreign language classroom: A social-interactive view of learning and three fundamental pedagogical principles. *Revista Canaria de estudios ingleses, 38*, 78–87.

Little, D. (2004). Constructing a theory of learner autonomy: Some steps along the way. In K. Mäkinen, P. Kaikkonen and V. Kohonen (eds), *Future Perspectives in Foreign Language Education* (pp. 15–25). Tutkimuksia: Oulun Yliopiston Kasvatustieteiden Tiedekunnan.

Little, D. (2007). Language learner autonomy: Some fundamental considerations revisited. *Innovation in Language Learning and Teaching, 1*, 14–29.

Little, D. (2010). Learner autonomy, inner speech and the European Language Portfolio. In A. Psaltou-Joycey and M. Mattheoudaki (eds), *Advances in Research on Language Acquisition and Teaching: Selected Papers* (pp. 27–38). Thessaloniki: Greek Applied Linguistics Association.

Littlewood, W. (1996). 'Autonomy': An anatomy and a framework. *System, 24*, 427–35.

Loyens, S. M., Magda, J. and Rikers, R. M. (2008). Self-directed learning in problem-based learning and its relationships with self-regulated learning. *Educational Psychology Review, 20*(4), 411–27.

Luckin, R. (2008). The learner centric ecology of resources: A framework for using technology to scaffold learning. *Computers & Education, 50*, 449–62.

Luckin, R. (2010). *Re-designing Learning Contexts: Technology-rich, Learner-centered Ecologies*. Oxon: Routledge.

Luckin, R., Clark, W. and Underwood, J. (2013). The ecology of resources: A theoretical grounded framework for designing next generation technology-rich learning. In R. Luckin, S. Puntambekar, P. Goodyear, B. L. Grabowski, J. Underwood and N. Winters (eds), *Handbook of Design in Educational Technology* (pp. 33–43). New York: Routledge.

Lund, A. (2006). The multiple contexts of online language teaching. *Language Teaching Research, 10*, 181–204.

Macaro, E. (1997). *Target Language, Collaborative Learning and Autonomy*. Clevedon: Multilingual Matters Ltd.

Macaro, E. (2008). The shifting dimensions of language learner autonomy. In T. Lamb and H. Reinders (eds), *Learner and Teacher Autonomy: Concepts, Realities and Responses* (pp. 47–62). Philadelphia: John Benjamins Publishing Company.

Malcolm, J., Hodkinson, P. and Colley, H. (2003). The interrelationships between informal and formal learning. *Journal of Workplace Learning, 15*, 313–18.

Maranto, G., and Barton, M. (2010). Paradox and promise: MySpace, Facebook, and the sociopolitics of social networking in the writing classroom. *Computers and Composition, 27*, 36–47.

Marefat, F., and Barbari, F. (2009). The relationship between out-of-class language learning strategy use and reading comprehension ability. *Porta Linguarum, 12*, 91–106.

Margaryan, A., and Littlejohn, A. (2008). Repositories and communities at cross-purposes: Issues in sharing and reuse of digital learning resources. *Journal of Computer Assisted Learning, 24*, 333–47.

Markus, H. R., and Kitayama, S. (1991). Culture and the self: Implications for cognition, emotion, and motivation. *Psychological Review, 98*, 224–53.

Marsick, V. J., and Watkins, K. E. (2001). Informal and incidental learning. *New Directions for Adult and Continuing Education, 89*, 25–34.

Maton, K. (2008). Habitus. In M. Grenfell (ed.), *Piere Bourdieu: Key Concepts* (pp. 49–65). London: Acumen.

McCaslin, M. A. R. Y. (2009). Co-regulation of student motivation and emergent identity. *Educational Psychologist, 44*, 137–46.

McCaslin, M., and Hickey, D. T. (2001). Self-regulated learning and academic achievement: A Vygotskian view. In B. Zimmerman and D. Schunk (eds), *Self-Regulated Learning and Academic Achievement: Theory, Research, and Practice*, 2nd edn (pp. 227–52). Mahwah, NJ: Erlbaum.

McGill, T. J., and Klobas, J. E. (2009). A task – technology fit view of learning management system impact. *Computers & Education, 52*, 496–508.

McGrath, I. (2000). Teacher autonomy. In B. Sinclair, I. McGrath and T.E. Lamb (eds), *Learner Autonomy, Teacher Autonomy: Future Directions* (pp. 100–10). Harlow: Addison Wesley Longman.

Mercer, S. (2011). Understanding learner agency as a complex dynamic system. *System, 39*, 427–36.

Merriam, S. B., Caffarella, R.S. and Baumgartner, L. M. (2007). *Learning in Adulthood: A Comprehensive Guide*. New York, US: John Wiley & Sons.

Meyers, E. M., Erickson, I. and Small, R. V. (2013). Digital literacy and informal learning environments: an introduction. *Learning, Media and Technology, 38*, 355–67.

Middleton, A. (2011). Audio active: discovering mobile learner-gatherers from across the formal-informal continuum. *International Journal of Mobile and Blended Learning, 3*, 31–42.

Mishra, P., and Koehler, M. J. (2006). Technological pedagogical content knowledge: A framework for teacher knowledge. *Teachers College Record, 108*, 1017–54.

Motteram, G. (1997). Learner autonomy and the web. In V. Darleguy, A. Ding and M. Svensson (eds), *Educational Technology in Language Learning: Theoretical Considerations and Practical Applications* (pp. 17–24). Lyon, France: National Institute of Applied Sciences.

Mozzon-McPherson, M. (2007). Supporting independent learning environments: An analysis of structures and roles of language learning advisers. *System, 35*, 66–92.

Murray, G. L. (1999). Autonomy and language learning in a simulated environment. *System, 27*, 295–308.

Murray, G. (2014). Exploring the social dimensions of autonomy in language learning. In G. Murray (ed.), *Social Dimensions of Autonomy in Language Learning* (pp. 3–11). Basingstoke, UK: Palgrave Macmillan.

Nakata, Y. (2011). Teachers' readiness for promoting learner autonomy: A study of Japanese EFL high school teachers. *Teaching and Teacher Education, 27*, 900–10.

Nardi, B. A., and O'Day, V. (1999). *Information Ecologies: Using Technology with Heart*. Cambridge, US: Massachusetts Institute of Technology.

National Research Council (2009). *Learning Science in Informal Environments: People, Places and Pursuits*. Washington, DC: The National Academies Press.

Neville, D. O., Shelton, B. E. and McInnis, B. (2009). Cybertext redux: Using digital game-based learning to teach L2 vocabulary, reading, and culture. *Computer Assisted Language Learning, 22*, 409–24.

Nguyen, L. T. C., and Gu, Y. Q. (2013). Strategy-based instruction: A learner-focused approach to developing learner autonomy. *Language Teaching Research, 17*, 19–30.

Nielson, K. B. (2011). Self-study with language learning software in the workplace: What happens. *Language Learning* & *Technology, 15*, 110–29.

North, S., Snyder, I. and Bulfin, S. (2008). DIGITAL TASTES: Social class and young people's technology use. *Information, Communication* & *Society, 11*, 895–911.

Nunan, D. (1996). Towards autonomous learning: Some theoretical, empirical and practical issues. In R. Pemberton, E. S. L., Li, W. W. F. Or and H. D. Pierson (eds), *Taking Control: Autonomy in Language Learning* (pp. 13–26). Hong Kong: Hong Kong University Press.

Nunan, D. (1997). Strategy training in the language classroom: An empirical investigation. *RELC Journal, 28*, 56–81.

O'Bryan, A. (2008). Providing pedagogical learner training in CALL: Impact on student use of language-learning strategies and glosses. *CALICO Journal, 26*, 142–59.

O'Dowd, R. (2007). Evaluating the outcomes of online intercultural exchange. *ELT Journal, 61*, 144–52.

Oliveira, T., and Martins, M. F. (2011). Literature review of information technology adoption models at firm level. *The Electronic Journal Information Systems Evaluation, 14*, 110–21.

Olmedo, M. I. (2015). *English Language Learning Beyond the Classroom Walls* (Unpublished doctoral dissertation). Barcelona: University of Barcelona.

Olsson, E. (2012). 'Everything I read on the Internet is in English': On the impact of extramural English on Swedish 16-year-old pupils' writing proficiency (Unpublished doctoral dissertation). Göteborgs: University of Göteborgs.

Oxford, R. L. (2003). Toward a more systematic model of L2 learner autonomy. In D. Palfreyman and R. C. Smith (eds), *Learner Autonomy Across Cultures* (pp. 75–91). Basingstoke, UK: Palgrave Macmillan.

Oxford, R. L. (2008). Hero with a thousand faces: Learner autonomy, learning strategies and learning tactics in independent language learning. In S. Hurd and T. Lewis (eds), *Language Learning Strategies in Independent Settings* (pp. 41–63). New York, USA: Multilingual Matters.

Oxford, R. L. (2011). *Teaching and Researching Language Learning Strategies.* Harlow: Person Longman.

Oxford, R. L. (2015). Expanded perspectives on autonomous learners. *Innovation in Language Learning and Teaching, 9*, 58–71.

Palfreyman, D. M. (2011). Family, friends, and learning beyond the classroom: Social networks and social capital in language learning. In P. Benson and H. Reinders (eds), *Beyond the Language Classroom* (pp. 17–34). Basingstoke, UK: Palgrave Macmillan.

Palfreyman, D. M. (2014). The ecology of learner autonomy. In G. Murray (ed.), *Social Dimensions of Autonomy in Language Learning* (pp. 175–91). Basingstoke, UK: Palgrave Macmillan.

Palfreyman, D. M., and Smith, R. C. (2003). *Learner Autonomy Across Cultures.* New York: Palgrave Macmillan.

Palviainen, Å. (2012). Lärande som diskursnexus: finska studenters uppfattningar om skoltid, fritid och universitetsstudier som lärokontexter för svenska. *Nordisk tidskrift for andrespråksforskning, Nr 1-2012*, 7–36.

Panadero, E., and Alonso-Tapia, J. (2014). How do students self-regulate? Review of Zimmerman's cyclical model of self-regulated learning. *Anales de Psicología/Annals of Psychology, 30*, 450–62.

Parrish, P., and Linder-VanBerschot, J. (2010). Cultural dimensions of learning: Addressing the challenges of multicultural instruction. *The International Review of Research in Open and Distributed Learning, 11*, 1–19.

Patall, E. A., Dent, A. L., Oyer, M. and Wynn, S. R. (2013). Student autonomy and course value: The unique and cumulative roles of various teacher practices. *Motivation and Emotion, 37*, 14–32.

Percival, A. (1996). Invited reaction: An adult educator responds. *Human Resource Development Quarterly, 7*, 131–9.

Pintrich, P. R. (2000). The role of goal orientation in self-regulated learning. In M. Boekaerts, P. Pintrich and M. Zeidner (eds), *Handbook of Self-Regulation* (pp. 451–502). San Diego, US: Academic Press.

Prichard, C. (2013). Training L2 learners to use SNSs appropriately and effectively. *CALICO Journal, 30*, 204–25.

Pusack, J. P. (1999). The Kontakte multimedia project at the University of Iowa. *CALICO Journal, 17*, 25–42.

Putnam, R. D. (1993). The prosperous community. *The American Prospect, 4*, 35–42.

Putnam, R. D. (2000). Bowling alone: America's declining social capital. In J. E. Lane and U. Wagschal (eds), *Culture and Politics* (pp. 223–34). Basingstoke, US: Palgrave Macmillan.

Qi, A. (2012). On the theoretical framework of autonomous learning. *International Journal of Education and Management Engineering, 11*, 35–40.

Rahimi, M., and Katal, M. (2012). The role of metacognitive listening strategies awareness and podcast-use readiness in using podcasting for learning English as a foreign language. *Computers in Human Behavior, 28*, 1153–61.

Ranalli, J. (2013). Online strategy instruction for integrating dictionary skills and language awareness. *Language Learning & Technology, 17*, 75–99.

Rankin, Y. A., McNeal, M., Shute, M. W. and Gooch, B. (2008). User centered game design: evaluating massive multiplayer online role playing games for second language acquisition. In *Proceedings of the 2008 ACM SIGGRAPH Symposium on Video Games* (pp. 43–9). ACM.

Ray, J. M. (2009). A template analysis of teacher agency at an academically successful dual language school. *Journal of Advanced Academics, 21*, 110–41.

Raya, M. J., Lamb, T. and Vieira, F. (2007). *Pedagogy for Autonomy in Language Education in Europe*. Dublin: Authentik.

Raz, J. (1986). *The Morality of Freedom*. Oxford: Clarendon Press.

Reeve, J. (2006). Teachers as facilitators: What autonomy-supportive teachers do and why their students benefit. *Elementary School Journal, 106*, 225–36.

Reeve, J. (2016). A grand theory of motivation: Why not?. *Motivation and Emotion, 40*, 31–5.

Reid, J. M. (1987). The learning style preferences of ESL students. *TESOL Quarterly, 21*, 87–111.

Reinders, H. (2010). Towards a classroom pedagogy for learner autonomy: A framework of independent language learning skills. *Australian Journal of Teacher Education, 35,* 40–55.

Reinders, H. (2011). Materials development for learning beyond the classroom. In P. Benson and H. Reinders (eds), *Beyond the Language Classroom* (pp. 175–89). Basingstoke: Palgrave Macmillan.

Reinders, H. (2012). Advising in context: Towards pedagogical and institutional integration. In J. Mynard and L. Carson (eds), *Advising in Language Learning* (pp. 170–84). Harlow, United Kingdom: Pearson Education Limited.

Reinders, H. (2013). Self-Access and Independent Learning Centers. In C. A. Chapelle (ed.), *The Encyclopedia of Applied Linguistics. Blackwell Publishing Ltd.* DOI:10.1002/9781405198431.wbeal1059.

Reinders, H., and White, C. (2010). The theory and practice of technology in materials development and task design. In N. Harwood (ed.), *Materials in ELT: Theory and Practice* (pp. 58–80). Cambridge: Cambridge University Press.

Reinders, H., and Pegrum, M. (2015). Supporting Language Learning on the Move. An evaluative framework for mobile language learning resources. In B. Tomlinson (ed.), *Second Language Acquisition Research and Materials Development for Language Learning* (pp. 116–41). London: Taylor & Francis.

Resnick, P. (2001). Beyond bowling together: Sociotechnical capital. *HCI in the New Millennium, 77,* 247–72.

Richards, J. C. (2015). The changing face of language learning: Learning beyond the classroom. *RELC Journal, 46,* 5–22.

Richardson, A. (2002). An ecology of learning and the role of elearning in the learning environment. *Global Summit of Online Knowledge Networks* (pp. 47–51). Australia: Education. Au Limited.

Rogers, A. (2016). '115 million girls …': Informal learning and education, an emerging field. In. S. McGrath and Q. Gu (eds), *Routledge Handbook of International Education and Development* (pp. 260–75). Oxon: Routledge.

Rosell-Aguilar, F. (2013). Podcasting for language learning through iTunes U: The learner's view. *Language Learning & Technology, 17,* 74–93.

Rubin, J. (1975). What the 'good language learner' can teach us. *TESOL Quarterly, 9,* 41–51.

Rubin, J., Chamot, A. U., Harris, V. and Anderson, N. J. (2007). Intervening in the use of strategies. *Language Learner Strategies, 30,* 29–45.

Rule, A. C. (2006). The components of authentic learning. *Journal of Authentic Learning, 3,* 1–10.

Saad, N. S. M., Yunus, M. M. and Embi, M. A. (2013). Research on international students in traditional host countries and Malaysia: Some potential areas in Malaysia. *Procedia-Social and Behavioral Sciences, 90,* 488–96.

Saadatmand, M., and Kumpulainen, K. (2012). Emerging technologies and new learning ecologies: learners' perceptions of learning in open and networked environments. In V. Hodgson, C. Jones, M. de Laat, D., McConnell, T. Ryberg and P. Sloep (eds), *Proceeding of the 8th International Conference on Networked Learning 2012* (pp. 266–75), Lancaster University.

Sackey, D. J., Nguyen, M. T., and Grabill, J. T. (2015). Constructing learning spaces: What we can learn from studies of informal learning online. *Computers and Composition, 35*, 112–24.

Sagarra, N., and Abbuhl, R. (2013). Optimizing the noticing of recasts via computer-delivered feedback: Evidence that oral input enhancement and working memory help second language learning. *The Modern Language Journal, 97*, 196–216.

Sawchuk, P. H. (2008). Theories and methods for research on informal learning and work: Towards cross-fertilization. *Studies in Continuing Education, 30*, 1–16.

Schunk, D. H., and Zimmerman, B. J. (1997). Social origins of self-regulatory competence. *Educational psychologist, 32*, 195–208.

Schunk, D. H., and Ertmer, P. A. (2000). Self-regulation and academic learning: Self-efficacy enhancing interventions. In M. Boekaerts, P. P. Pintrich and M. Zeidner (eds), *Handbook of Self-Regulation* (pp. 631–49). San Diego, US: Academic Press.

Schwandt, T. A. (2000). Three epistemological stances for qualitative inquiry. In N. Denzin and Y. Lincoln (eds), *Handbook of Qualitative Research*, 2nd edn (pp. 189–213). Thousand Oaks: Sage Publications.

Schwartz, D. L., and Arena, D. (2013). *Measuring what Matters Most: Choice-based Assessments for the Digital Age*. Boston, MA: MIT Press.

Scribner, S., and Cole, M. (1973). Cognitive consequences of formal and informal education. *Science, 182*, 553–9.

Sefton-Green. J. (2006). *Literature Review in Informal Learning with Technology Outside School.* Bristol, UK: Futurelab.

Selwyn, N. (2008). An investigation of differences in undergraduates' academic use of the internet. *Active Learning in Higher Education, 9*, 11–22.

Selwyn, N. (2011). *Education and Technology: Key Issues and Debates.* London: Continuum International Publishing Group.

Shahsavari, S. (2014). Efficiency, feasibility and desirability of learner autonomy based on teachers' and learners' point of views. *Theory and Practice in Language Studies, 4*, 271–80.

Shakarami, A., and Abdullah, M. H. (2011). Management of language learning strategies: The case of Net-Generation ESL tertiary learners. *Journal for International Business and Entrepreneurship Development, 5*, 287–98.

Sharples, M. (2009a). Methods for evaluating mobile learning. In G. Vavoula, N. Pachler and A. Kukulska-Hulme (eds), *Researching Mobile Learning: Frameworks, Tools and Research Designs* (pp. 17–39). Oxford: Peter Lang.

Sharples, M., Arnedillo-Sánchez, I., Milrad, M. and Vavoula, G. (2009b). Mobile learning. In N. Balacheff, S. Ludvigsen, T. D. Dong, A. Lazonder & S. Barnes (eds), *Technology-Enhanced Learning* (pp. 233–49). Berlin, Netherlands: Springer.

Shih, Y. C., and Yang, M. T. (2008). A collaborative virtual environment for situated language learning using VEC3D. *Educational Technology & Society, 11*, 56–68.

Siemens, G. (2003). Learning ecology, communities, and networks: Extending the classroom. *Elearnspace*. Retrieved from http://cop.rdmc.ou.nl/sites/bieb/Bibliotheek%20%20Publicaties/elearnspace.doc.

Sinclair, B. (2000). Learner autonomy: The next phase. In I. McGrath, B. Sinclair and T. Lamb (eds), *Learner Autonomy, Teacher Autonomy: Future Directions* (pp. 4–14). Harlow: Longman.

Skule, S. (2004). Learning conditions at work: A framework to understand and assess informal learning in the workplace. *International Journal of Training and Development, 8*, 8–20.

Sockett, G., and Toffoli, D. (2012). Beyond learner autonomy: A dynamic systems view of the informal learning of English in virtual online communities. *ReCALL, 24*, 138–51.

Spear, G. E., and Mocker, D. W. (1981). *The Organizing Circumstance: Environmental Determinants in Self-Directed Learning*. Washington: National Institute of Education.

Spector, J. M. (2001). An overview of progress and problems in educational technology. *Interactive Educational Multimedia, 3*, 27–37.

Steel, C. H. (2012). *Fitting Learning into Life: Language Students' Perspectives on Benefits of Using Mobile Apps*. Retrieved from http://www.ascilite.org/conferences/Wellington12/2012/images/custom/steel,_caroline_-_fitting_learning.pdf.

Steel, C. H., and Levy, M. (2013). Language students and their technologies: Charting the evolution 2006–2011. *ReCALL, 25*, 306–20.

Stefanou, C. R., Perencevich, K. C., DiCintio, M. and Turner, J. C. (2004). Supporting autonomy in the classroom: Ways teachers encourage student decision making and ownership. *Educational Psychologist, 39*, 97–110.

Stern, H. H. (1983). *Fundamental Concepts of Language Teaching: Historical and Interdisciplinary Perspectives on Applied Linguistic Research* (Unpublished doctoral dissertation). Oxford: Oxford University Press.

Stevens, R. H., and Thadani, V. (2007). Quantifying students' scientific problem solving efficiency and effectiveness. *Technology, Instruction, Cognition and Learning, 5*, 325–37.

Stevenson, M. P., and Liu, M. (2010). Learning a language with Web 2.0: Exploring the use of social networking features of foreign language learning websites. *CALICO Journal, 27*, 233–59.

Stickler, U., and Hampel, R. (2015). Qualitative research in CALL. *CALICO Journal, 32*, 380–95.

Stockwell, G. (2013). Tracking learner usage of mobile phones for language learning outside of the classroom. In P. Hubbard, M. Schultz and B. Smith (eds), *Human-Computer Interaction in Language Learning: Studies in Honor of Robert Fischer*. CALICO Monograph Series (pp. 118–36). San Marcos, TX: CALICO.

Stolk, J., Martello, R., Somerville, M. and Geddes, J. (2010). Engineering students' definitions of and responses to self-directed learning. *International Journal of Engineering Education*, *26*, 900–13.

Straub, E. T. (2009). Understanding technology adoption: Theory and future directions for informal learning. *Review of Educational Research*, *79*, 625–49.

Stubbé, H. E., and Theunissen, N. C. M. (2008). Self-directed adult learning in a ubiquitous learning environment: A meta-review. In *Proceedings of the First Workshop on Technology Support for Self-Organized Learners* (pp. 5–28).

Šumak, B., Polancic, G. and Hericko, M. (2010). An empirical study of virtual learning environment adoption using UTAUT. *Mobile, Hybrid, and On-Line Learning, 2010. ELML'10. Second International Conference on*. IEEE.

Sun, Y., Franklin, T. and Gao, F. (2015). Learning outside of classroom: Exploring the active part of an informal online English learning community in China. *British Journal of Educational Technology*, *45*, 1–14.

Sundqvist, P. (2009). *Extramural English Matters: Out-of-School English and its Impact on Swedish Ninth Graders' Oral Proficiency and Vocabulary* (Unpublished doctoral dissertation). Karlstad: Karlstad University Studies.

Sundqvist, P. (2011). A possible path to progress: Out-of-school English language learners in Sweden. In P. Benson and H. Reinders (eds), *Beyond the Language Classroom* (pp. 106–18). New York: Palgrave Macmillan.

Sundqvist, P., and Sylvén, L. K. (2014). Language-related computer use: Focus on young L2 English learners in Sweden. *ReCALL*, *26*, 3–20.

Sundqvist, P., and Wikström, P. (2015). Out-of-school digital gameplay and in-school L2 English vocabulary outcomes. *System*, *51*, 65–76.

Sykes, J. M., Reinhardt, J. and Thorne, S. L. (2010). Multiuser digital games as sites for research and practice. In F. M. Hult (ed.), *Directions and Prospects for Educational Linguistics* (Vol. 11, pp. 117–35). Dordrecht: Springer Netherlands.

Sylvén, L. K., and Sundqvist, P. (2012). Gaming as extramural English L2 learning and L2 proficiency among young learners. *ReCALL*, *24*, 302–21.

Taiwo, A. A., and Downe, A. G. (2013). The theory of user acceptance and use of technology (UTAUT): A meta-analytic review of empirical findings. *Journal of Theoretical & Applied Information Technology*, *49*, 48–58.

Tang, L. L. (2014). Technology Integration by Teachers and its Impact on Students' Technology Integration in Learning Chinese as a Second Language (Unpublished master thesis). Hong Kong: University of Hong Kong.

Teo, T. (2009). Modelling technology acceptance in education: A study of pre-service teachers. *Computers & Education*, *52*, 302–12.

Teo, T., and van Schaik, P. (2012). Understanding the intention to use technology by preservice teachers: An empirical test of competing theoretical models. *International Journal of Human-Computer Interaction*, *28*, 178–88.

Thanasoulas, D. (2000). What is learner autonomy and how can it be fostered. *The Internet TESL Journal*, *6*, 37–48.

Thanh, V. N. (2011). Language learners' and teachers' perceptions relating to learner autonomy-Are they ready for autonomous language learning? *VNU Journal of Science, Foreign Languages, 27*, 41–52.

The Swedish National Agency of Education. (2012). Internationella språkstudien 2011. Rapport 375, 2012. Stockholm: The Swedish National Agency of Education.

Thorne, S. L., and Reinhardt, J. (2008). 'Bridging activities', new media literacies, and advanced foreign language proficiency. *CALICO Journal, 25*, 558–72.

Thornton, K. (2010). Supporting self-directed learning: a framework for teachers. *Language Education in Asia, 1*, 158–70.

Toffoli, D., and Sockett, G. (2010). How non-specialist students of English practice informal learning using web 2.0 tools. *ASp. la revue du GERAS, 58*, 125–44.

Toffoli, D., and Sockett, G. (2015). University teachers' perceptions of online informal learning of English (OILE). *Computer Assisted Language Learning, 28*(1), 7–21.

Toh, Y., So, H. J., Seow, P., Chen, W. and Looi, C. K. (2013). Seamless learning in the mobile age: A theoretical and methodological discussion on using cooperative inquiry to study digital kids on-the-move. *Learning, Media and Technology, 38*, 301–18.

Tomlinson, B. (2011). Principles and procedures for self-access materials. *Studies in Self-Access Learning Journal, 1*, 72–86.

Tough, A. (1971). *The Adult's Learning Projects. A Fresh Approach to Theory and Practice in Adult Learning*. Ontario: The Ontario Institute for Studies in Education.

Trinder, R. (2016). Blending technology and face-to-face: Advanced students' choices. *ReCALL, 28*, 83–102.

Truebridge, S. (2014). *Resilience Begins with Beliefs: Building on Student Strengths for Success in School*. New York: Teachers College Press.

Ucko, D. A., and Ellenbogen, K. M. (2008). Impact of technology on informal science learning. In D. W. Sunal, E. Wright and C. Sundberg (eds), *The Impact of the Laboratory and Technology on Learning and Teaching Science K-16* (pp. 239–66). Charlotte, NC: Information Age Publishing.

Underwood, J., Luckin, R. and Winters, N. (2012). Managing resource ecologies for mobile, personal and collaborative self-directed language learning. *Procedia-Social and Behavioral Sciences, 34*, 226–9.

Ürün, M. F., Demir, C. E. and Akar, H. (2014). A study on ELT high school teachers' practices to foster learner autonomy. *Journal of Language Teaching and Research, 5*, 825–36.

Van Deurzen, E. (2012). *Existential Counselling and Psychotherapy in Practice*. Los Angeles: Sage Publications.

Van Dijk, J. A. G. M. (2005). *The Deepening Divide: Inequality in the Information Society*. Los Angeles: Sage Publications.

Vannini, P., and Burgess, S. (2009). Authenticity as motivation and aesthetic experience. In P. Vannini and J. P. Williams (eds), *Authenticity in Culture, Self, and Society* (pp. 103–19). Burlington: Ashgate Publishing Company.

Veenman, M. V. J. (2007). The assessment and instruction of self-regulation in computer-based environments: A discussion. *Metacognition Learning, 2*, 177–83.

Veenman, M. V. J., Van Hout-Wolters, B. H. A. M. and Afflerbach, P. (2006). Metacognition and learning: Conceptual and methodological considerations. *Metacognition and Learning, 1*, 3–14.

Venkatesh, V., Davis, F. D. and Morris, M. G. (2007). Dead or alive? The development, trajectory and future of technology adoption research. *Journal of the Association for Information Systems, 8*, 267–86.

Venkatesh, V., Thong, J. Y. and Xu, X. (2012). Consumer acceptance and use of information technology: extending the unified theory of acceptance and use of technology. *MIS Quarterly, 36*, 157–78.

Venkatesh, V., Morris, M. G., Davis, G. B. and Davis, F. D. (2003). User acceptance of information technology: Toward a unified view. *MIS Quarterly, 27*, 425–78.

Viberg, O., and Grönlund, Å. (2013). Cross-cultural analysis of users' attitudes toward the use of mobile devices in second and foreign language learning in higher education: A case from Sweden and China. *Computers & Education, 69*, 169–80.

Vieira, F., Barbosa, I., Paiva, M. and Fernandes, I. S. (2008). Teacher education towards teacher (and learner) autonomy: What can be learnt from teacher development practices? In T. Lamb and H. Reinders (eds), *Learner and Teacher Autonomy: Concepts, Realities, and Responses* (pp. 217–36). Amsterdam, Netherland: John Benjamins Publishing Company.

Villanueva, M. L., Ruiz-Madrid, M. N. and Luzón, M. J. (2010). Learner autonomy in digital environments: Conceptual framework. In M. J. Luzón, N. Ruiz-Madrid and M. L. Villanueva (eds), *Digital Genres, New Literacies, and Autonomy in Language Learning* (pp. 1–19). Newcastle, UK: Cambridge Scholars Publishing.

Voller, P. (1997). Does the teacher have a role in autonomous language learning? In P. Benson and P. Voller (eds), *Autonomy and Independence in Language Learning* (pp. 98–113). London: Longman.

Volman, M., van Eck, E., Heemskerk, I. and Kuiper, E. (2005). New technologies, new differences. Gender and ethnic differences in pupils' use of ICT in primary and secondary education. *Computers & Education, 45*, 35–55.

Wall, S. (2003). Freedom as a political ideal. *Social Philosophy and Policy, 20*, 307–34.

Wallace, L. (2015). Reflexive photography, attitudes, behavior, and CALL: ITAs improving spoken English intelligibility. *CALICO Journal, 32*, 449–79.

Wehmeyer, M. L., Agran, M. and Hughes, C. (2000). A national survey on teachers' promotion of self-determination and student-directed learning. *Journal of Special Education, 34*, 58–68.

Weinstein, C. E., Woodruff, T. and Awalt, C. (2002). *Becoming a Strategic Learner: LASSI Instructional Modules*. Clearwater, FL: H&H Publishing.

White, C. (1995). Autonomy and strategy use in distance foreign language learning: Research findings. *System, 23*, 207–21.

White, C. (2009). Towards a learner-based theory of distance language learning: The concept of the learner-context interface. In P. Hubbard (ed.), *Computer Assisted Language Learning: Critical Concepts in Linguistics. Volume IV: Present Trends and Future Directions in CALL* (pp. 97–112). London: Routledge.

Whitworth, A. (2009). Whose context is it anyway? Workplace e-learning as a synthesis of designer-and learner-generated contexts. *Impact: Journal of Applied Research in Workplace E-learning, 1*, 27–42.

Widdowson, H. G. (1979). The authenticity of language data. Paper presented at the Georgetown University Round Table, *Explorations in Applied Linguistics* (pp. 163–72). Oxford: Oxford University Press.

Wiklund, I. (2002). Social networks from a sociolinguistic perspective: The relationship between characteristics of the social networks of bilingual adolescents and their language proficiency. *International Journal of the Sociology of Language, 153*, 53–92.

Williams, M. D., Rana, N. P. and Dwivedi, Y. K. (2015). The unified theory of acceptance and use of technology (UTAUT): a literature review. *Journal of Enterprise Information Management, 28*, 443–88.

Winke, P. M. (2013). The effects of input enhancement on grammar learning and comprehension. *Studies in Second Language Acquisition, 35*, 323–52.

Winke, P. M., and Goertler, S. (2008). Did we forget someone? Students' computer access and literacy for CALL. *Calico Journal, 25*, 482–509.

Winke, P., Goertler, S. and Amuzie, G. L. (2010). Commonly taught and less commonly taught language learners: are they equally prepared for CALL and online language learning?. *Computer Assisted Language Learning, 23*, 199–219.

Winnie, P. H., and Hadwin, A. F. (1998). *Using CoNoteS2 to Study and Support Self-Regulated Learning*. San Francisco, CA: International Association of Applied Psychology.

Winne, P. H., and Perry, N. E. (2000). Measuring self-regulated learning. In M. Boekaerts, P. Pintrich, and M. Zeidner (eds), *Handbook of Self-Regulation* (pp. 531–66). San Diego, US: Academic Press.

Wong, L. H. (2012). A learner-centric view of mobile seamless learning. *British Journal of Educational Technology, 43*, E19–E23.

Wong, L. H., and Looi, C. K. (2011). What seams do we remove in mobile-assisted seamless learning? A critical review of the literature. *Computers & Education, 57*, 2364–81.

Wong, L. H. and Looi, C. K. (2012). *Enculturing Self-Directed Seamless Learners: Towards a Facilitated Seamless Learning Process Framework Mediated by Mobile Technology*. 7th IEEE International Conference on Wireless, Mobile and Ubiquitous Technology in Education, Takamatsu.

Wong, L. H., Chai, C. S., Aw, G. P. and King, R. B. (2015). Enculturating seamless language learning through artifact creation and social interaction process. *Interactive Learning Environments, 23*, 130–57.

Wong, L. L., and Nunan, D. (2011). The learning styles and strategies of effective language learners. *System*, *39*, 144–63.

Wu, M. M. F. (2012). Beliefs and out-of-class language learning of Chinese-speaking ESL learners in Hong Kong. *New Horizons in Education*, *60*, 35–52.

Yan, W. (2007). What do autonomous language learners expect their teachers to do? – A study on teacher's roles in autonomous learning project. *Foreign Language World*, *4*, 005.

Yıldırım, Ö. (2008). Turkish EFL learners' readiness for learner autonomy. *Journal of Language and Linguistic Studies*, *4*, 65–80.

Young, R. (1986). *Personal Autonomy: Beyond Negative and Positive Liberty*. London: Croom Helm.

Yowell, C. M., and Smylie, M. A. (1999). Self-regulation in democratic communities. *The Elementary School Journal*, 469–90.

Zenotz, V. (2012). Awareness development for online reading. *Language Awareness*, *21*, 85–100.

Zhan, Y., and Andrews, S. (2014). Washback effects from a high-stakes examination on out-of-class English learning: insights from possible self theories. *Assessment in Education: Principles, Policy & Practice*, *21*, 71–89.

Zhang, L. F., and Sternberg, R. J. (2011). Learning in a cross-cultural perspective. In V. G. Aukrust (ed.), *Learning and Cognition in Education* (pp. 16–22). Cambridge: Academic Press.

Zimmerman, B. J. (2000). Attaining self-regulation: A social cognitive perspective. In M. Boekaerts, P. R. Pintrich and M. Zeidner (eds), *Handbook of Self – Regulation: Theory, Research, and Applications* (pp. 13–29). San Diego: Academic Press.

Zimmerman, B. J. (2011). Motivational sources and outcomes of self-regulated learning and performance. In B. Zimmerman and D. H. Schunk (eds), *Handbook of Self-Regulation of Learning and Performance* (pp. 49–64). New York: Routledge.

Zimmerman, B. J. and Risemberg, R. (1997). Becoming a self-regulated writer: A social cognitive perspective. *Contemporary Educational Psychology*, *22*, 73–101.

Zimmerman, B. J., and Kitsantas, A. (2002). Acquiring writing revision and self-regulatory skill through observation and emulation. *Journal of Educational Psychology*, *94*, 660–8.

Zimmerman, B. J., and Campillo, M. (2003). Motivating self-regulated problem solvers. In J. E. Davidson and R. J. Sternberg (eds), *The Psychology of Problem Solving* (pp. 233–62). Cambridge: Cambridge University Press.

Index

Lightning Source UK Ltd.
Milton Keynes UK
UKHW010450220119
335981UK00003B/88/P